OECD Public Governance Reviews

Second Public Procurement Review of the Mexican Institute of Social Security (IMSS)

RESHAPING STRATEGIES FOR BETTER HEALTHCARE

OECD
BETTER POLICIES FOR BETTER LIVES

Please cite this publication as:
OECD (2018), *Second Public Procurement Review of the Mexican Institute of Social Security (IMSS): Reshaping Strategies for Better Healthcare*, OECD Public Governance Reviews, OECD Publishing, Paris.
http://dx.doi.org/10.1787/9789264190191-en

ISBN 978-92-64-19017-7 (print)
ISBN 978-92-64-19019-1 (PDF)

Series: OECD Public Governance Reviews
ISSN 2219-0406 (print)
ISSN 2219-0414 (online)

Photo credits: Cover © De watchara/Shutterstock.com; © Orin zuu/thenounproject.com; © Garagestock / Shutterstock.com; ©Adrien Coquet/thenounproject.com

Corrigenda to OECD publications may be found on line at: *www.oecd.org/about/publishing/corrigenda.htm*.

Foreword

Overall, OECD countries have improved the quality of their healthcare, but the price tag has been high – on average amounting to 9% of gross domestic product (GDP) in 2016. While healthcare has also improved in Mexico, the country persistently ranks low for health spending, a reliable determinant of a population's health status. Furthermore, at just above 50% of total health expenditure, the share of public financing of healthcare in Mexico is the second lowest in the OECD. In addition, Mexico is facing pressing social challenges that have substantial implications for health such as an ageing population, pollution, sedentary lifestyles and obesity. To improve value for money and reduce health inequities, the country needs to further invest in cost-effective programmes that affect the personal, environmental and social determinants of health. This includes more effective public services that use health budgets – particularly public funds – more efficiently.

As one of the biggest government expenditures in OECD countries (around one-third of total government budgets), public procurement is increasingly recognised as a means of ensuring the efficiency and effectiveness of public service delivery. In the health sector, the public procurement of goods, services and infrastructure all contribute to meeting patients' needs; from receiving cost-effective and efficient medicines to being hospitalised in the most appropriate setting.

The Mexican Institute for Social Security (*Instituto Mexicano de Seguro Social*, IMSS) is the largest social security institute in Latin America. As a key actor in Mexico's healthcare system and largest public buyer, IMSS strives to be a leader in the strategic use of public procurement. IMSS recently called on the OECD to monitor its progress in implementing previous OECD policy recommendations on the integrity and efficiency of its procurement framework. It also asked for its procurement strategies and practices to be assessed against the 2015 OECD Recommendation of the Council on Public Procurement.

The *'Second Public Procurement Review of the IMSS, Reshaping Strategies for Better Healthcare'* is the result of an OECD peer review on public governance. Such reviews help governments at all levels to design and implement strategic, evidence-based and innovative policies to strengthen their governance; respond effectively to diverse and disruptive economic, social and environmental challenges; and deliver on their commitments to citizens.

IMSS has made significant progress in transforming its procurement operations. It has improved efficiency by creating a strong procurement function that is adapted to its organisational structure. It has successfully led the largest procurement scheme in the Mexican public sector, not only saving more than MXN 14 billion between 2013 and 2016 for the benefit of all participating institutions, but also supporting productivity growth with an 18% increase between 2012 and 2017 in the number of medicines procured with the same amount of resources. A strengthened risk management system is also allowing IMSS to address systemic issues in healthcare and procurement, such as fraud, corruption and the waste of public funds.

Alongside this progress, further avenues exist for IMSS to achieve procurement excellence and provide effective healthcare to citizens. For example, it could make better use of procurement data in developing future procurement strategies. By comparing alternative procurement strategies and their long-term impact, IMSS could also ensure sustained benefits. The Institute could contribute more to achieving national priorities, such as better access to healthcare, by aligning procurement strategies with national health policies. IMSS can also develop mechanisms to attract more small and medium-sized enterprises to public markets, such as dividing contracts into lots or increasing bidding periods, thus contributing to inclusive growth.

In the last few years, IMSS has made significant progress in reforming its procurement function to address some of its most pressing challenges. However, a wealth of opportunities still remains for IMSS to champion the Mexican health system and to reshape its procurement policies.

Angel Gurría

OECD Secretary-General

Acknowledgements

Under the direction and oversight of Marcos Bonturi, OECD Director for Public Governance, and János Bertók, Head of the Public Sector Integrity Division, this review was co-ordinated by Matthieu Cahen, Senior Policy Analyst, with the support of Paulo Magina, Head of the OECD Public Procurement Unit. The authors of the report were Rosana Aragon-Plaza, Kjersti Berg, Andy Cochrane, Kenza Khachani, Gavin Ugale and Jacobo Garcia Villareal.

Valuable comments and suggestions were received from Ian Forde, Antonio Capobianco and Matt Tavantzis. Editorial assistance was provided by Thibaut Gigou, Meral Gedik, Fiona Hinchcliffe and Juan Pablo Bolaños. Pauline Alexandrov, Alpha Zambou, Edwina Collins and Nadjad Bacar provided administrative assistance.

The OECD expresses its gratitude to IMSS leadership for its fruitful co-operation and leadership. In particular, the OECD would like to thank Tuffic Miguel Ortega, IMSS General Director and the following individuals who held the identified positions at the time of this review: Mikel Arriola Peñalosa, IMSS General Director; Ricardo Cavazos, Director for Institutional Outreach and Delegations Evaluation; and Patricio Caso, Director for Administration. Héctor Francisco Fernández Carpio, Regulatory Coordinator, served as the point of contact for OECD and led the collection of information and data for the review. The co-operation of their teams and all IMSS units were critical for the successful completion of this review.

Ambassador Mónica Aspe and Maya Alejandra Camacho Dávalos, of the Permanent Delegation of Mexico to the OECD, were instrumental in supporting the OECD in this project.

This review is part of a series of peer reviews on public procurement in OECD, G20 and non-member economies. It benefited from input from senior public procurement officials who participated in the OECD Meeting of the Working Party of Leading Practitioners on Public Procurement held in Paris on 16-18 October 2017, chaired by Dag Stromsnes, Chief Procurement Officer, Agency for Public Management and e-Government (Difi) in Norway. Special thanks go to the lead reviewers: Bruno Carrière, General Director, *UniHa* and Francisco Valero Bonilla, Coordinator, *Instituto Nacional de Gestion Sanitaria.*

The OECD Mexico Centre, under the leadership of Roberto Martinez, and its publications staff, notably Alejandro Camacho, co-ordinated the editorial process for the Spanish publication.

The review was approved by the OECD Working Party of the Leading Practitioners on Public Procurement (LPP) on 27 November 2017 and declassified by the Public Governance Committee on 15 December 2017.

Table of contents

Tables

Figures

Boxes

Abbreviations and Acronyms

ANDIS	National Association of Medical Supplies Distributors *(Asociación Nacional de Distribuidores de Insumos para la Salud)*
ALOS	Average length of stay in hospitals
ARI	Institutional Risk Management *(Administración de Riesgos Institucionales)*
ASF	Mexican Supreme Audit Institution *(Auditoria Superior de la Federación)*
BUO	Single registry of suppliers *(Bolsa Unica de Ofertas)*
CABCS	Co-ordination of Procurement of Goods and Contracting for Services area *(Coordinación De Adquisición de Bienes y Contratación de Servicios)*
CANIFARMA	National Chamber of the Pharmaceutical Industry *(Cámara Nacional de la Industria Farmaceútica)*
CCA	Co-ordination of Supply Control department *(Coordinación de Control de Abasto)*
CCE	Business Co-ordination Council *(Consejo Coordinador Empresarial)*
CCNPMIS	Coordinating Commission for the Negotiation of Medicines Prices and other Health Products *(Comisión Coordinadora para la Negociación de Precios de Medicamentos y otros Insumos para la Salud)*
CFE	Federal Electricity Commission *(Comisión Federal de Electricidad)*
COCODI	Institutional Development and Control Committee *(Comité de Control y Desempeño Institucional)*
COFECE	The Mexican Competition Commission *(Comisión Federal de Competencia Económica)*
COFEMER	Federal Commission for Regulatory Improvement *(Comisión Federal de Mejora Regulatoria)*
CONCAMIN	Industry Chambers Confederation *(Confederación de Cámaras Industriales)*
COPARMEX	Mexico's Exployers Confederation *(Confederación Patronal de la República Mexicana)*

COSO	Committee of the Sponsoring Organisation of the Treadway Commission
DIDT	Directorate of Innovation and Technological Development *(Dirección de Innovación y Desarrollo Tecnológico)*
HR	Human resources
HPV	Health Purchasing Victoria
IMSS	Mexican Institute of Social Security *(Instituto Mexicano del Seguro Social)*
INAI	National Institute for Transparency, Freedom of Information, and Personal Data Protection *(Instituto Nacional de Transparencia, Acceso a la Información y Protección de Datos Personales)*
ISSSTE	State Employees' Social Security and Social Services Institute *(Instituto de Seguridad y Servicios Sociales de los Trabajadores del Estado)*
KPI	Key performance indicator
LAASSP	Law on Acquisitions, Leases and Services by the Public Sector *(Ley de Adquisiciones, Arrendamientos y Servicios del Sector Público)*
LFPA	Federal Law of Administrative Procedure *(Ley Federal de Procedimiento Administrativo)*
LGRA	General Law on Administrative Responsibilities *(Ley General de Responsabilidades Administrativas)*
LGTAIP	General Law on Transparency and Access to Public Information *(Ley General de Transparencia y Acceso a la Información Pública)*
LOPSRM	Law on Public Works and Associated Services *(Ley de Obras Publicas y Servicios Relaciando con la Misma)*
LSS	Social Security Law *(Ley del Seguro Social)*
MAAGMAASSP	Procurement Manual *(Manual Administrativo de Aplicación General en Materia de Adquisiciones, Arrendamientos y Servicios del Sector Público)*
MAAG-CI	Manual of Internal Control System *(Acuerdo por el que se emiten las Disposiciones y el manual Administrativo de Aplicacion General en material de Control Interno)*
MC	The Coordination of Modernisation and Competitiveness Unit
MECI	Standard Model of Internal Control *(Modelo Estándar de Control Interno)*
NACS	National Anti-Corruption System
NHS	United Kingdom's National Health Service
OCDS	Open Contracting Data Standard

OIC	Internal Control Office *(Órgano Interno de Control)*
PAAAS	Annual procurement plan *(Programa Anual de Adquisiciones, Arrendamientos y Servicios)*
PEMEX	Petróleos Mexicanos
POT	Transparency Duties Portal *(Portal de Obligaciones de Transparencia)*
PREI	Institutional Resources Planning *(Planeacion de Recursos Institucionales)*
PTAR	Working Programme of Risk Management *(Programa de Trabajo de Administracion de Riesgos)*
RIA	Regulatory Impact Assessment
RLAASSP	Bylaws of the Law on Acquisitions, Leases and Services by the Public Sector *(Reglamento de la Ley de Adquisiciones, Arrendamientos y Servicios del Sector Público)*
ROPSRM	Bylaws of the Law on Public Works and Associated Services *(Reglamento de la Ley de Obras Publicas y servicios relaciando con la misma)*
SAI	Internal procurement system *(Systema de Abasto Institucional)*
SCII	System of Institutional Internal Control
SDO	Subsequent Discount Offer
SEDENA	Ministry of Defence *(Secretaría de la Defensa Nacional)*
SEI	Executive Information System *(Sistema Ejecutivo de Información)*
SFP	Ministry of Public Administration *(Secretaria de la Función Pública)*
SHCP	Ministry of Finance and Public Credit *(Secretaria de Hacienda y Crédito Publico)*
UMAE	Highly-specialised Medical Units *(Unidades Médicas de Alta Especialidad)*
UNIHA	*Union des Hôpitaux pour les Achats*

Executive summary

In ageing societies, the quality and efficiency of healthcare services are increasingly attracting governments' attention and citizens' interest. While the amount of healthcare spending per capita is a baseline indicator, it is not the only determinant of how well a health system functions. Governments must also be careful to spend effectively. The Mexican Institute of Social Security (*Instituto Mexicano de Seguro Social*, IMSS) provides healthcare services to over 75 million inhabitants and is a key institution in Mexico's fragmented health system. Public procurement – which represents almost one-third of government expenditure in OECD countries – provides sizeable opportunities for maximising the efficiency of healthcare spending. In Mexico, one of the lowest per-capita spenders in healthcare in the OECD, efficiency is even more vital.

In 2012, IMSS asked the OECD to peer review its procurement organisation and practices. Implementing the OECD's policy recommendations has brought tangible benefits to the Institute. However, strengthening public procurement requires continuous assessment of the effectiveness of strategies and processes to ensure that they remain relevant and have an optimal impact on public service delivery. IMSS therefore invited the OECD to review progress made in implementing the previous policy recommendations and suggest improvements, taking into account evolutions of the healthcare system and organisational changes in the Institute.

This second peer review highlights IMSS's achievements in a number of areas that are pivotal for transforming its procurement operations. Overall, IMSS has improved its procurement efficiency and developed strong competition in the markets in which it operates, allowing it to lead the largest consolidated procurement scheme in the Mexican public sector.

Consolidated tenders for medicines – begun in 2011 – have demonstrated their efficiency, increasing participation by public institutions at all levels and extending the coverage of products. Between 2013 and 2016, these institutions saved more than MXN 14 billion, 60% of which can be attributed to IMSS. This procurement technique also supported productivity growth, with 18% more medicines procured with the same amount of resources between 2012 and 2017.

IMSS's has begun to develop a skilled procurement workforce able to implement complex procurement strategies in a highly technical environment. Centralised procurement information and dashboards provide crucial data on trends and patterns to help IMSS take informed decisions.

IMSS has also reinforced its supplier management. Following the OECD's recommendation to strengthen sanctions for contract non-compliance, IMSS has increased its oversight of contractor performance, allowing it to avoid costs of MXN 275 million in 2016 alone. IMSS has also matched medicine delivery strategies to the local practices and constraints identified in the previous review. A "consumption on demand" strategy implemented in 2016 to prevent medicine supply disruption in its pharmacies and hospitals now allows patients to receive their prescribed medicines in 99.4% of cases.

To ensure that the market responds to the Institute's needs and patients' demands, IMSS regularly involves pharmaceutical institutes and business associations in the design of procurement strategies and tender documentation.

Healthcare and procurement are both particularly vulnerable to corruption, fraud, waste and mismanagement, ultimately affecting patients. IMSS has therefore brought its internal control system and risk management activities in line with Mexican and international standards. It has dedicated entities that champion risk management activities, refined its risk assessments and improved training to raise awareness about corruption and fraud risks.

Despite the progress achieved, the review found areas where IMSS can further improve procurement in order to provide high-quality, cost-effective healthcare services to citizens.

Key recommendations

IMSS should continue to **develop a skilled and motivated procurement workforce** able to carry out complex procurement operations efficiently. Actions required include a skills gap analysis and a continuous training action plan. An attractive professional career path would also reduce excessive staff turnover, which is undermining investments in professionalisation programmes.

IMSS could use data better to inform decisions, starting with the **consistent and structured collection of procurement information** from all its entities. IMSS should also ensure that current technological developments are aligned with procurement practices and that they support strategic public procurement. This would require greater co-ordination and co-operation with the Ministry of Public Administration, and between the national e-Procurement system CompraNet and IMSS's internal procurement platform.

Despite the benefits of IMSS's current procurement strategies, they need **constant adjustment**. For example, aggressive procurement strategies such as reverse auctions are starting to show diminishing returns and are tainting suppliers' perceptions of IMSS's objectives. Opportunities to maximise savings should be explored, such as integrating lifecycle costing assessments and measuring the impact of procurement outcomes on patients' length of stay in hospitals. There are also opportunities to minimise the risks of excessive market concentration or collusion in certain procurement strategies, such as large, repetitive and predictable consolidated tenders.

IMSS could improve the quality of its healthcare services through better supplier management, for example **shifting from ensuring compliance to promoting performance**. Transparent interactions with suppliers and business associations at all stages of the procurement cycle will provide a better understanding of opportunities and challenges.

The IMSS risk management framework should include clear responsibilities, critical areas in the procurement cycle and its tolerance for risk. In addition to reinforcing oversight by the Ministry of Public Administration and the Mexican Supreme Audit Institution, these measures would support **strategic risk-taking** and the development of innovative procurement strategies.

Being the largest public buyer in Mexico, IMSS's procurement decisions could **support broader national policy objectives**. Greater alignment of procurement strategies with national health priorities would provide sizeable benefits. For instance, IMSS could increase bidding periods and production lead time to allow smaller manufacturers of generic drugs to participate. Doubling the penetration rate of generic drugs would save Mexican households more than MXN 2.2 billion a year, contributing to the objective of universal access to healthcare.

Finally, IMSS could benefit from international experience to **promote innovation**. In OECD countries, such as the United Kingdom or France, innovative technological solutions have provided better healthcare services. IMSS has recently made progress but would need to develop output-based technical specifications or engage earlier with markets to promote innovative solutions.

Chapter 1. Public procurement in the context of Mexico's health challenges

Mexico's health system is marked by persisting significant challenges despite recent reforms. This Chapter discusses a number of these challenges and which role public procurement can play in addressing these systemic issues. Since health expenditure per capita is one of the most crucial variables affecting health status, public procurement represents a powerful lever to maximise the value for money arising out this public spending.

The statistical data for Israel are supplied by and under the responsibility of the relevant Israeli authorities. The use of such data by the OECD is without prejudice to the status of the Golan Heights, East Jerusalem and Israeli settlements in the West Bank under the terms of international law.

In a country marked by the health challenges of an ageing population, a sedentary lifestyle and geographical differences in healthcare access and quality, it is essential for Mexico's national healthcare system to improve its efficiency. Although public investment in Mexico's healthcare system increased from 2.4% to 3.2% of gross domestic product (GDP) between 2003 and 2013, it is unclear whether this is translating into tangible health gains (OECD, 2016[1]).

At the same time, the share of the national health budget spent on administration, which is the highest in the OECD at almost 10%, is accompanied by high out-of-pocket spending on health care by citizens.

Although many health indicators are improving in Mexico, the country has the lowest life expectancy in the OECD (Box 1.1). This is largely explained by the prevalence of lifestyles leading to higher risk factors for chronic diseases and mortality. Access barriers to high-quality healthcare services are also at the root of this situation. These key indicators suggest that the Mexican health system is not fully effective, and possibly signal a failure of the system to provide effective insurance, high-quality services, or both (OECD, 2016[1]).

Box 1.1. Health issues in Mexico

In 2013, life expectancy in Mexico was the lowest of all OECD countries at 74.6 years, compared to the OECD average of 80.5 years.

Mexico has the second highest obesity rate among OECD countries, after the United States, with one out of three adults in Mexico being obese. Obesity is a known risk factor for cardiovascular diseases, diabetes and some forms of cancer.

The quality of care in Mexico is also generally lower than in most other OECD countries. This is notably the case for hospital care provided for patients admitted for acute conditions such as a heart attack or stroke. The percentage of patients surviving these life-threatening conditions is much lower in Mexico than in other OECD countries. For reasons such as low supply of health workers (i.e. nurses) and unequal geographical distribution of doctors, barriers in access to high-quality health care services are prevalent.

Since 2012, health expenditure in Mexico has increased more rapidly than in most other OECD countries, driven by increases in government (public) expenditure. Still, overall health expenditure per capita in Mexico remains much lower than in nearly all other OECD countries (except Turkey).

Source: (OECD, 2015[2])

Mexico's healthcare system must change to deliver people-centred, high-quality care. Without far-reaching reforms, Mexico runs the risk of maintaining a fragmented health care system with challenges such as marked inequalities in access and quality, further entrenching socioeconomic disadvantage. An inefficient, unresponsive health care system will hold Mexico back from achieving the health, prosperity and progress of which it is certainly capable in the coming years.

While tackling some of these challenges requires structural reforms to the healthcare system, boosting the effectiveness and efficiency of public health procurement could also play a major role in shaping better public health care. Indeed, across OECD countries public spending on health accounts for approximately 30% of public procurement expenditure (OECD, 2017[3]).

Universal access to quality health care, supported by adequate budgeting, is necessary to achieve more inclusive economic growth. Efficient healthcare spending through strategic public procurement practices is therefore essential.

How does Mexico compare to other OECD countries on health spending?

Health spending per capita is a crucial variable of health status in OECD countries. According to the most recent statistics, Mexico ranks the lowest across the OECD, with USD 1 080 spent per capita in 2016 (OECD, 2017[4]). In 2013 Mexico spent 6.2% of its GDP on health (Figure 1.1), somewhat less than the OECD average of 8.9% (OECD, 2016[1]). Therefore the delivery of high-quality, yet cost-effective healthcare services to Mexican citizens is becoming increasingly challenging.

Figure 1.1. Health spending as a share of GDP

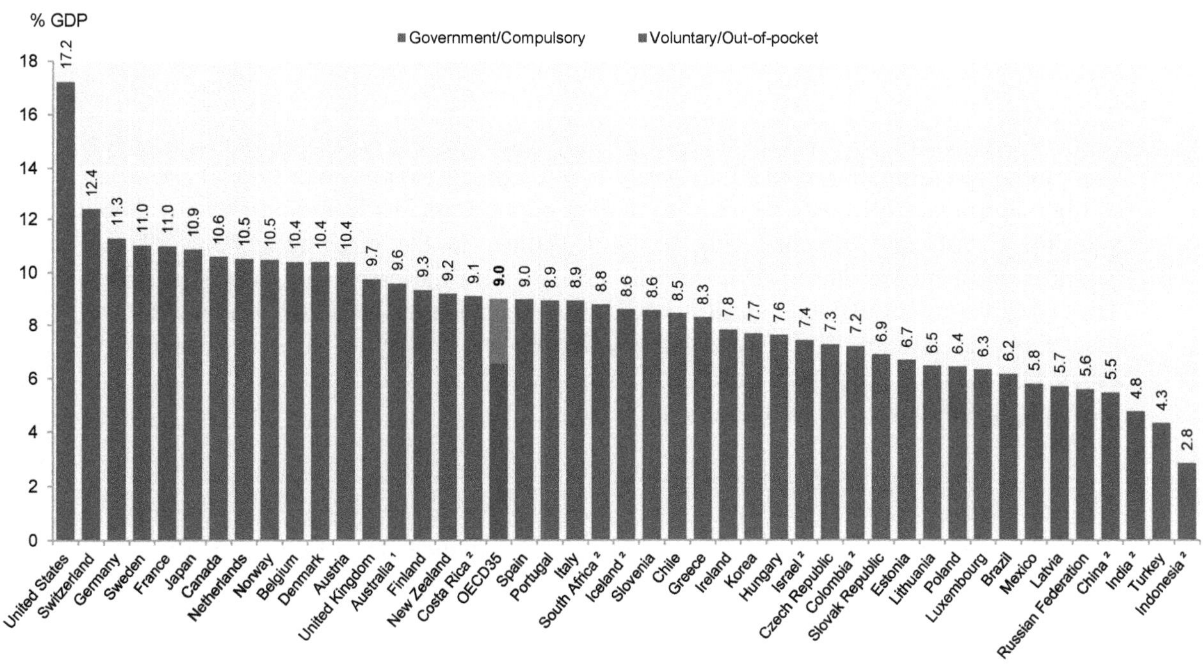

Note: Expenditure excludes investments, unless otherwise stated.

1. Australian expenditure estimates exclude all expenditure for residential aged care facilities in welfare (social) services.

2. Includes investments.

Source: (OECD, 2017[4])

The share of this spend coming from public funding sources is particularly low. In OECD countries, only the United States (49%) reports a share of public spending on health lower than Mexico (51%), the average being 72.5% (OECD, 2017[4]). An OECD study on *Tackling Wasteful Spending on Health* (OECD, 2017[3]), showed that the proportion of funding allocated to administering health services in Mexico, at 5.7% of total health spending, was the third highest in the OECD (Figure 1.2). This study identified high administrative costs in all three forms of financing scheme (government schemes, compulsory health insurance schemes, and voluntary prepayment schemes).

Figure 1.2. Administration as a share of current health expenditure by financing scheme, 2014 (or nearest year)

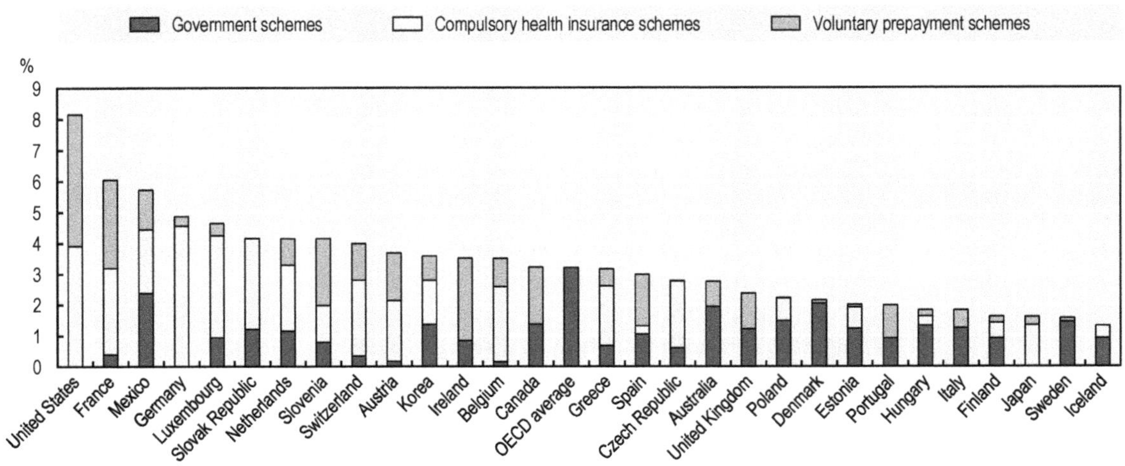

Source: (OECD, $2017_{[3]}$)

With public spending on health care already low in comparison to other OECD countries, the high administrative costs required to deliver services means less funding is available to frontline staff and patient-facing services. Added to the ongoing impacts of cost pressures on spending due to demographic changes and the increasing cost of services, Mexican government officials, health professionals, academics and other stakeholders all agree that the country faces renewed challenges in improving the performance of healthcare services, in particular the efficiency and quality of service provision, and ultimately health outcomes (Secretaría de Salud, $2013_{[5]}$).

Where does procurement fit into the picture?

Public procurement is a crucial pillar of strategic governance, and of government service delivery, and is a key economic activity for governments. In recent years, public procurement has been recognised as a strategic tool to achieve value for money along with other policy objectives. This holds true for the health sector, where procurement spending is a crucial element to enhance health status. As shown in Figure 1.3, health is the largest sector for government procurement expenditure in almost all OECD countries (OECD, $2017_{[6]}$).

Figure 1.3. Structure of public procurement spending, 2015

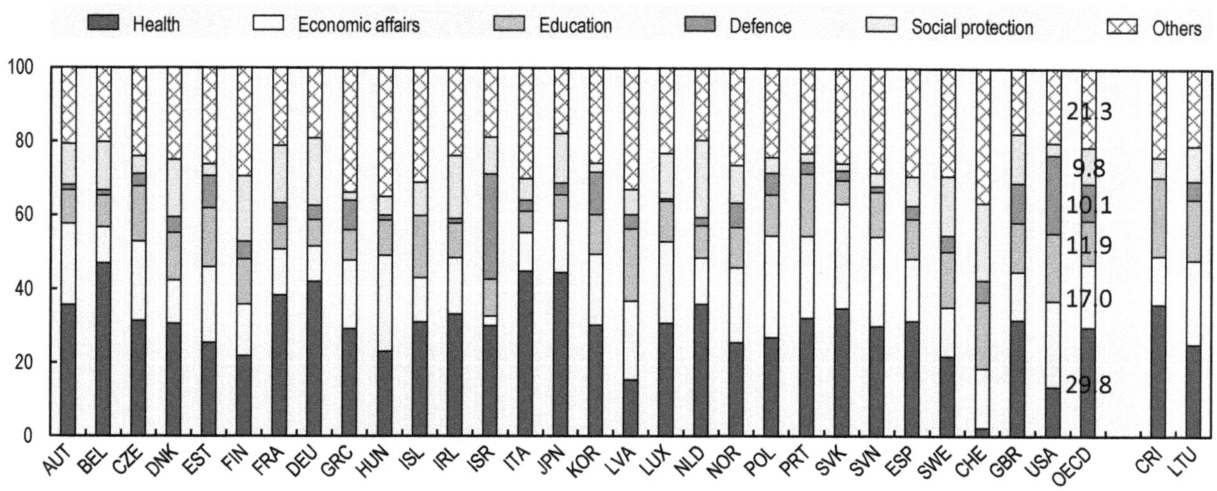

Source: (OECD, 2017[6])

Currently, health services in Mexico are provided through a variety of sub-systems – multiple private and public insurers employing their own staff to deliver health care, with an individual's affiliation usually determined by their employer. The Mexican Institute of Social Security (*Instituto Mexicano del Seguro Social*, IMSS) is the largest public institution, providing health insurance and healthcare services (as well as pensions and a range of other benefits) principally for Mexicans in salaried private (formal) employment.

As shown in national public procurement reports, IMSS is in fact the largest public buyer in Mexico (Figure 1.4), thus initiatives and efforts to further strengthen the strategic dimension of its procurement practices would not only directly benefit the institution, but could also diffuse across the entire federal administration. Being one of the OECD countries to spend the most on medical goods (at around 30% of total health expenditure; (OECD, 2015[2])), increasing the effectiveness of this spending could also strengthen IMSS's financial sustainability, allowing it to replenish reserves previously used to finance operating costs.

The acquisition of medical products, services and physical assets by IMSS is subject to the Mexican public procurement framework and notably its two laws: the Law on Acquisitions, Leases and Services of the Public Sector (*Ley de adquisiciones, arrendamientos y servicios del sector público,* LAASSP) and the Law on Public Works and Associated Services (*Ley de Obras Publicas y servicios relaciando con la misma,* LOPSRM). Increased efficiencies will have to be found within this framework, which delimits IMMS's scope to use its public procurement strategically.

Figure 1.4. The top five procurement spenders (in Million MXN) of the Mexican federal public administration, 2016

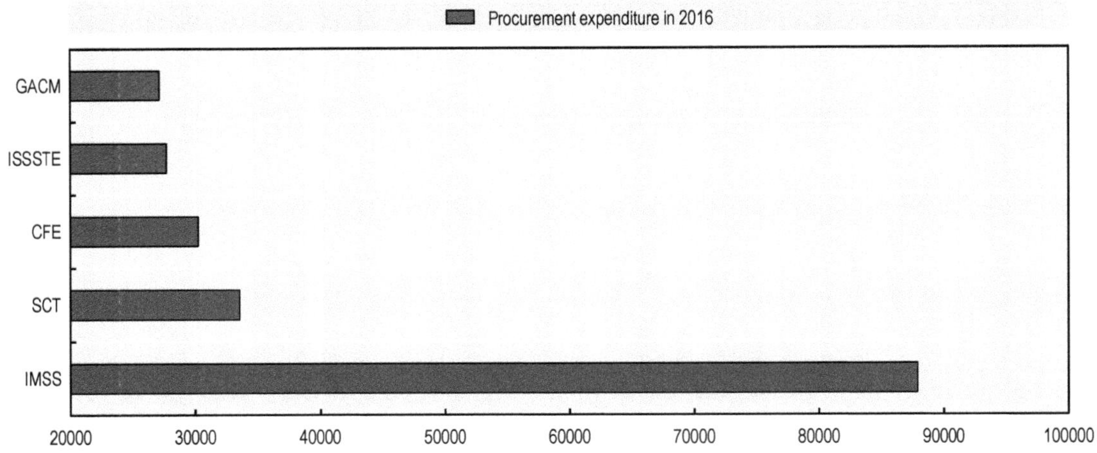

Note: GACM (Grupo Aeroportuario de la Ciudad de Mexico), ISSSTE (Instituto de Seguridad y Servicios Sociales de los Trabajadores del Estado), CFE (Comision Federal de Electrica), SCT (Secretaria de Comunicaciones y Transportes).
Source: Calculations based on CompraNet, accessible here:
https://compranetim.funcionpublica.gob.mx/Compranet/AnaliticoDependenciaEntidad.faces;jsessionid=07BC20AFFE8EE908322DD1DFFFF86FFB

In 2012 the OECD carried out a review of IMSS's procurement processes and practices, and made several recommendations in crucial dimensions (OECD, 2013[7]). These included the capacity of the procurement workforce, the information technology environment and the management of suppliers.

The review also made recommendations aimed at reducing the risk of disruption in the supply of medicines, which would ultimately affect Mexican citizens. In the years since the review, IMSS has made significant efforts to ensure that drugs are delivered in a timely and efficient manner to patients. In 2017 (up until August) this resulted in an all-time high ratio of 99.2% of medical prescriptions being fulfilled (Figure 1.5).

Figure 1.5. Number and share of prescriptions satisfied, 2013-2017

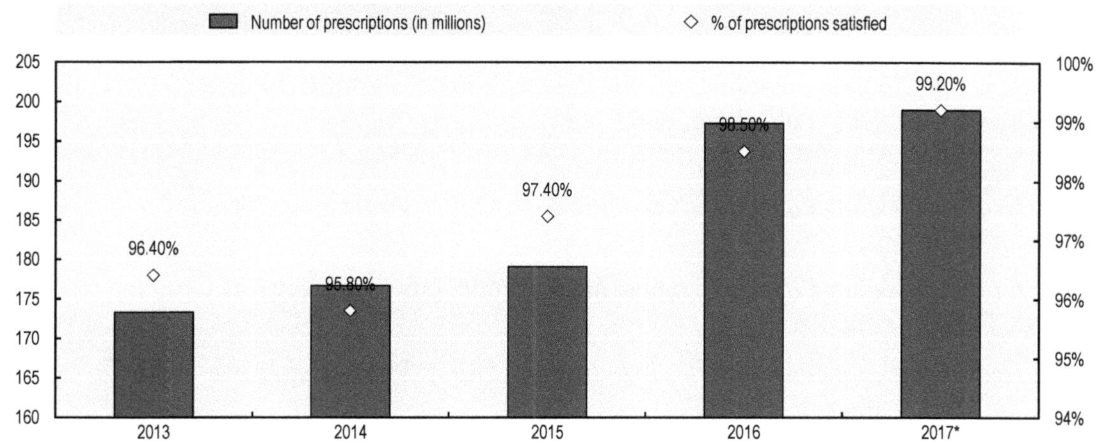

Note: Projection for 2017 based on data from January to August
Source: Information provided by IMSS

All these recommendations were meant to pave the way for better healthcare procurement practices and to support IMSS in achieving transformational reforms. This review assesses progress made, while also identifying additional improvements that will continue to increase the effectiveness of the procurement practices and strategies of Mexico's largest public buyer.

The review is structured into three main parts which provide a holistic assessment of IMSS's procurement framework and practices. It first discusses progress made and the impacts stemming from procurement reforms based on previous recommendations (OECD, 2013[7]). It then identifies further opportunities to transform IMSS's procurement function into a successful strategic governance tool. Finally, it analyses efforts and suggests additional initiatives to put IMSS at the forefront of the Mexican health system.

References

OECD (2013), *Public Procurement Review of the Mexican Institute of Social Security: Enhancing Efficiency and Integrity for Better Health Care*, OECD Public Governance Reviews, OECD Publishing, Paris, http://dx.doi.org/10.1787/9789264197480-en. [7]

OECD (2015), *Health at a Glance 2015: OECD Indicators*, OECD Publishing, Paris, http://dx.doi.org/10.1787/health_glance-2015-en. [2]

OECD (2016), *OECD Reviews of Health Systems: Mexico 2016*, OECD Reviews of Health Systems, OECD Publishing, Paris, http://dx.doi.org/10.1787/9789264230491-en. [1]

OECD (2017), *Health at a Glance 2017: OECD Indicators*, OECD Publishing, Paris, http://dx.doi.org/10.1787/health_glance-2017-en. [4]

OECD (2017), *Tackling Wasteful Spending on Health*, OECD Publishing, Paris, http://dx.doi.org/10.1787/9789264266414-en. [3]

OECD (2017), *Government at a Glance 2017*, OECD Publishing, Paris, http://dx.doi.org/10.1787/gov_glance-2017-en. [6]

Secretaría de Salud (2013), *Programa Sectorial de Salud 2013-2018, [Sectoral Health Programme 2013-2018]*, http://dof.gob.mx/nota_detalle.php?codigo=5326219&fecha=12/12/2013. [5]

Part I. Human and technological capital, enablers of strategic public procurement: Progress made and existing opportunities

Chapter 2. Strengthening the capabilities of IMSS procurement staff

Building the capability of the procurement workforce will help IMSS achieve its strategic objectives, enabling it to deliver cost-effective services to patients. This chapter explores how, by building on the work already done following the previous review, the implementation of a capability-building strategy can make a tangible difference to the effectiveness of front-line services. By learning from international best practice and implementing an attractive career path for procurement staff, IMSS will be more successful in attracting, retaining, developing and engaging its workforce.

The vision of IMSS is "to be the basic instrument of social security, established as a national public service, for workers and their families" (IMSS, 2016[1]). To achieve this objective, IMSS must provide a diverse range of products and services to support patients, including medical supplies and equipment, medication, and the general goods and services required to operate a large number of medical centres and hospitals. To provide well-performing and cost-effective health services, IMSS must be able to rely on a sound procurement system, which is able to maximise the effectiveness of outsourced or purchased goods and services in order to deliver patient outcomes. However, to deliver on IMSS's complex and technical procurement needs, and its more strategic objectives (Box 2.1), requires a skilled and competent workforce.

The demands on procurement professionals are constantly growing and diversifying, particularly as procurement is increasingly required to play a more strategic role and manage a range of complex issues. This is in addition to, as opposed to instead of, the fundamental procurement skills of developing tender documents, understanding market factors, and overseeing a fair and compliant process.

Box 2.1. The elements of strategic procurement

While efficiency and cost effectiveness are among the primary objectives of public procurement, governments are also increasingly using it to pursue additional secondary policy objectives. These refer to any of a variety of environmental and socio-economic objectives such as green growth, the development of small and medium-sized enterprises (see Chapter Eight), innovation or standards for responsible business conduct achieved through the use of public procurement. Governments increasingly use procurement as a policy lever to support such objectives, in addition to the primary objectives of public procurement: delivering the goods and services necessary to accomplish the government's mission in a timely, economical and efficient manner.

Green public procurement is defined by the European Commission as "a process whereby public authorities seek to procure goods, services and works with a reduced environmental impact throughout their life cycle when compared to goods, services and works with the same primary function that would otherwise be procured."

Innovative goods/services are those characterised by a new or significantly improved product or process. For an innovation to be considered as such, it needs to have been implemented, which is interpreted as having been introduced on the market (see Chapter Nine).

Source: (OECD, 2015[2])

The OECD's experience in its work with many countries has shown that capability is a key pillar of a sound public procurement system (OECD, 2016[3]). An efficient system includes:

1. procurement rules and procedures that are simple and clear, ensuring access to procurement opportunities
2. effective institutions to conduct procurement plans and procedures, and conclude, manage and monitor public contracts
3. appropriate electronic tools
4. suitable human resources, in numbers and skills, to plan and carry out procurement processes
5. competent contract management.

The 2015 OECD Recommendation of the Council on Public Procurement calls upon countries to develop a procurement workforce with the capacity to continually deliver value for money efficiently and effectively (OECD, 2015[4])(Box 2.2).

This chapter looks at what IMSS has done so far to implement the capability-related recommendations made by the previous OECD review and makes suggestions for further steps that could be taken to develop a workforce that is well equipped to achieve IMSS's goals (OECD, 2013[5]). The chapter outlines a path for developing and implementing a capability strategy that will not only build the skills required to deliver cost-effective and strategic procurement, but also develop a more engaged workforce.

Box 2.2. The OECD Recommendation on Public Procurement – principle on capacity

IX. RECOMMENDS that Adherents develop a procurement workforce with the capacity to continually deliver value for money efficiently and effectively.

To this end, Adherents should:

i) Ensure that procurement officials meet high professional standards for knowledge, practical implementation and integrity by providing a dedicated and regularly updated set of tools, for example, sufficient staff in terms of numbers and skills, recognition of public procurement as a specific profession, certification and regular trainings, integrity standards for public procurement officials and the existence of a unit or team analysing public procurement information and monitoring the performance of the public procurement system.

ii) Provide attractive, competitive and merit-based career options for procurement officials, through the provision of clear means of advancement, protection from political interference in the procurement process and the promotion of national and international good practices in career development to enhance the performance of the procurement workforce.

iii) Promote collaborative approaches with knowledge centres such as universities, think tanks or policy centres to improve skills and competences of the procurement workforce. The expertise and pedagogical experience of knowledge centres should be enlisted as a valuable means of expanding procurement knowledge and upholding a two-way channel between theory and practice, capable of boosting application of innovation to public procurement systems.

Source: (OECD, 2015[4])

Professionalising the IMSS procurement workforce is worth the investment

To reinforce its organisational structure and address systemic weaknesses, IMSS should consider resuming its efforts to develop a sustained, long-term procurement professionalisation programme

The previous OECD review had recommended that, to enhance the capability of procurement in IMSS, the central procurement unit should engage in strategic workforce planning in a way that addresses gaps and disseminates the institute's vision to develop a common understanding across its procurement functions (OECD, 2013[5]).

At the time of the previous review, IMSS had just transitioned from a decentralised to a centre-led model, which allowed the central procurement unit to administer more than half of the total value of all IMSS contracts, as well as establishing procurement policies and procedures for decentralised units (the Highly Specialised Medical Units – *Unidades Médicas de Alta Especialidad* or UMAEs – and regional offices, known as delegations). The transition was an opportunity to leverage the centre-led model to improve the strategic management of the IMSS workforce so as to increase procurement capability, efficiency and workforce engagement and satisfaction.

Following the OECD review, IMSS initiated a programme of work, "Strengthen the Institutional Vision and Strategically Position the Purchasing Function", to implement the recommendations. The programme included the development and rollout of a procurement strategy, and a professionalisation and accreditation action plan.

The programme made some progress, delivering several concrete actions. For example, an awareness campaign was launched for staff, entitled "*Tú Vales Mil*" ("You are worth a thousand") featuring posters and notices which highlighted the importance of the work of IMSS's procurement staff. This was reinforced through the delivery of an induction course, attended by 1 800 IMSS procurement staff (around 59% of the 3 030 IMSS staff who carry out purchasing functions nationally). It was run by in-house instructors, who ensured that participants were made aware of the overall IMSS strategic direction and procurement's supporting role. The programme was estimated to cost MXN 4 million (EUR 193 700[1]) to implement.

However, before fully implementing the recommendations of the previous review, IMSS undertook an analysis of the anticipated cost of rolling out a broad professionalisation programme. For example, one tranche of the action plan was to "Implement a System of Professionalization and Certification of Purchasing Personnel: Recruitment, Selection, Training, Evaluation of Performance, Promotion", which was broken into sub-actions and was expected to cost MXN 33.2 million (approximately EUR 1.6 million). This tranche was due to take place between April 2012 and August 2013, and to include the following components:

- working with the Ministry of Public Administration (*Secretaria de la Función Publica*, SFP) to design a buyer certification model
- providing courses and workshops to 2 280 workers on issues such as combating collusion or the public procurement law on goods, leases and services of the public sector
- strengthening managerial skills and abilities
- running a training programme on specialisation in public procurement for 600 buyers
- designing, developing and implementing a programme that identified gaps in staff skills and knowledge, and delivered targeted training to close those gaps.

However, a change in leadership and an increased focus on cost reduction meant that delivery of the action plan was halted. This was despite the initial investment to establish a plan and build the foundations of a capability strategy and action plan (see below). While the cost assessment provided IMSS with a greater understanding of the extent of investment necessary to implement the professionalisation programme, it could have been complemented by an assessment of the likely benefits deriving from such an effort.

Indeed, investing in building the capability of the public procurement workforce has been found in a variety of contexts to bring both direct and indirect benefits. According to the literature, investing in capability-building programmes provides substantial returns on investment, such as increased savings, as well as longer-term advantages. In the field of health care in the United States, one study found that investing in building the capability of procurement staff to implement improved procurement processes translated into a return on investment of 177%, meaning that for every one dollar invested, 1.77 dollars would be returned (McLinden et al., 2010[6]). Focusing on the impact of professionalisation of the procurement workforce, another study found it led to the direct ability to achieve greater cost savings and an overall maturity in category management, strategic sourcing and supplier relationship management (KPMG, 2012[7]).

Besides direct benefits, implementing a comprehensive and attractive professionalisation programme could help IMSS address a systemic weakness already identified in the previous review, which is a high rate of staff turnover. At an average of 31% per year, turnover for IMSS procurement staff continues to be high, particularly when compared to the average turnover across the rest of the organisation (11.5%), as demonstrated in Table 2.1.

Table 2.1. Turnover rate at IMSS, 2015-2016

	Average	Employees	Management
IMSS staff total	11.50%	11.34%	23.14%
IMSS procurement staff	31.66%	26.60%	38.66%

Source: Data provided by IMSS

Studies by leading research organisations in this field show that providing development and career advancement opportunities, and ensuring employees are able to connect with the organisation's strategy and goals, are among the key drivers of employee satisfaction, engagement and retention (Milich, 2014[8]; Young, 2014[9]). There is also a strong correlation between employee engagement and high organisational productivity and performance (Rayton et al., 2012[10]). The challenges of engaging and retaining staff can be exacerbated within a centre-led environment. Ensuring that employees remain focused and connected to the organisation becomes more difficult without senior management being able to regularly deliver messages to their teams in face-to-face meetings.

A high rate of turnover is costly, requiring extra expenditure on recruitment and training, and implying a loss of productivity and effectiveness. Research estimates that the cost of directly replacing an employee can be as high as 50 to 60% of their annual salary, and total associated costs of turnover can rise to 90 to 200% (Mitchell et al., 2001[11]). Given that the rate of employee turnover among procurement staff at IMSS is currently 31%, which is significantly higher than the average across the organisation (11.5%), ongoing investment in a capability strategy that can increase engagement and reduce employee turnover should lift individual and organisational performance across IMSS and ultimately result in a more efficient organisation.

However, to ensure that investment in capability-building programmes delivers tangible and lasting benefits, focus needs to be maintained on continuously encouraging employees to develop skills by institutionalising learning. According to OECD research on developing skills to lift global productivity, it is imperative that employees are given access to flexible on-the-job training and education opportunities alongside work, in order to develop and adapt their skills (OECD, 2015[12]).

The need for a well-communicated and sustained procurement capability development strategy is also emphasised by feedback received from IMSS employees who were undertaking skills assessments in 2014. IMSS identified a degree of resistance to the diagnostic exercises that they were carrying out (described later in the chapter), mainly through the low turnout of employees for the sessions. For example, of the 46 staff working at the central procurement unit who were invited, only 3 participated in the diagnostic sessions, and of the 420 staff in the delegations, only 168 participated (Figure 2.1). The reasons provided by staff pointed to a negative attitude towards the evaluation process, including the project's "lack of credibility" given "that there is no continuity in these types of programmes".

Figure 2.1. Staff participation in IMSS capability diagnostic exercises, 2014

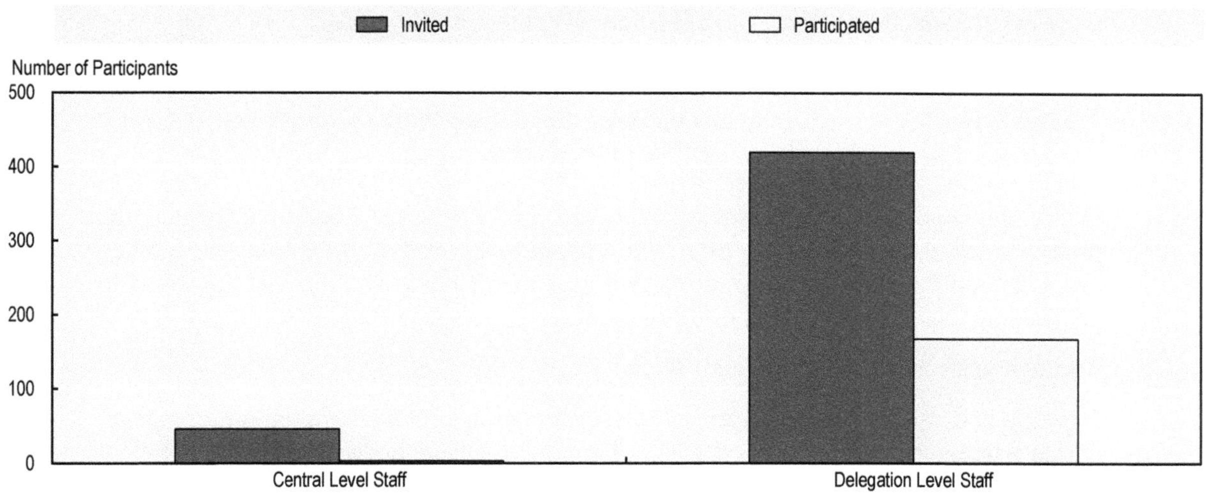

Source: Data provided by IMSS

In summary, investing in a comprehensive, far-reaching professionalisation programme could achieve tangible benefits that largely outweigh implementation costs. This programme should however be developed with a long-term perspective and not be perceived as an isolated initiative. To achieve this, IMSS needs to align the procurement capability development programme with the institution's objectives.

Creating a capability-building strategy that is aligned with IMSS's objectives

By effectively implementing a procurement capability development strategy, IMSS will be able to align human resources (HR) activity and staff performance with the institution's objectives

In an economic environment where public spending is constrained while the demands on health services and costs of providing them are increasing, an effective centre-led procurement function could help IMSS to contain cost increases, improve specifications and unlock innovation. Elevating the central procurement unit (the Administration Unit) to a position where the procurement workforce can provide strategic support to the delivery of its business objectives would therefore enable IMSS to provide better public services for its customers.

Public procurement, conducted by individuals with the requisite skills and training, can be an enabler for lowering the cost and increasing the quality and impact of public service delivery. According to Deloitte's Global Chief Procurement Officer Survey 2017, which surveyed 480 procurement leaders from 36 countries, procurement is playing an increasingly strategic role for organisations, and is using levers such as consolidating spend (40%), increasing competition (35%), specification improvement (28%), increasing levels of supplier collaboration (26%) and reducing total ownership costs (26%) in order to deliver value to their organisations. However, 60% of chief procurement officers recognised that their teams do not have all the skills required to deliver their procurement strategy, and therefore struggle to fully take advantage of this opportunity (Deloitte, 2017[13]).

An increasing number of countries are realising that the effectiveness and impact of strategic public procurement relies significantly on the skills and competencies of the procurement workforce. For example, the European Union has focussed on defining a framework for successful professionalisation programmes (Box 2.3).

Box 2.3. Draft European Commission recommendations on the professionalisation of public procurement

While developing recommendations for member states on how to approach the professionalisation of the workforce, the European Commission mapped out ten key areas, including compliance, training and systems. Taking a "Strategic approach to professionalisation" is the first of those areas.

Strategic approach to professionalisation

Develop and implement long-term professionalisation strategies, based on a strategy, an inclusive approach, improved data collection, a "needs assessment", and efficient deployment.

a) Adopt a strategy document describing the organisational approach and containing specific action plans.
b) Define strategies and action plans based on inclusive processes at national and local level.
c) Conduct thorough needs assessments based on better use of data sources.
d) Ensure professionalisation initiatives are differentiated and tailored to recipients.
e) Take into account developments in other Member States and at an international level.
f) Leverage tools and networks at national, European and international level.

Source: (European Commission, 2017[14])

A report by PricewaterhouseCooper's Public Sector Research Centre also concludes that "addressing the various factors needed to create empowered institutions to deliver public services calls for a comprehensive approach to capability-building (PwC: Public Sector Research Centre, 2007[15]). This means focusing on the following:

- Developing a clear strategy
- Ensuring commitment from leadership
- Organisational and process design
- Technology
- People and culture."

Within a large and complex organisation like IMSS, the development of a long-term procurement capability strategy would build a greater connection between the institution's overall objectives and the work done by the procurement workforce, and help to align all procurement-related HR activity.

This approach has been taken in a number of different contexts, including by the Mexican oil company, PEMEX (Box 2.4).

Box 2.4. Launching a professionalisation strategy for procurement at PEMEX

In reviewing public procurement practices at PEMEX, the OECD identified that in a challenging economic environment, the positioning of the procurement function in the organisation could create synergies with the business's strategic objectives. The decision taken by the PEMEX Board of Directors to conduct a review of the procurement function was made following an analysis of existing practices in 14 different oil companies worldwide. They took the view that by creating value, the procurement team at PEMEX could generate savings, quality and opportunity in goods, services and works acquired by PEMEX.

PEMEX is one of the main sources of business for the private sector in Mexico; it is thus critical that the company is endowed with the right number of procurement officials with a fit-for-purpose set of competencies and skills to fulfil the company's objectives. PEMEX recognises that the development of the strategic role of the procurement function will be a gradual process. In particular, PEMEX has identified three main challenges:

- completing the setup of the organisational structure and encouraging its efficient and transparent operation, with incremental added value
- developing the required competencies to adopt best practices in a timely and effective manner
- developing the personnel to facilitate the continuity of operations in key posts.

The strategy "Professionalising to Transform" (Profesionalizar para Transformar) is the first intensive effort by the Corporate Directorate for Procurement and Supply to establish a basic platform of standardised knowledge relative to the business practices that will advance the feasibility of the procurement business model, where the guiding criterion is value creation. As part of Professionalising to Transform, seven e-learning courses have been delivered to procurement staff that concentrated on the basic procurement concepts, methodologies, and strategies. These courses provide harmonised knowledge to incorporate good practices and standardise the procurement function.

Source: (OECD, 2017[16])

IMSS has already begun to develop a strategic plan for procurement overall, as part of the improvement programme that followed the previous OECD review. This included a mission statement, vision and objectives which outline how the procurement function would support IMSS's strategic objectives (Table 2.2).

Table 2.2. Draft IMSS strategic plan for improving purchasing

Title	Statement
IMSS mission	To be the basic instrument of social security, established as a public service of a national character, for workers and their families (rightful residence).
IMSS procurement vision	To be a strategic function, with personnel specialised in the subject matter, that guarantees supply at a national level, under the standards of efficiency, impartiality, transparency and regulations.
IMSS procurement mission statement	To meet the demands of the requesting areas of IMSS, through the acquisition and supply of products and services, adhering to the principles of efficiency, honesty, effectiveness and value, as well as the applicable regulatory framework, contributing to the fulfilment of the institution's strategic objectives.
IMSS procurement strategic objectives	Contribute to the achievement of IMSS's strategic objectives by satisfying the demand for goods and services in the best conditions (opportunity, quality, price) with a modern, efficient, and transparent regulatory process. Procurement adopts best practices, methodologies and systems related to supply chain in order to offer users products and services of the highest quality, standard of delivery, price, in accordance with the current legislation and regulations. It has a highly motivated, professional and certified purchasing workforce and organizational infrastructure that regulates and operates the supply process efficiently, transparently and effectively, constantly seeking to maximize the benefits of the entire value chain, with a broad sense of social responsibility that ensures that IMSS is a sustainable institution.

Source: Information provided by IMSS

This includes many of the key aspects that one would expect to be included in a mission and vision statement. However, the strategic objectives section would need to be refined if targets are to be quantifiable and measurable. Similarly, the measurable benefits that the capability strategy could deliver should be clearly defined. The lack of these elements makes monitoring and measurement of progress very difficult, while the failure to advertise the tangible benefits may explain the reticence to invest in the programme.

While this is a notable first attempt to develop a procurement capability-building strategy, it now needs to be complemented by several additional actions to ensure its effective implementation. Provided that IMSS wishes to continue with this approach, its next step is to translate the above statements into a plan. This plan should ensure alignment between the organisation's overall objectives (listed in the table) and the strategies put in place to develop the workforce to deliver them (Figure 2.2).

Figure 2.2 illustrates how the organisation's objectives should serve as a point of reference with which the capability strategy should be aligned. The capability strategy should lead to a series of activities required to implement it:

- a competency model that maps out the skills required of the procurement workforce in order to deliver the strategy
- a needs analysis to identify the largest gaps between the capabilities of the workforce and those required by the competency model
- an action plan which identifies the steps required to close the capability gaps in a sustainable way – this would include recruitment, training and succession planning
- ongoing performance management of the workforce and notably the achievement of its objectives.

Figure 2.2. The linkages between IMSS's strategic objectives and capability strategy

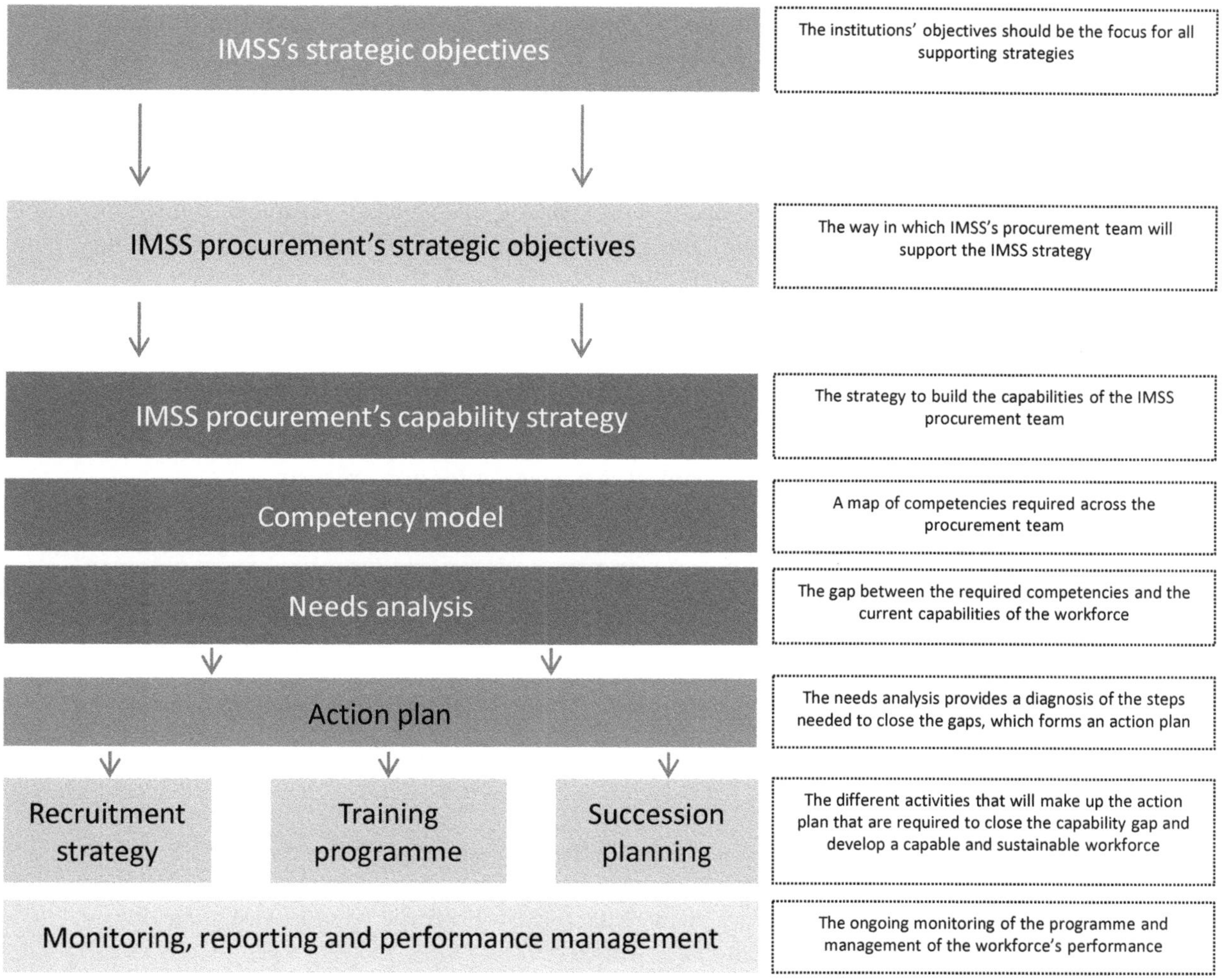

By ensuring that each of these steps is aligned to each other and the overall IMSS strategy, the central procurement unit can ensure greater coherence in achieving IMSS's institutional objectives, even with a dispersed procurement workforce.

Developing a competency model that reflects the diversity of procurement's role

To ensure that the procurement workforce can demonstrate the diverse skills required to execute the IMSS strategy, a comprehensive competency model could be developed which reflects the strategic role of procurement and defines a career path through the organisation

Competencies can be described as "the skills, knowledge and behaviours that lead to successful performance" (Civil Service and The Rt Hon Lord Maude of Horsham, 2012[17]). The previous OECD review already highlighted the need to develop a performance management system, including a competency model, in order to improve organisational effectiveness and help to connect employees to the agency's mission and goals (OECD, 2013[5]). In 2014, IMSS undertook work to establish competencies for its procurement function. The 19 competencies were grouped into four categories, and are outlined below:

- Directive competencies: administrative process; decision making; negotiation; effective communication; leadership.
- Competencies of action and teamwork: results-focused; initiative; tenacity; innovation; collaborative working.
- Competencies of personal effectiveness: stress management; self-awareness; self-control; emotional intelligence; flexibility.
- Technical competencies: contract planning; contracting; contract administration.

The technical competencies listed above are expanded in Table 2.3. However, while they include important activities within the procurement lifecycle, they do not reflect the strategic nature of procurement activities. For example, there are no references to activities related to managing relationships with suppliers, or working closely with medical professionals on technical specifications. Neither is there an indication to staff of the skills, knowledge or behaviours required to carry out these activities, or how they should be applied in their daily work.

Table 2.3. IMSS's technical competencies for procurement

Planning	Procurement	Contract management
Identify needs and stocks	Conduct market research	Determine and dictate early termination and / or suspension
Estimate prices	Select procurement methods and carry out the procedure	Determine termination of contracts
Integrate and generate the demand needs analysis	Award contracts	Prepare settlements and cancel guarantees

Source: Information provided by IMSS

Given that progress in implementing many initiatives stemming from the OECD review has waned, despite the initial work in this area, there is currently no agreed set of procurement-specific competencies or a recognised job profile for the vast majority of employees within the IMSS procurement workforce.

Some work has been done at the federal level in Mexico to establish core competency skills and develop certification for procurement professionals. The "Executive Action to Prevent Corruption and Avoid Conflicts of Interest" organised training and certification of public servants involved in public procurement in order to ensure their honesty and to establish a base-level of performance (Secretaría de la Función Pública, 2015[18]). However, it is unclear how the skills included in that certification programme or the competencies related to honesty and performance are factored into IMSS's work on competencies.

Interviews carried out during the field mission stressed the need for general training to build skills such as the use of Microsoft Excel and proficiency in writing. While commonly required for many different positions, the absence of these skills could hinder the development of a workforce geared towards strategic procurement. Indeed, proficiency in writing is instrumental in developing or reviewing technical specifications and ensuring their clarity. These skills have not been identified in the competency model. If they were included, recruitment and training processes could target skills in this area.

The content of a fully developed competency model ideally includes: categories or clusters of competencies (i.e. a group to which homogeneous and/or similar competencies belong); the competencies that make up each cluster; a definition of each competency;

and several behavioural indicators of each competency (i.e. behavioural examples that an individual should demonstrate if they possess that competency) (Draganidis and Mentzas, 2006[19]). Furthermore, the competency model can be divided into tiers so as to demonstrate the standards expected at each level of the organisation (see Box 2.5 for a UK example). This will also serve to enhance the level of professionalisation at IMSS by demonstrating the standards expected of individuals undertaking procurement even at the lowest levels of the organisation. Demonstrating that staff are being given opportunities to develop and progress is also likely to reduce employee turnover.

A tiered competency model could set the standard for employees throughout the IMSS procurement workforce, with training programmes, job profiles, performance management and recruitment processes all aligned to these standards, and to the overall IMSS mission. If developed effectively, a competency model will outline the behaviours that are (and are not) expected of IMSS staff (Box 2.5), and will demonstrate that staff throughout the organisation have the opportunity to progress, providing a "line of sight" to senior roles within the organisation.

One additional area that can be clarified through the competency model relates to the technical skills and knowledge required of procurement practitioners. Discussions during the fact-finding mission highlighted the importance of the role of clinicians in developing specifications for tenders and in evaluating tender responses. This makes IMSS heavily reliant on clinicians and other individuals with technical knowledge to conduct many of the critical steps during the procurement process. However, medical professionals do not typically have a full understanding of the procurement cycle or an appreciation of how procurement activities should be delivered, and so a partnership with procurement professionals is required to deliver the best outcomes. This means identifying a number of individuals with the ability to develop high levels of technical proficiency, who can also communicate with authority when dealing with clinicians. This may involve developing a specialist role for procurement professionals who are capable of delivering complex medical procurement projects. It may also mean building into the IMSS competency model a requirement for certain procurement professionals to develop a sufficient level of technical knowledge to be able to review and validate the work of clinicians in developing technical specifications and in evaluating tender documents.

Providing an objective viewpoint during the development of specifications and the evaluation of tenders is a critical part of procurement's role in fighting corruption. An OECD report on Preventing Corruption in Public Procurement found that corrupt tactics were sometimes employed by the technical service responsible for comparing the offers during the evaluation phase (OECD, 2016[20]). These included tailoring technical specifications for specific companies and revising bids upwards. By building their technical and negotiation skills, procurement practitioners will be more able to hold internal colleagues to account and ensure that procurement processes are fair and objective.

Box 2.5. "Behavioural people" in the UK's civil service competency model

The UK Government's competency model for its civil service is a generic model that is applicable to all types of government roles. Civil servants are told that if they "work as part of a profession with a separate framework this complements (their) professional framework and should be used alongside it", meaning that these standards are required of all employees and more specific standards may be applicable to certain roles.

The model focuses on ten competencies, grouped into three "clusters", with each one broken down into six levels, from Director General/Director at Level 6 to Administrative Officer at Level 1. The model describes six behaviours that effective employees are likely to demonstrate, and six behaviours that ineffective employees are likely to demonstrate. These behaviours are provided for each level for each of the ten competencies.

Source: (Civil Service and The Rt Hon Lord Maude of Horsham, 2012[17])

Outlining a needs-driven capability-building action plan for the entire employee lifecycle

To be sure that appropriate staff capabilities are developed, maintained and recognised, IMSS should develop a targeted capability-building action plan that covers the whole employee lifecycle

In order to implement a long-term, sustainable approach to employee development, IMSS should implement an action plan that considers all parts of the employee lifecycle, ensuring that from recruitment to performance management, a common set of competencies is identified and reinforced. Such an action plan could be more targeted and efficient if investment is focussed on the capabilities that are most lacking in the procurement workforce, and roles and responsibilities of those implementing the action plan are clearly defined.

Conducting a capability needs analysis to develop targeted training

The European Commission recommends that as part of taking a strategic approach to professionalisation, institutions "conduct thorough needs assessments based on better use of data sources" (European Commission, 2017[14]). This is in line with the recommendation of the previous OECD review, which suggested that IMSS "carry out a diagnosis, at the local entity level, of potential areas of opportunity in technical and staff skills" (OECD, 2013[5]).

A diagnostic exercise was carried out in 2014 to implement this recommendation. The exercise was conducted electronically using two psychometric tools that were distributed to staff by email. The tools measured employees against the 16 non-technical competencies that formed part of the procurement competency model developed by IMSS. This provided IMSS with data on the average levels of capability across its workforce. As an example, Figure 2.3 provides the findings of the capability assessment for one particular IMSS team.

Figure 2.3. Competency diagnostic of the Coordination of Purchasing Goods and Contracting Services Team

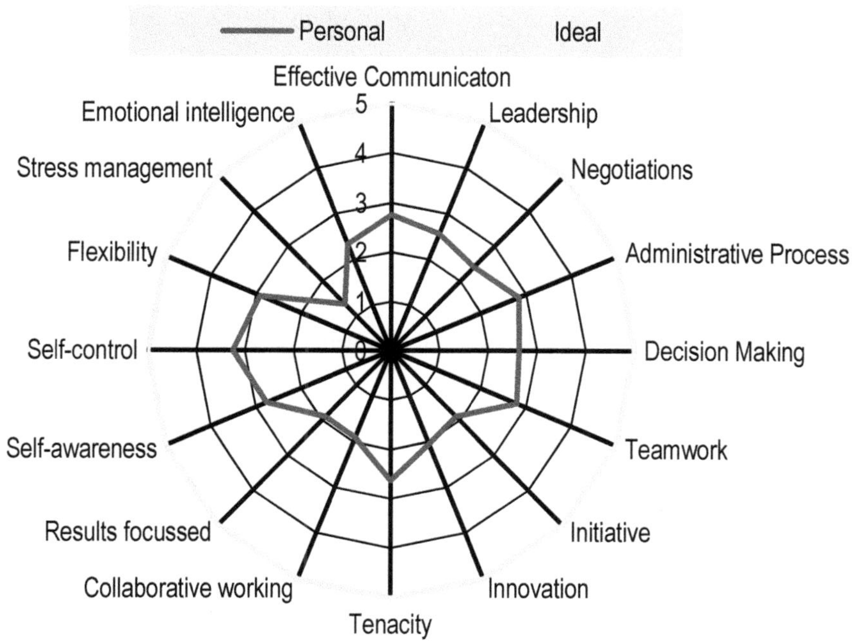

Source: Information provided by IMSS

However, this diagnostic exercise focused on "soft skills" and personal traits, as opposed to technical or procurement-specific skills. Therefore, it has not been able to provide IMSS with a full picture of capability levels across the range of skills required of procurement professionals. Neither did the diagnostic seek to identify the training methods that were most effective, the processes that could alert staff to training events, or the different levels of training that would be required by the various staff grades. However, running additional diagnostic sessions to fill these information gaps would be costly and could add to staff frustration.

Slovakia recently conducted a targeted training gap analysis exercise featuring detailed discussions with key individuals (Box 2.6). The analysis was not restricted to the capability gaps of the workforce – it also explored the effectiveness of the institution's entire training programme, including the employees who were targeted, the training methods used, and how applicable the training content was for the areas in greatest need of development.

Box 2.6. Gap analysis of training needs in Slovakia

To develop a training action plan to strengthen the capacities of the procurement workforce in the Slovak Republic, a gap analysis was conducted using a questionnaire that sought to capture the current training situation. The questionnaire focused on three dimensions, each identified as being significant in determining the capability of the procurement workforce. Sample questions have been provided for each of the three dimensions below:

- Characteristics of the procurement workforce:
  - Is the procurement workforce clearly identified?
  - How is the workforce composed?
  - What is the typology of the public procurement workforce in terms of professional experience?
- The performance of the procurement system:
  - What is the share of procurement operations subject to open tender?
  - How many instances are there of irregularities leading to financial corrections?
  - What are the main grounds for objections and complaints?
  - Which secondary policy objectives are most frequently implemented (green procurement, innovation, support to SMEs, etc.)?
- The training system in place:
  - Are there eligibility criteria for training participants?
  - How visible are training opportunities to staff members?
  - Are training courses structured according to seniority or according to different roles in procurement lifecycle?
  - What subjects are currently included in the training curriculum?
  - What types of delivery models are available (in-class, e-learning, distance learning) and are classes a mix of theory and practical?
  - What is the frequency of trainings and are there mandatory hours/events for staff to attend?
  - Is feedback collected from training participants?

This analysis enabled a thorough assessment of the existing training on offer, its content and structure, and perceptions both from trainers and trainees' perspectives. Fifty responses were gathered from trainers and participants, allowing for the identification of areas in greatest need of focus. Thirty-five individuals from 20 different entities were interviewed to discuss responses in more detail and investigate further training needs.

Source: (OECD, 2016[21])

Conducting a similar exercise at IMSS would avoid the need for a costly analysis of the entire workforce. The analysis could evaluate the average skill levels and the areas of greatest need across a cross-section of the workforce. This would provide a sufficient benchmark to enable a targeted action plan to be developed. To enable its effective implementation, the plan would also need to allocate clear roles and responsibilities to the multiple actors involved.

Defining roles and responsibilities to ensure coordination of HR activities

Within IMSS, HR responsibilities are spread across several units. Should an action plan be developed without having the roles and responsibilities of the different HR teams clearly defined, there is a risk that a lack of accountability and coordination will impede the plan's delivery. Table 2.4 gives a non-exhaustive indication of how responsibilities for HR matters are currently spread among just three of the different units.

Table 2.4. Sample of HR responsibilities of three IMSS units

Unit	Administration Unit (*Unidad de Admistracion*)	Personnel Unit (*Unidad de Personal*)	Organisation, Capability and Competitiveness Unit (*Unidad de Organizacion, Capacitacion y Competitividad*)	
Team	Co-ordination of the Aquisition of Goods and Contracting Services(*Coordinaction de Adquisicion de Bienes Y Contratacion de Servicios*)	Co-ordination of the Management of Human Resources (*Coordinaction de Gestion de Recursos Humanos*)	Co-ordination of the Modernisation of the Administration (*Coordinacion de Modernizacion Administrativa*)	Co-ordination of Competency and Training (*Coordinaction de Competetividad y Capacitacion*)
Responsibility	To approve the selection, appointment and changes in the secondment of the personnel in positions; structure the services that make up coordination at a national level, based on institutional norms and policies.	Co-ordinate, control, evaluate and inform the processes, plans, programmes, projects, systems, strategies, mechanisms and actions in the field of management and administration of the institute's human resources.	Check that the regulations and guidelines issued regarding the issuance and control of specific rules, procedures and methods of work are complied with by the Decentralised Operational and Administrative Bodies, in administrative modernisation procedures, studies, organisational, management and regulatory improvement.	Co-ordinate the implementation of training needs preparation, and preparation of the preliminary draft of the training budget, in order to formulate the Annual Institutional Training Programme.
	Validate and sanction specific training programmes for "basic' and "trustworthy' personnel.	Determine the plans and programmes for selection of personnel both for new entrants and when promoting existing "basic" and "trustworthy" staff, for decentralised administrative operations and regulatory bodies, in order to implement the policies and institutional guidelines, verifying compliance.	Co-ordinate actions to measure and promote improvements in organisational culture.	Approve the Annual Institutional Training Programme so that training aligns with the institution's strategy and complies with applicable regulations.
		Supervise the achievement of goals in the areas of workforce planning, human resources and personnel services for centralised staff, in accordance with Personnel Unit policies.	Co-ordinate the performance of organisational effectiveness studies for the different administrative units of the institute, to identify areas with opportunities for improvement.	Implement measures for the issuance of training plans for internal training and supporting documentation.

Source: Information provided by IMSS

Co-ordinating HR activity across so many departments reinforces the need for a well-articulated action plan that is agreed by all key stakeholders. It also means that responsibilities for implementing the various elements of the action plan must be clearly allocated. Clear accountability for the plan's delivery through the assignment of actions to different teams will also lead to a more efficient use of resources. For example, a procurement training programme would need to align with SFP's own training programme in order to take advantage of the SFP professionalisation programme and avoid duplication. It would also need to align with the Annual Institutional Training Programme developed by the Organisation, Capability and Competitiveness Unit (see Table 2.4).

Developing a multi-faceted action plan to hire, develop and retain procurement staff

However, training is just one part of the "employee lifecycle", and just one part of the coordinated activity that is required to ensure that staff are well-trained, engaged and effective. Competency frameworks, job profiles, certification systems and training should all be focused on providing attractive, competitive and merit-based career options for public procurement professionals.

This section has been broken into different elements of the "employee lifecycle" in order to assess initiatives in each area and suggest areas for improvement.

Recruitment processes

Public procurement systems need to attract motivated and skilled individuals in order to build their effectiveness. Public procurement is a multidisciplinary profession that requires, among other things, the knowledge of law, economics, public administration, accounting, management, and marketing. These interdisciplinary skills are increasingly required, given the growing complexity of public procurement processes and the shift to strategic procurement.

Effective recruitment processes will not only identify suitable applicants from outside of the organisation, but also increase the engagement of internal applicants. By demonstrating a commitment to open, fair and transparent processes for recruiting and hiring individuals into roles based on merit, IMSS would also motivate internal staff, thus reducing employee turnover rates.

According to current recruitment practices, the hiring process is managed centrally, including for the recruitment of individuals within the delegations. The assessment of employees is based on a number of factors, including the use of voice analysis to assess responses to a telephone interview on integrity. The assessment process does not currently test the level of an applicant's technical skills, however, and is based on interview performance as opposed to an examination.

A more rounded and diverse assessment process, that includes a technical skills component or role-play situations focused on negotiation or stakeholder engagement skills, could lead to the appointment of candidates more suited to the diverse skillsets required of procurement practitioners. A broader assessment process may also be less likely to discriminate against individuals from technical backgrounds who are applying for management roles for the first time.

Training programmes

In Mexico, responsibilities for procurement training programmes lie with several entities and are based on different objectives. At the federal level, the Ministry of Public Administration (*Secretaria de la Función Publica*, SFP) is responsible for establishing guidelines for the responsibilities of public servants in relation to public procurement.

The SFP provides free training for public servants of the Federal Public Administration to support the effective execution of their duties. Table 2.5 summarises SFP's training programme, which combines topics on general procurement with the use and administration of centrally-developed framework agreements.

Table 2.5. SFP's procurement-related training courses

	Courses on acquisition, leasing and services	Courses on public works and related services
General	Best practices in public procurement	
	Basic course on CompraNet	
Specific	The social witness in public procurement procedures	
	Provisions applicable to contracts financed with external credits	
	Market research in LAASSP	Market research for public works
	Use of framework contracts	Hiring of public works under the condition of payment at an elevated price
	Consolidated contracts	Hiring of public works under the condition of payment at unit prices
	Criteria for evaluating proposals in the LAASSP	Mechanisms for evaluating proposals for public works
	Modification of contracts in the LAASSP	Modification of contracts in the public works law
	Subsequent discount offers	Recruitment of contracts in the public works law
	Workshop on economic tools applied to public procurement	Review of indirect costs and financing in PUs
Video courses	Consolidated contracts	
	Use of framework contracts	
	Importance of the promotion of good practices in public procurement for the improvement of public management	
	Global procurement initiative: achieving value in public works and infrastructure procurement procedures	
	Law of acquisitions, leases and services of the public sector	
	Methodology for market research	
	Public procurement strategies	

Source: Information provided by SFP

Training at IMSS is currently delivered in an ad hoc way, and is typically delivered to senior staff, unionised staff, or to induct new staff. Training is targeted at specific issues, for example to support the implementation of a new information system. Users of CompraNet (the Mexican national e-procurement system, see Chapter 3) also receive training on the use of the system. However, general procurement training is only delivered to limited cohorts of staff. In 2016, only 80 members of staff received training on procurement-specific issues, focusing on procurement laws. The training was delivered in-person and was co-ordinated centrally, taking place in Mexico City. The duration of the course was three days per week for four hours each day over a period of a month.

Besides ad-hoc training, a professionalisation course was initiated in 2014, which resulted in 13 individuals achieving a Diploma in Competence Development for Public Procurement following a three-year training programme. The course was targeted at "General Directors, Directors, Commissioners responsible for monitoring the Auditors,

Administrators, Consultants, Managers and Directors in the Public Sector" and featured 4 modules of 32 hours each

According to research by McKinsey, organisations are now shifting their spending on capability-building to focus both on functional roles and "frontline" employees (McKinsey & Company, 2015[22]). While leadership roles are obviously still targeted for leadership development training, more technical procurement training should be focused on the larger majority of the workforce that is engaged in procurement activities as part of their day-to-day role.

The make-up of the IMSS procurement workforce does not necessarily lend itself to centrally-administered and located training, with 72 staff employed at the central level, and 300 employed at the local level. This does not include individuals in Operative Vulnerability Positions, of which there were 1 038 positions in 2016 (870 of which were occupied). These employees conduct the vast majority of purchasing activity, but are not typically invited to participate in training activity. While targeting the staff directly involved in purchasing activity would be a worthwhile objective, the cost of administering training to a large and geographically dispersed workforce can be high. Traditional methods involve engaging third parties to deliver in-person courses in different regions.

However, methods such as e-learning are increasingly being used to deliver training to a broader audience in a cost-effective way while keeping track of progress achieved by participants (OECD, 2016[21]). The use of such training methods would open access to training beyond the cohort that currently has the opportunity to participate, leading to the broader professionalisation of the IMSS procurement workforce.

Other than e-learning, a large number of other training methods and formats exist, many of which would be less costly and equally as effective as delivering in-person training to decentralised units. These new methods include formal and informal coaching, mobile learning exercises (e.g. podcasts, videos, job aids), off-site experiential learning programmes (e.g. model factories or offices), job-shadowing (potentially with IMSS medical staff), partnerships and networks, and distance learning programmes. Different training methods are also likely to have different levels of effectiveness according to the subject that is being delivered.

At the time of the field mission, the training programme for 2017 had not yet been approved, but it was proposed to feature courses on transparency and the implementation of the procurement-related aspects of laws related to anti-corruption (the *Ley General del Sistema Nacional Anticorrupción* and the *Ley General de Responsabilidades Administrativas)*). While these are topics with which IMSS's procurement workforce are often confronted, a more tailored approach to training matched to specific roles would bring additional efficiencies. This can be done either through conducting the aforementioned needs assessment process to target identified skill deficiencies across the workforce, or through allowing managers to develop training programmes that are based on the development needs of their employees or teams.

The training programme can be a blend of topics, methods and sources. For example, IMSS has partnered with other institutions to provide courses on the fundamentals of procurement. This course will allow public procurement individuals from different institutions that are at the early stages of their procurement careers to share experiences, while the institutions share the training costs. Providing choice to staff and managers will allow training courses and other learning opportunities to be brought together into individual development plans that are tailored for each employee.

Performance management and succession planning

The previous review identified the implementation of a performance management system as a key deliverable of the improvement programme (OECD, 2013[5]). This system was implemented in 2015. However, for procurement professionals, much of the focus of the performance review is on soft skills, and does not cover technical or procurement-specific skills. This is certainly down to the fact that, as previously noted, there is currently no agreed set of procurement-specific competencies or a recognised job profile for the vast majority of employees within the IMSS procurement workforce.

Beginning to formally measure employee performance unlocks a wealth of HR management data. This can be used for a number of activities, including workforce planning (in the tracking and measurement of employee satisfaction, engagement and retention); assessing management performance and the success of training programmes; and transparently sharing performance progress with employees. Figure 2.4 details how these data are currently used in OECD member countries.

Figure 2.4. Use of HR management data in OECD countries

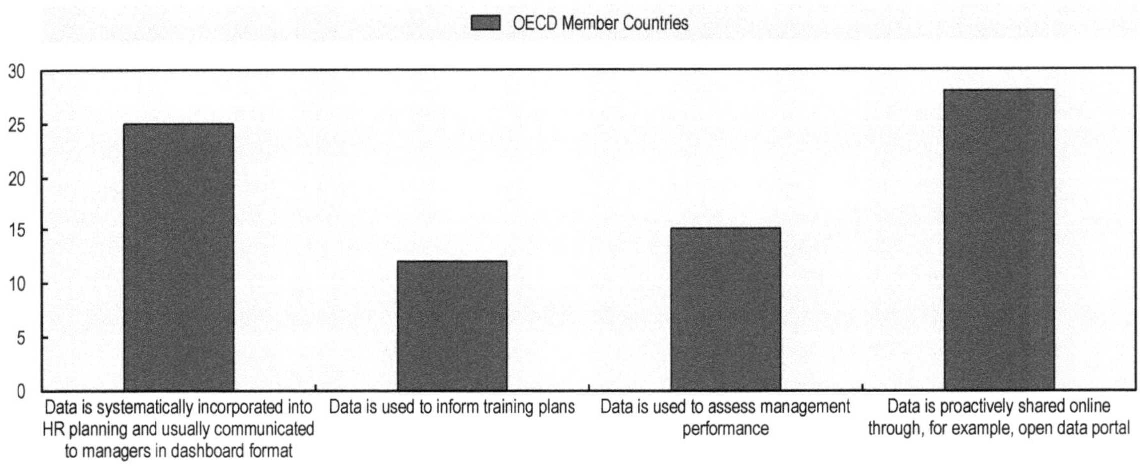

Source: (OECD, 2017[23])

As previously discussed, a set of measurable objectives must be developed to monitor the achievement of IMSS's procurement strategy to develop "a highly motivated, professional and certified purchasing workforce and organizational infrastructure that regulates and operates the supply process efficiently, transparently and effectively, constantly seeking to maximize the benefits of the entire value chain, with a broad sense of social responsibility that ensures that IMSS is a sustainable institution" (see Table 2.2). These objectives can then be translated from an organisational to an individual level, so that employees can be encouraged to deliver the strategy by including relevant performance objectives in their individual performance agreements or development plans. Figure 2.5 illustrates how these objectives can "cascade" through the organisation, using the example of reducing IMSS's carbon footprint.

Figure 2.5. How objectives flow from organisational to individual

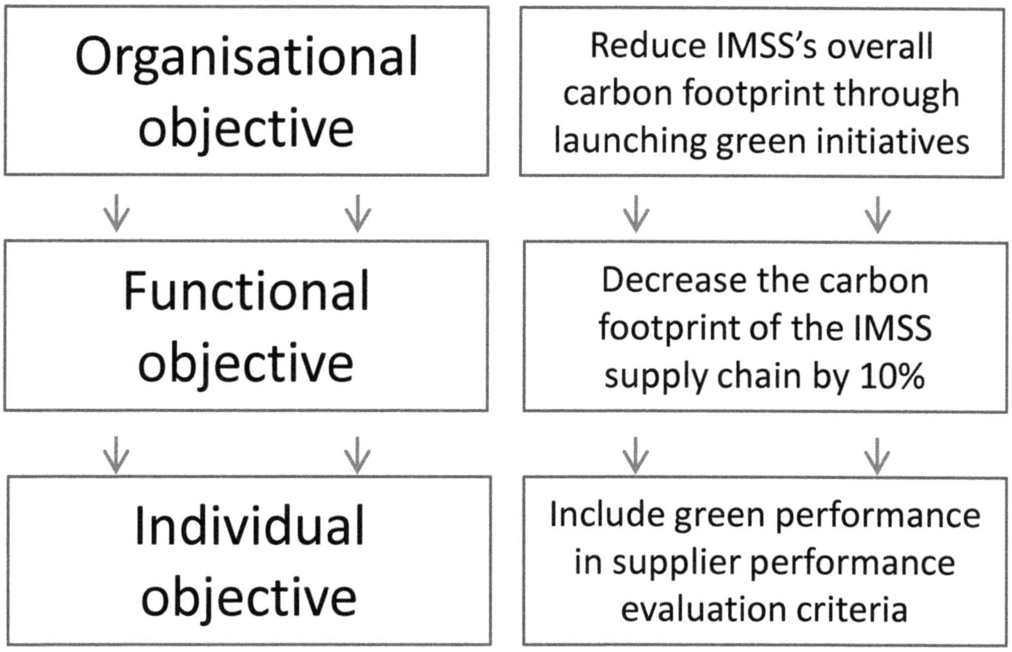

Source: Authors' analysis based on information provided by IMSS

By aligning strategies, objectives and competencies, IMSS can ensure that staff have the incentives to deliver against IMSS's overall objectives, as well as ensuring that HR practices and policies provide officials with the skills and motivation needed to deliver against those objectives.

As part of a performance management system, individuals within IMSS should be encouraged to develop and progress through the organisation. This can then lead to the systematised identification of individuals with the potential to progress to senior leadership roles should they receive the necessary training and development opportunities. The evolution of lower-level staff to take on senior roles at IMSS represents a significant opportunity to reduce recruitment costs and build a pipeline of staff who have developed an understanding of IMSS from the lowest levels of the organisation. A visible commitment to succession planning can also assure staff that opportunities exist to rise up the ranks within the organisation.

Proposals for action

IMSS should address systemic weaknesses by resuming efforts to develop a procurement capability strategy. This would take advantage of the work already done to centralise procurement activities, and would be a worthwhile, long-term investment with tangible benefits that largely outweigh implementation costs. This programme should however be developed with a long-term perspective and not be perceived as an isolated initiative. To achieve this, IMSS needs to align the procurement capability development programme with the institution's objectives. Specific steps required include the following:

Develop a capability development strategy designed to support the achievement of IMSS's institutional objectives

- Frame the capability strategy around the role of procurement as a strategic tool for delivering public services.
- Articulate the role of procurement practitioners in containing cost and unlocking innovation.
- Clearly identify the benefits that can be expected from building procurement capability in order to secure the investment required to implement the strategy.
- Outline how achievement of the objectives and benefits will be carried out and how progress will be monitored, ensuring clear links to the organisation's vision for strategic procurement.

Establish a comprehensive competency model that lists the diverse skills required, is tailored to the strategic role of procurement and defines a career path through the organisation

- Group the competences required at different levels of the organisation.
- Provide behavioural examples that demonstrate to staff how they can exhibit the skills required.
- Include the technical, practical and strategic skillsets that enable procurement practitioners to effectively perform their jobs.
- Focus competency frameworks, job profiles, certification systems and training on providing attractive, competitive and merit-based career options for public procurement professionals.

Develop a targeted capability-building action plan with clear roles and responsibilities

- Ensure the action plan looks at the whole employee lifecycle to ensure that capacities are developed, maintained and recognised from recruitment onwards. This can be done by aligning job profiles, recruitment selection criteria and performance agreements with a common competency model.
- Conduct a high-level review of the capabilities of a cross-section of the IMSS workforce.
- Ensure the action plan clearly outlines the roles and responsibilities of various human resources teams and other actors in order to maximise the return on investment.
- Include any relevant (and achievable) objectives in employees' performance agreements to incentivise performance.
- Make a visible commitment to succession planning to assure staff that opportunities exist to rise up the ranks within the organisation.

Note

[1] At 1 EUR = MXN 21.0697.

References

Civil Service and The Rt Hon Lord Maude of Horsham (2012), *Civil Service competency framework*, https://www.gov.uk/government/publications/civil-service-competency-framework (accessed on 09 November 2017). [17]

Deloitte (2017), "Growth: the cost and digital imperative The Deloitte Global Chief Procurement Officer Survey 2017", http://www.deloitte.co.uk/cposurvey2017 (accessed on 08 September 2017). [13]

Draganidis, F. and G. Mentzas (2006), "Competency based management: a review of systems and approaches", *Information Management & Computer Security*, Vol. 14/1, pp. 51-64, http://dx.doi.org/10.1108/09685220610648373. [19]

European Commission (2017), *Commission Recommendation on the professionalisation of public procurement: Building an architecture for the professionalisation of public procurement*, http://ec.europa.eu/docsroom/documents/25614 (accessed on 09 November 2017). [14]

IMSS (2016), *Acerca del IMSS*, http://www.imss.gob.mx/conoce-al-imss (accessed on 09 November 2017). [1]

KPMG (2012), "The Power of Procurement: A global survey of Procurement functions", https://assets.kpmg.com/content/dam/kpmg/pdf/2012/07/the-power-of-procurement-a-global-survey-of-procurement-functions.pdf (accessed on 09 November 2017). [7]

McKinsey & Company (2015), *Building capabilities for performance*, https://www.mckinsey.com/business-functions/organization/our-insights/building-capabilities-for-performance. (accessed on 09 November 2017). [22]

McLinden, D. et al. (2010), "Evaluating the future value of educational interventions in a health care setting", *Performance Improvement Quarterly*, Vol. 22/4, pp. 121-130, http://dx.doi.org/10.1002/piq.20071. [6]

Milich, V. (2014), *A key driver of employee engagement*, Hay Group, http://blog.haygroup.com/a-key-driver-of-employee-engagement/ (accessed on 09 November 2017). [8]

Mitchell, T. et al. (2001), "How to keep your best employees: Developing an effective retention policy", http://www.csus.edu/indiv/s/sablynskic/documents/keepingyourbest_000.pdf (accessed on 09 November 2017). [11]

OECD (2013), *Public Procurement Review of the Mexican Institute of Social Security: Enhancing Efficiency and Integrity for Better Health Care*, OECD Public Governance Reviews, OECD Publishing, Paris, http://dx.doi.org/10.1787/9789264197480-en. [5]

OECD (2015), *Government at a Glance 2015*, OECD Publishing, Paris, http://dx.doi.org/10.1787/gov_glance-2015-en. [2]

OECD (2015), "OECD Recommendation of the Council on Public Procurement", https://www.oecd.org/gov/ethics/OECD-Recommendation-on-Public-Procurement.pdf (accessed on 14 September 2017). [4]

OECD (2015), *The Future of Productivity*, OECD Publishing, Paris, http://dx.doi.org/10.1787/9789264248533-en. [12]

OECD (2016), *Roadmap: How to Elaborate a Procurement Capacity Strategy*, http://www.oecd.org/governance/ethics/Roadmap-Procurement-Capacity-Strategy.pdf (accessed on 09 November 2017). [3]

OECD (2016), "Preventing Corruption in Public Procurement", http://www.oecd.org/gov/ethics/Corruption-in-Public-Procurement-Brochure.pdf (accessed on 09 November 2017). [20]

OECD (2016), "Developing Administrative Capacity for Public Procurement in the Slovak Republic: A Training Action Plan for 2016 - 2019", http://www.oecd.org/gov/public-procurement/publications/capacity-public-procurement-slovak-republic-training.pdf (accessed on 09 November 2017). [21]

OECD (2017), *Public Procurement Review of Mexico's PEMEX: Adapting to Change in the Oil Industry*, OECD Public Governance Reviews, OECD Publishing, Paris, http://dx.doi.org/10.1787/9789264268555-en. [16]

OECD (2017), *Government at a Glance - 2017 edition*, https://stats.oecd.org/Index.aspx?DataSetCode=GOV_2017 (accessed on 11 September 2017). [23]

PwC: Public Sector Research Centre (2007), "The road ahead for public service delivery", https://www.pwc.com/gx/en/psrc/pdf/the_road_ahead_for_public_service_delivery.pdf (accessed on 09 November 2017). [15]

Rayton, B. et al. (2012), "THE EVIDENCE: Employee Engagement Task Force - Nailing the evidence workgroup", http://engageforsuccess.org/wp-content/uploads/2015/09/The-Evidence.pdf (accessed on 09 November 2017). [10]

Secretaría de la Función Pública (2015), *8 Acciones ejecutivas para prevenir la corrupción y evitar posibles conflictos de interés | Secretaría de la Función Pública | Gobierno | gob.mx*, https://www.gob.mx/sfp/acciones-y-programas/acciones-ejecutivas-para-prevenir-la-corrupcion-y-evitar-posibles-conflictos-de-interes (accessed on 09 November 2017). [18]

Young, S. (2014), *What are the top drivers of employee attraction, retention and sustainable engagement?*, WillisTowersWatson, https://www.towerswatson.com/en-GB/Insights/Newsletters/Europe/HR-matters/2014/12/What-are-the-top-drivers-of-employee-attraction-retention-and-sustainable-engagement (accessed on 09 November 2017). [9]

Chapter 3. Relying on comprehensive information to inform public procurement decisions at IMSS

Fully exploiting comprehensive information from different sources will help IMSS to develop tailored strategies aiming at enhancing its procurement outcomes while delivering cost-effective services to its beneficiaries. Given the potential offered by the digitalisation of procurement processes, this chapter explores how IMSS could further leverage on existing IT tools to enhance the overall efficiency of its procurement system. Furthermore, this chapter analyses how procurement intelligence could support IMSS in delivering on its strategies. Last, this chapter discusses how IMSS could further evidence the added-value and impact of its procurement strategies.

The statistical data for Israel are supplied by and under the responsibility of the relevant Israeli authorities. The use of such data by the OECD is without prejudice to the status of the Golan Heights, East Jerusalem and Israeli settlements in the West Bank under the terms of international law.

As every policy area, public procurement is governed by a specific regulatory framework which includes the set of rules each contracting authority should follow. The legislative framework however doesn't in itself provide those entities with all means to ensure efficient and effective public spending. To do so, besides legislative provisions and manuals, procurement officials need to rely on information available from a variety of sources to tailor specific strategies ensuring efficient outcomes. This is not less central in health procurement. Indeed, efficient spending through sound public procurement practices provides the opportunity to improve the quantity and quality of health products and services and ensure their delivery in a timely manner Information to define procurement strategies and measure the performance of the system could be provided by an enabling technological environment. Therefore, this chapter will assess the degree to which the digitalisation of IMSS procurement system contributes to its overall efficiency. Furthermore, this chapter also identify opportunities to further strengthen the collection, structuring and use of procurement-related information at the different stages of the procurement cycle. The analysis refers also to the recommendations provided by the OECD in the previous review of IMSS including recommendations on the e-procurement system (OECD, 2013[1]). It will therefore assess the implementation and impact of the various OECD recommendations

Digitalising procurement to improve efficiency

To further streamline procurement operations, IMSS could leverage on existing information systems, both internal and external

Given the sheer volumes of money involved in public procurement, and recognising the benefits of e-procurement, many countries (OECD and also non-member countries) have developed e-procurement systems in recent years. E-procurement systems can significantly simplify the way procurement is conducted, reduce waste and deliver better procurement outcomes (European Commission, 2016[2]).

E-procurement refers to the integration of digital technologies in the replacement or redesign of paper-based procedures throughout the procurement process. It is an effective tool to increase transparency, facilitate access to public tenders, increase efficiency through automation of tasks, reduce direct interaction between procurement officials and companies, increase outreach and foster competition. The OECD Recommendation on Public Procurement calls upon countries to improve public procurement systems by harnessing the use of digital technologies to support appropriate e-procurement innovation throughout the procurement cycle (OECD, 2015[3]). A well-functioning e-procurement system can advance many of the other pillars of a sound public procurement system. It is a pivotal instrument to generate information to inform future public procurement decisions.

The digitalisation of the procurement process includes two main aspects: (1) digitalising the external platforms publicising tendering processes; and (2) digitalising the internal systems supporting whole-of-procurement activities, including tender preparation and contract management till the completion of the contract. As shown in Table 3.1, all OECD countries have e-procurement systems with various functionalities covering the whole procurement cycle.

Table 3.1. Provision of e-procurement functionalities

	Announcing tenders	Provision of tender documents	E-submission of bids	E-reverse auctions	Notification of award	E-submission of invoices	Online catalogue
Australia	●	●	●	○	●	○	○
Austria	●♦	●♦	●♦	♦	●	●	♦
Belgium	●	●	●	●	●	♦	●
Canada	●	●	○	○	●	♦	♦
Chile	●	●	●	○	●	○	●
Denmark	●♦	♦	●♦	♦	●♦	●♦	○
Estonia	●♦	●♦	●	●	●	♦	○
Finland	●	●	●	●	●	●	♦
Germany	●♦	●♦	●♦	○	●♦	○	○
Greece	●	●	●	●	●	○	○
Hungary	●	●	○	○	●	○	○
Iceland	●	●	○	○	●	●	○
Ireland	●	●	●	○	●	○	○
Israel	●♦	●♦	○	●	●	●	○
Italy	●♦	●♦	●♦	♦	●♦	●	●
Japan	●♦	●♦	●♦	○	●♦	●♦	●♦
Korea	●	●	●	○	●	●	●
Latvia	●♦	●♦	●	○	●♦	○	○
Mexico	●	●	●	●	●	○	○
Netherlands	●	●	●	○	●	○	●
New Zealand	●	●	●	●	●	♦	●
Norway	●	●	♦	○	●	♦	♦
Poland	●	♦	○	●	●	○	●
Portugal	●	●	●	●	●	○	●
Slovak Republic	●	●	●	●	●	○	○
Slovenia	●	●	○	●	●	●	●
Spain	●	●	●	○	●	●	●
Sweden	♦	♦	♦	♦	♦	♦	○
Turkey	●	●	●	○	●	○	○
United Kingdom	●	♦	♦	♦	●	♦	♦
OECD Total							
● In a national central e-procurement system	29	26	21	11	29	10	11
♦ Only in e-procurement systems of some specific procuring entities	1	4	3	5	1	7	5
○ No	0	0	6	14	0	13	14

Source: (OECD, 2017[4])

Much fewer countries have e-procurement systems covering the entire procurement cycle, including electronic submission of bids, contract management or provision of invoices. Yet greater digitalisation of the procurement process can act as a commercial incentive for suppliers which impacts on productivity through for instance time savings and costs savings (EBRD, 2015[5]). It could also impact internal productivity, one of the five goals of IMSS's institutional programme for 2014-2018, by automating repetitive administrative tasks.

In Mexico SFP is in charge of implementing the federal e-procurement system CompraNet. The system has been launched since 1996 and has been continuously improving. The use of CompraNet is mandated by the two public procurement laws:, the law of Acquisitions, Leases and Services of the Public Sector (*Ley de adquisiciones, arrendamientos y servicios del sector público* – LAASSP) and the Law of Public Works and related services (*Ley de Obras Publicas y servicios relaciando con la misma* – LOPSRM); and their regulations: the Regulation of the LAASSP (Reglamento de la Ley de Adquisiciones, Arrendamientos y Servicios del Sector Público- RLAASSP) and the Regulation of the LOSRM (*Reglamento de la Ley de Obras Publicas y servicios* – ROPSRM).

CompraNet's main objectives are:

- contributing to harmonised policies for public procurement in the federal public administration
- promoting transparency in the procurement process
- generating the necessary information for the adequate planning, scheduling and budgeting of public procurement activities.

Although all functionalities in CompraNet are supporting those objectives, the electronic submission of bids provides multidimensional benefits. The submission of electronic bids facilitates data analysis and retrieving information. As described in Table 3.1, Compranet includes this functionality; however according to article 26 of LAASSP, this functionality is not mandatory. Contracting authorities can decide whether to allow electronic submissions or not and can ask economic operators to submit their bids either on paper, electronically, or both (mixed or hybrid procedure)).

When tenders are submitted in hybrid or paper form, contracting authorities have to organise clarification meetings and bid opening sessions that involve the physical presence of all bidders. For electronic processes, on the other hand, bidders can participate virtually, reducing the direct costs for both contracting authorities and suppliers relating to the organisation and attendance of those mandatory meetings. Some electronic bidding information, such as prices, can also be automatically integrated into IMSS's internal procurement system, the SAI. When IMSS receives paper based bids, minimum information is manually reported in the SAI by IMSS officials. The manual process includes a risk of error which can affect data quality and harm the quality and efficiency of the system.

According to data provided by SFP, in 2016, less than half (46%) of bids were submitted electronically, representing 59% in terms of procurement volume. There has been a remarkable increase in the use of full electronic procedures in the last five years – from 7% of procedures in 2012 to 46% in 2016. While mixed procedures decreased from 2012 to 2015, it is worth noting that this decrease was not only in favour of electronic procedures, but also paper-based procedures (Figure 3.1).

Figure 3.1. Number of procurement tenders by type of submission

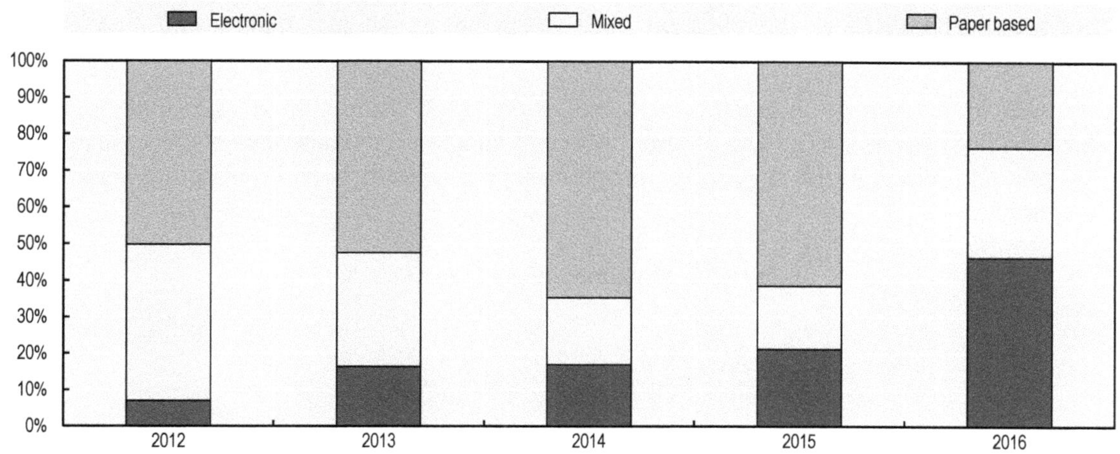

Source: Data provided by SFP

Among the challenges usually identified when implementing an end-to-end mandatory e-procurement system are stakeholder's objections (EBRD, 2015[5]). These include objections from the private sector, linked to concerns about the lack of remote connectivity, the low level of computer literacy, data security etc. However, despite the Internet penetration rate in Mexico (around 56% of the population in 2016 according to (Internet World Stats, 2016[6])), representatives of the private sector interviewed during the fact-finding mission clearly indicated their preference for electronic procedures, while noting potential issues with the upload of heavy documents. Taking these views into account, IMSS could benefit from further promoting e-submission in its procurement procedures, not only to eliminate red tape costs, but also to enhance data quality in supporting future public procurement decisions.

With increased electronic information, IMSS could build on the benefits of direct integration with its internal IT systems. These systems are mainly used for managing the entire procurement cycle, in particular the pre-tendering and contract management phase. They are often based on Enterprise Resource Planning (ERP) tools, which are used not only for procurement activities, but also for the management of human resources, finance and other areas, ensuring increased visibility, automated processes, improved efficiency and productivity. Being off-the-shelf solutions, those systems could however be further customised to fit specific strategies and legislative environments. Table 3.2 describes the benefits of an effective IT system for procurement activities.

Table 3.2. Benefits of a strong IT system

Functionality	Benefits
Spend visibility	View spend by procurement categories/ suppliers/ units, etc
Stock management	Management of stocks on a regular basis to ensure meeting the needs
Electronic purchase orders	Issue electronic orders taking into account available stocks
Automatic workflows	Faster validation process and transparency
Data collection	Development of indicators

Source: adapted from (Australian Government,(n.d.)[7])

IMSS has two systems in place to manage procurement activities: the SAI and the Institutional Resources Planning (*Planeacion de Recursos Institucionales* – PREI). The SAI has been developed in 1997 and implemented in 2000 to support IMSS procurement activities. The PREI is the platform used by IMSS to manage budget and financial information.

In line with its strategy of technical modernisation, IMSS decided in 2008 to incorporate SAI modules to the PREI. This migration would enable to enhance the efficiency of the system and have a full visibility on procurement activities and budgeting aspects (Figure 3.2).

Figure 3.2. Functionalities of the new SAI

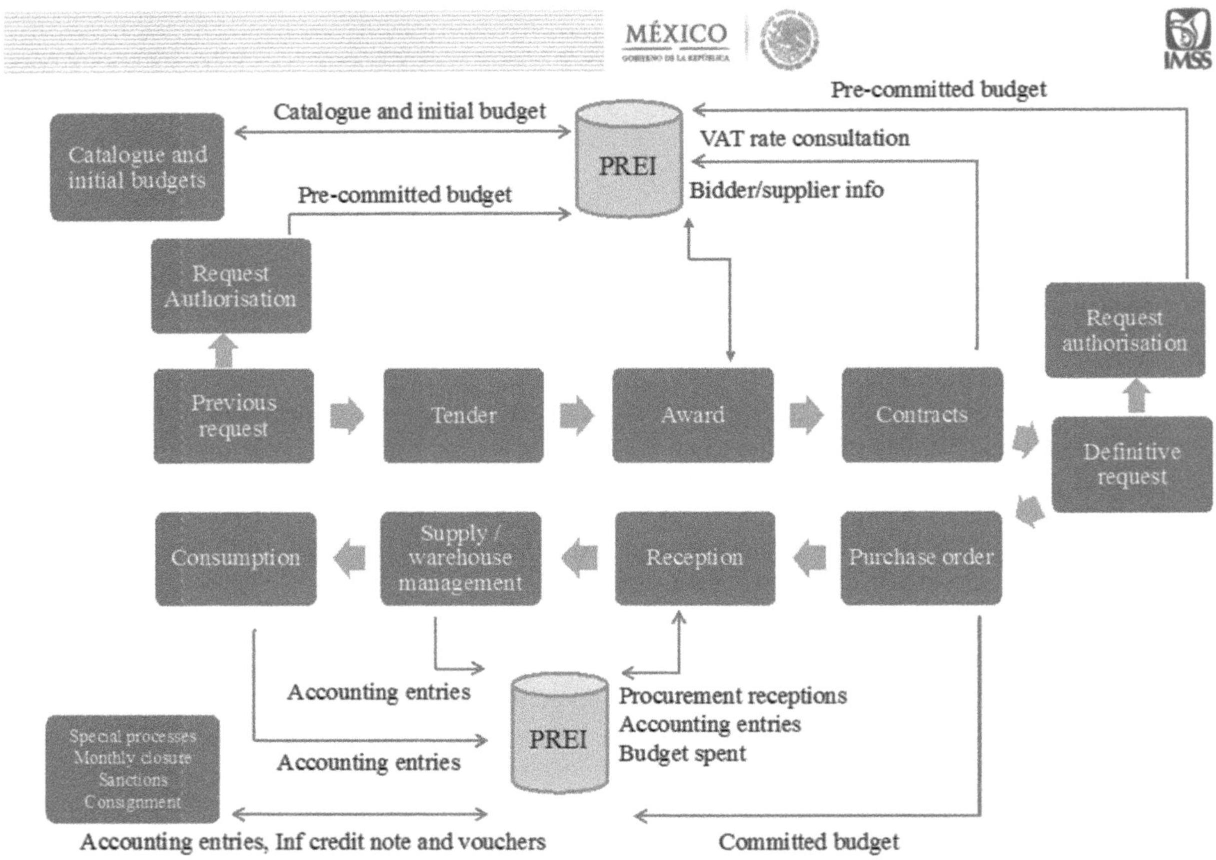

Source: Information provided by IMSS

Doing more to align IMSS's IT systems with current procurement strategies

IMSS used to have another IT tool to carry out some procurement processes – the single registry of suppliers (*Bolsa Unica de Ofertas*-BUO). It was used by delegations and UMAEs to address immediate needs based on prior authorisation from the central level. These immediate needs might include a supplier's non-performance, unsuccessful tenders or unforeseen exceptional needs. Interested potential suppliers had to register in this platform and provide information on the categories of goods and services they could supply and with what conditions. To enhance the efficiency of the system and to reduce duplications, the last OECD review recommended that IMSS enhance the BUO by integrating it with CompraNet (OECD, 2013[1]). However, IMSS did not manage to integrate the BUO with Compranet due to the cost of the technological modifications required. Instead, IMSS carried out further investigations into the efficiency of the system and decided to stop using the BUO platform in 2014. The institute realised that the system did not promote competition or encourage suppliers to give their best offers since they knew that IMSS entities would not risk a supply disruption. Suppliers used to set high reference prices which were harming the efficiency of the system.

Following this decision, IMSS then introduced a new process called "Local procurement" (*Compras locales*). The main goal of this scheme is to determine terms and characteristics that UMAEs and delegations have to follow when undertaking a procurement procedure. Unlike the BUO, the local procurement scheme has to be undertaken through CompraNet and requires budget validation by the central area.

As IT tools should support organisations' strategic objectives, IMSS could benefit from pursuing the analysis of its information system to assess whether it is supporting its procurement strategies. For example, IMSS could assess whether the current functions of its systems are aligned with its daily procurement practices.

While the integration of the SAI modules to the PREI and the "Local procurement" process represent a clear improvement for IMSS, it could be further improved to meet international best practices and to be in line with the legal framework for procurement. For example, for the bid evaluation, Article 36 of the LAASSP only allows for the use of the "pass or fail" or binary method (*criterio binario*) if it is not possible to use the points and percentage evaluation mechanism. However, the new system is built to support procurement processes using only the binary method.

The current system also only includes sections on prices submitted by bidders. It doesn't allow for the entry of points associated with other criteria (technical, environmental, etc.) or the weights associated to each criterion. This prevents procurement officials from using other evaluation methods to undertake a comprehensive bid analysis based on multi-award criteria. This limitation of the current system is maintained in the new system integrating SAI modules to the PREI harming the overall efficiency of the procurement system. IMSS should consider bringing its information system in line with the legal framework, which enables procurement officials to use the most appropriate evaluation method (award criteria, their weights and scoring method), which will support increased efficiency of the entire procurement system.

Having an automated process is crucial to ensure the efficiency of the system and to increase the productivity of the different stakeholders involved in the procurement process; however to reap the benefits of automation, stakeholders need to be informed about the process stages. Following the tender procedure and the notification of contracts, the new system does not include automatic notification to Requiring Areas of the availability of contracts. This means that Requiring Areas need to check regularly to see if contracts are available in order to issue purchase orders. This undermines the productivity and efficiency of the system.

In addition, while IMSS has developed a specific web interface for suppliers, the system does not include an automatic notification to alert suppliers of the issuance of purchase orders. From January to September 2017, IMSS issued on average 3 081 purchase orders per day. Again, suppliers need to regularly check the web interface to make sure they are aware of all purchase orders issued, increasing the risk of delays of urgent purchasing.

IMSS should consider adding notifications to its IT system for relevant stakeholders involved in the procurement process.

Besides additional opportunities in the management of tenders and contract execution, IMSS's internal system should also be flexible and scalable enough to ensure it serves different procurement strategies. As an example, procurement strategies identifying leasing schemes as opposed to buying might require different accounting rules. No less important is to adapt the internal system to the organisational structure of IMSS's procurement function.

Improving internal sharing of information would inform IMSS procurement strategies

Procurement takes place at different levels: at the national level through consolidated tenders, centrally and by the UMAEs and the delegations. Around 57.5% of IMSS's procurement activities, representing around USD 2.27 billion,[1] are undertaken by the delegations and UMAEs. While all entities are using the same system, they each have dedicated servers which provide information to the central database. When goods and services are not procured under the centralised scheme, each IMSS entity undertakes its own procurement procedure. In this system, officials from a specific entity only have access to information related to procurement activities undertaken at their entity level. If they want to consult contractual conditions or prices offered or paid by other IMSS entities, for instance, officials need to access the information through CompraNet, though this information may not even be available there. Indeed, as discussed later in this chapter, data on CompraNet are not always harmonised and are rarely reusable.

Sharing information among IMSS's different entities would help the decentralised entities define the most appropriate procurement strategy. The internal information system does not include a "read-only" mode, which implies that if IMSS's central procurement unit gives access to information on a specific entity to officials from other entities, data could be modified. Enabling all officials involved in procurement activities to access to IMSS-wide procurement information in a "read-only" mode would be useful to tailor procurement strategies and ensure consistent practices across all entities.

In addition, critical documents – such as market analysis undertaken by each delegation and UMAE, as well as at the central level – are not integrated into the internal IT systems. Each official in charge of a specific procedure keeps the documents on their own computer. This risk losing the information over time and duplication of effort by entities undertaking similar procurement procedures. IMSS could consider developing a platform for sharing such information among procurement officials from the different levels. Box 3.1 gives the example of an information system developed in France in 2016 by Resah, a public interest group aiming at supporting the performance of the health sector.

Box 3.1 Sharing procurement information in France

Resah aims at supporting the performance of the health sector through the aggregation of demand and the professionalisation of the procurement workforce. It has two main activities: a central procurement body and a centre of expertise. Considering that IT tools can be a lever for operational performance, in 2016 the Resah developed an IT platform with four modules: 1) aggregation of demand; 2) standardisation, 3) performance management; and 4) exchange.

The exchange module's main objective is to serve as a collaborative platform for procurement officials from the various entities and hospitals which form part of the group. It includes three main spaces:

- Communication: news, exchange fora
- Contact details: joint directory, organisation chart per hospital department, etc
- Work: Good practice sheets, satisfaction questionnaires, exchange of best practices

Beyond merely sharing procurement data, this information-sharing system creates a community of users who exchange ideas on procurement best practices and provide insights into strategic stages of the procurement cycle, such as information necessary to design procurement strategies.

Source: Adapted from (Resah, 2016[8])

Using procurement intelligence to help IMSS implement its strategies

Successful procurement activities require matching demand with supply. Demand analysis, also referred to as needs analysis, is the first step in procurement. However, it is not limited to analysing the quantities of goods and services required; it is also about understanding the needs in terms of performance and functionalities expected. Indeed, demand which is oriented towards solutions and not products has the potential to improve public service delivery (Chapter 9).

In addition, demand analysis should go hand in hand with a sound market analysis to identify the characteristics, capacity and capability of the supply market. This will enable an understanding of the extent to which the market can meet the needs of the procuring entities (Figure 3.3). These two steps affect the tender design and the whole procurement cycle since they shape the tender documentation. This is why – in line with international best practice – procurement entities should view these as strategic rather than administrative tasks. Market and demand analysis should no focus only on high value tenders at the central level; those are required steps to undertake for each procurement procedures taking place at all levels.

Figure 3.3. Functionalities of the new SAI

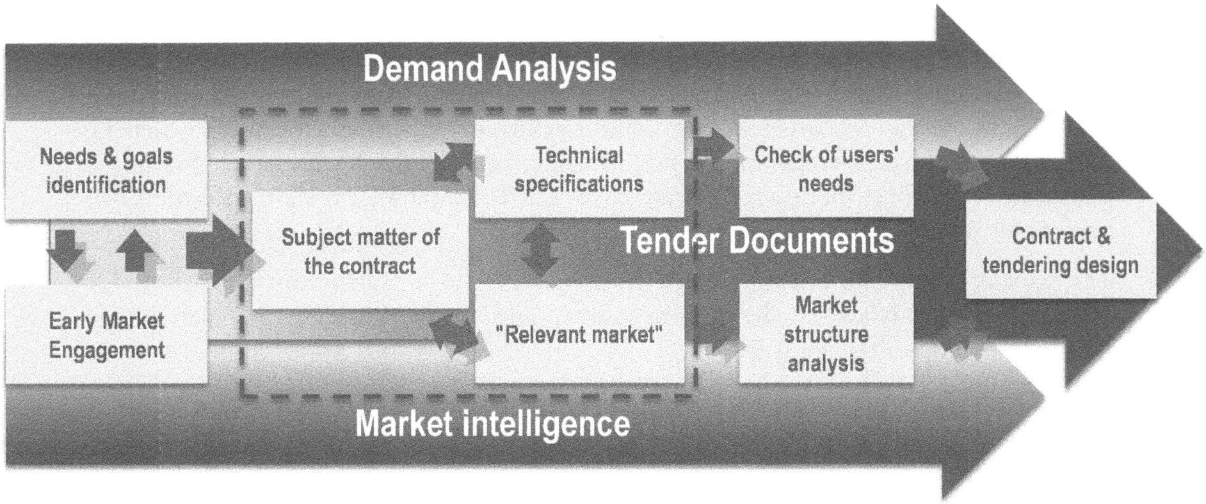

Source: (OECD, 2017[9])

To unleash the power of consolidated tenders, IMSS could better capture decentralised needs

IMSS procurement activities are performed at three levels: locally, by delegations and UMAEs; centrally, when aggregating the needs of delegations and UMAEs; and nationally, aggregating IMSS's needs with those of other entities of the health system through consolidated tenders. Demand analysis is typically performed over a two-week period and is based only on existing products and services and on historical procurement. Decentralised entities have to identify products and services included in the six internal catalogues derived from the national catalogues (*cuadros basicos*): drugs, healing material, food, auxiliary diagnostic, instruments and medical equipment, osteosynthesis and endoprotesis.

The Co-ordination of Supply Control department (CCA) is responsible for collecting and analysing the needs of the UMAEs and delegations. This demand analysis involves five steps:

1. The CCA disseminates guidelines to Delegations and UMAEs for determining needs and calculating demand based on the universal operative catalogue for therapeutic goods and services and the schedule of activities.
2. Delegations and UMAEs report their needs through the internal procurement system (SAI).
3. The CCA analyses and validates their needs, identifying variations based on the validated average consumption and the real consumption of the previous year.
4. The CCA informs delegations and UMAEs of the main variations to enable them to ask for further clarifications or to make the necessary adjustments before including them in the final version.
5. The CCA consolidates the final requirements and analyses the products and services to be procured through the centralised procurement scheme. Products and services with specific characteristics, or which are not commonly procured, will be procured directly by the local entities.

On the basis of this demand analysis, IMSS's central procurement unit decides on the level of aggregation of needs in the annual procurement programme-PAAAS. (Figure 3.4). These steps enable the annual procurement programme to be completed.

Figure 3.4. Impact of demand analysis on the procurement strategy

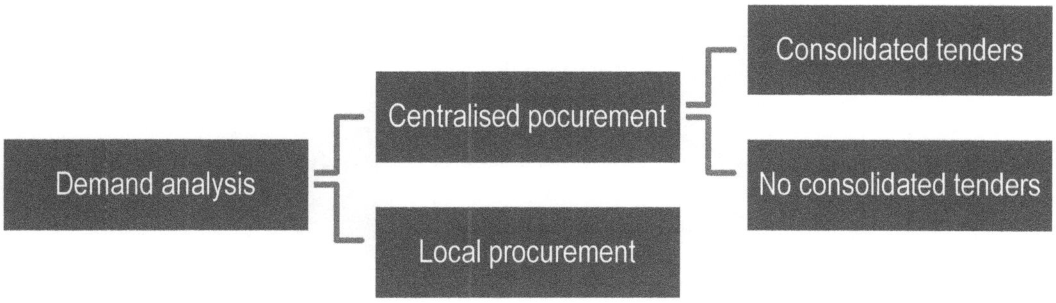

Source: Information provided by IMSS.

Demand analysis does not capture the performance or functions expected; each delegation and UMAE might also have specificities which will require solutions with specific characteristics or functions. Understanding the specific requirements of decentralised entities beyond the products or services required is central to the decision on the level of aggregation, however. This has been a problem in some consolidated tenders for medicines where different delivery requirements have hindered them from achieving their overarching objectives.

Consolidated tenders or joint procurement arrangements aggregate the demands of the various entities. This gives them increased purchasing power and offers opportunities for economies of scale and lower administrative costs for the entities that are part of the agreement ((Burns and Lee, 2008[10]) and ; (Nollet and Beaulieu, 2005[11])). IMSS started consolidated tenders in 2011 with one partner (SEDENA). By 2016 more than 40 partners were involved, dramatically scaling up the impact of the exercise. In order to achieve their objectives and their potential to generate savings and reduce transaction costs, initial demand analysis needs to be complemented by a more detailed assessment of public entities' requirements (Figure 3.5).

Figure 3.5. The process involved in consolidated tenders

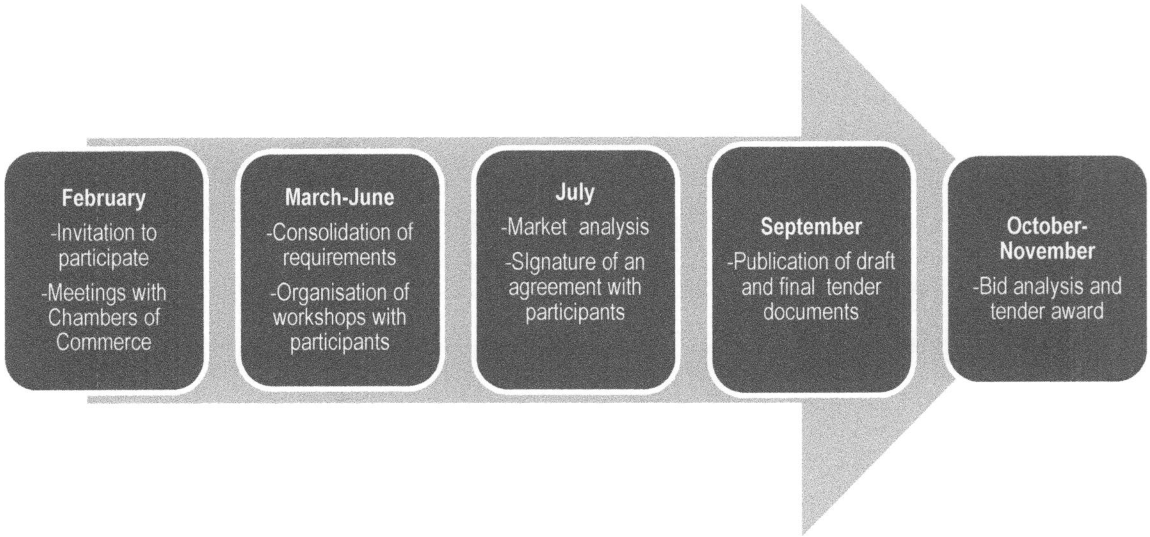

Source: Information provided by IMSS.

In order to reap the benefits of consolidated tenders and demand aggregation, according to accepted good practices, a number of criteria and parameters need to be taken into account:

- Homogenous needs: ensuring that entities have the same needs for products and services under the consolidated tender.
- Financial situation of each partner: including partners with financial issues might represent a risk for the suppliers, who then might apply a uniform premium for all prices of products and services under the consolidated tender.
- Delivery options (time, location and quantity) of each partner: the presence of several delivery options in the same contract can make it hard to disentangle the incremental value of a particular delivery option
- Timing of purchase: timings need to be aligned across entities, meaning that the starting date of the contract should be convenient for everyone.

In the consolidated tenders managed by IMSS, there is no specific process for selecting the entities to be part of the agreement. Indeed, any entity interested in joining the consolidated tender can do so if they fulfil basic requirements: providing the required information, having substantial needs and providing benefits to the tender. However, no further analysis is performed to analyse factors such as the different delivery options or the financial situation of entities part of the agreement. Given that suppliers have to set uniform prices, some entities may have to pay a premium because of other entities' specific requirements or financial situation. As the primary mission of health institutions is to provide universal health access, the analysis of partners' financial situation should not lead to their exclusion. However, entities should provide guarantees to reassure potential suppliers. IMSS should review its methodology for consolidated tenders to include a careful analysis of all the different parameters in order to implement mitigation measures if needed.

A better engagement with suppliers and understanding their capabilities would help IMSS in coping with concentrated markets

In addition to capturing internal demand, procurement strategies and tender design are also defined according to knowledge of the market (Figure 2.3). Effective communication channels are needed between the private sector and public officials in charge of procurement activities for two main reasons. First, it will enable potential bidders to better understand the entity's needs, and second it will provide officials in charge of drafting or reviewing technical specifications with a better understanding of market capabilities (see also Chapter 4).

Information asymmetries often arise in public procurement since potential suppliers often have more information than the contracting entity on their costs, prices, market trends, products or services, and their substitutes. Therefore, engaging with suppliers could help decrease the information gap for the contracting entity by allowing them to collect more reliable and up-to-date information on the market.

Engagement with the private sector could involve two elements, depending on the time at which it occurs. As mentioned above the public entity could provide general information on future procurement opportunities to alert potential suppliers on future tenders. It could also engage in more detailed exchanges with the market to shape a specific procurement strategy. Both types of effort could help to mitigate market concentration and attract new suppliers. As shown by a recent survey of procurement practice across the OECD, the private sector is consulted to varying degrees at different stages of tender design (Figure 3.6).

Figure 3.6. Supplier consultation at different stages of framework agreement (FA) preparation

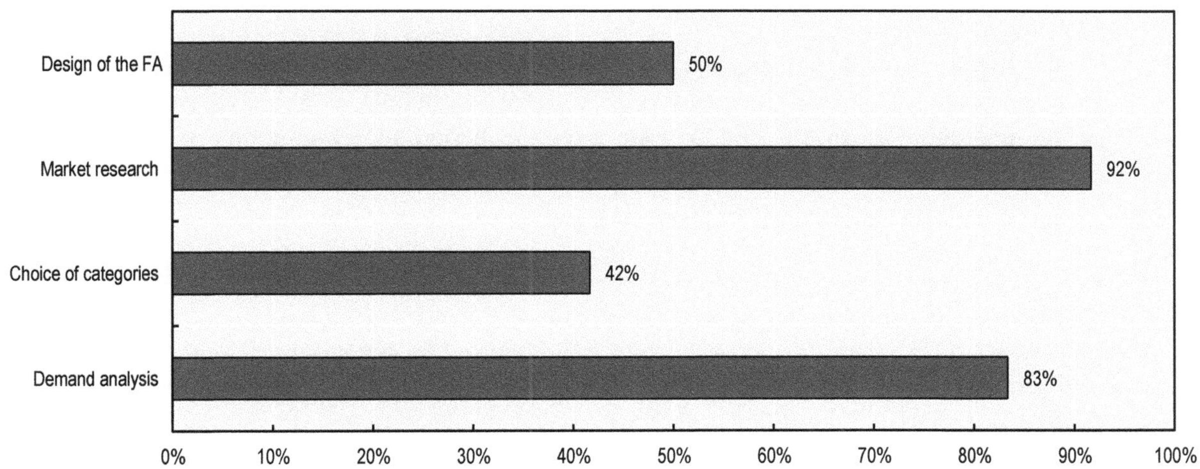

Note: The figure is based on responses received from 11 OECD countries—namely, Belgium, Canada, Chile, Finland, France, Greece, Hungary, Italy, New Zealand, Portugal and Spain—and 2 non-OECD countries—Colombia and Costa Rica.
Source: (OECD, 2017[12])

Every year the Mexican Ministry of Economy organises a public procurement fair ("*Expo Compra de Gobierno*") to raise supplier awareness. This fair serves as a platform for contracting authorities and potential suppliers to meet and discuss procurement opportunities and the existing solutions in the market. In 2015, 17 ministries and 93 public entities participated in this fair, including IMSS and other large contracting authorities such as PEMEX and the Federal Electricity Commission (*Comisión Federal de Electricidad*, CFE). Those IMSS officials who have participated reported clear benefits, though only officials from the central area of IMSS attended. IMSS could consider also involving and inviting procurement officials from UMAEs and delegations to give them a better sense of the market's capacity.

Some entities in other OECD countries organise similar meetings and events with suppliers, but on a more regular or sector-oriented basis. IMSS could benefit from organising similar events. Box 3.2 provides an example of "speed-dating events" in New Zealand.

Box 3.2. Procurement "speed dating" in New Zealand

"Meet the Buyer" is an event that brings small and medium-sized enterprises (SMEs) together with large purchasing organisations, giving them both an informal platform for engagement. The highlight of the Meet the Buyer event is the series of 15-minute pre-arranged meetings where small businesses (sellers) get to meet with the large purchasing organisations (buyers) and find out about their upcoming procurement activity and/or present their product/service offerings.

A typical Meet the Buyer setup will also have areas for a mini-expo and presentations where businesses can network with others, speak with exhibitors and access topical information and tools.

- Meet the Buyer is advertised through various channels: Potential suppliers will get to know the details of participating buyers and their interests, overviews of key projects or essential service needs.
- Sellers send in their expressions of interest to meet with particular buyers via a simple web form.
- Buyers shortlist businesses they want to meet: With a limited number of meetings available, buyers shortlist businesses based on their expressions of interest. The shortlisting is done after the period for expressions of interest closes so that the meetings arranged are beneficial to both parties.

Source: (New Zealand Government Procurement,(n.d.)[13])

The outreach of procurement opportunities can be extended through means other than annual fairs. IMSS has developed a microsite to provide updates on its procurement activities. It includes relevant information for suppliers such as: 1) What has IMSS procured in the past? ; 2) What is IMSS planning to procure; and 3) Who are IMSS's suppliers? The section on what IMSS is planning to procure provides information to all potential suppliers on future procurement opportunities. These are classified by categories of products and services, but not by IMSS entities. Information on IMSS's past procurement activities helps suppliers understand IMSS's previous procurement in terms of geographical distribution, which has a strong link with future procurement. Based on this information, potential suppliers can prepare for upcoming tenders, thus helping to increase competition.

However, two main issues with this microsite have been identified by the review team that hinder this objective. Firstly, the information is not regularly updated and contains information from previous years. Secondly, there is only information on procurement opportunities for the current year and not on a longer-term basis. Given the fact that IMSS is implementing multi-year contracts in certain product categories, it should be able to provide information to potential suppliers on procurement opportunities in the next few years. IMSS would therefore benefit from updating the information on its procurement activities as well as including information for the coming years.

In addition to raising general awareness on future procurement opportunities, market analysis in the pre-tendering phase helps to reduce information asymmetries and to understand market capacity, ultimately feeding into the design of tenders. It is a useful tool to adjust tender specifications so as to maximise competition (OECD, 2017[12]). Undertaking a sound market analysis has several advantages, such as:

- Increasing awareness of the characteristics of the market and recent market developments or trends that may affect competition for the tender or that may make collusion more likely (e.g. small number of suppliers, standardised or simple products, little or no entry, etc.).
- Collecting information on suppliers, their products, prices and cost structures. If possible, a comparison of prices offered in business-to-business procurement is recommended.
- Collecting information about recent price changes. This will help procurement practitioners to be informed about prices in neighbouring geographic areas and about prices of possible alternative products.

In Mexico, Article 2-X of the LAASSP defines market analysis as a process that provides information on the existence of goods and services; providers at the national and international level; and estimated prices based on historical prices, prices from other entities (public and private) and prices from potential suppliers. According to the law, market analysis is pivotal for defining reference prices and allowing for budget allocation. This could explain why the focus is heavily on comparative financial information and less on a structured analysis of the market, technological trends or alternative solutions.

To better grasp the costs and benefits of alternative solutions available on the market, market analysis should factor in associated costs with the purchase of a specific product. Market studies should be based on a comprehensive analysis that takes into account not only initial prices, but also the related functions, delivery conditions and product lifetime. This approach has been promoted in many countries, including in the European Union (Box 3.3).

Yet, encompassing these other elements in market analysis requires procurement officials with the necessary skills and specific training. The previous review identified market research as an area for improvement (OECD, 2013[1]). Following the reorganisation of IMSS, a market research unit was created in 2016 to support central procurement activities. The creation of the market unit is also in line with recommendations of COFECE, the Mexican Competition Commission (COFECE, 2016[14]). While this unit has developed a market research template, procurement officials remain dependent on the availability of information.

Box 3.3. The life cycle approach in the European Commission

Life cycle costing (LCC) is being applied by an increasing number of public authorities across the EU and in a range of sectors. Under the 2014 EU procurement rules a contract must be awarded based on the most economically advantageous tender (MEAT). Cost or price will form part of the assessment of any procedure, and is usually one of the most influential factors. Costs may be calculated on the basis of a product's life-cycle. But how do you define the cost? When you purchase a product, service or work, you always pay a price. Purchase price, however, is just one of the cost elements in the whole process of purchasing, owning and disposing. Life-cycle costing (LCC) means considering all the costs that will be incurred over the lifetime of the product, work or service:

- Purchase price and all associated costs (delivery, installation, insurance, etc.)
- Operating costs, including energy, fuel and water use, spares, and maintenance
- End-of-life costs, such as decommissioning or disposal

LCC may also include the cost of externalities (such as greenhouse gas emissions), under specific conditions laid out in the directives.

LCC makes good sense regardless of a public authority's environmental objectives. By applying LCC, public purchasers take into account the costs of resource use, maintenance and disposal which are not reflected in the purchase price. Often this will lead to 'win-win' situations whereby a greener product, work or service is also cheaper overall. The main potential for savings over the life cycle of a good, work or service are:

- Savings on use of energy, water and fuel
- Savings on maintenance and replacement
- Savings on disposal costs

The European Commission is developing a calculation tool for life-cycle costing which aims to facilitate its use amongst public procurers. The LCC calculation tool will be developed in accordance with Article 68 of the current (2014) public procurement directives. It will focus on specific product categories, such as office IT equipment, lighting (indoor lighting), white goods, vending machines and medical electrical equipment.

Source: (European Commission,(n.d.)[15])

The implementation of a lifecycle costing approach could be beneficial for IMSS for three reasons. First, building on recent efforts by the entity to improve its financial situation (González Anaya and García Cuéllar, 2015[16]), a comprehensive financial analysis of all the costs involved in purchasing a specific product would provide additional options to increase savings. Second, it could allow IMSS to procure products with a better overall performance, ultimately to the benefit of the final users: the patients. Third, it could serve to further ground the definition of estimated prices in market analysis which are used to assess tenders and to calculate savings. However, the benefits mentioned might be hindered by a provision of the legal framework. Indeed, according to Article 2 of the LAASSP, acceptable prices cannot be higher than 10% of median prices identified through market research. If the price is higher, offers are rejected. To avoid supply disruption, the current system might provide the wrong incentives to overestimate reference prices.

Information from sources other than historical spending included in CompraNet such as benchmarks with national and international entities could also help IMSS develop a more robust market analysis. This is particularly valid given that IMSS's procurement portfolio consists of markets characterised by high price volatility and rapid technological changes. In addition, it could also provide grounds for decisions on the application of multi-year contract schemes. In addition to financial and technical information, a risk management approach (as discussed in Chapter 7) could give IMSS insights into alternative solutions and the potential impacts of various risks. This would allow IMSS to compile relevant information available supporting tender design.

IMSS could consider systematically publishing draft tender documents in order to receive the views of the private sector (see also Chapter 5), as is the case in other Mexican institutions (OECD, 2015[17]). Article 29 of the LAASSP allows for contracting authorities to publish the draft tender documentation on CompraNet for at least ten days. According to Article 41 of the RLAASSP, contracting authorities should publish draft tender documents for tenders with a value larger than 50% of the whole tendered amount, and gives priority to important tenders based on the programme, priorities, needs and main objectives of each entity. During this study, IMSS mentioned that currently 60% of tender procedures include the publication of draft tender documentation.

To ensure consistent practice among its different entities and with the assistance of SFP, IMSS central procurement unit could consider further supporting decentralised pre-tendering activities.

Increasing the effectiveness of both centralised and decentralised procurement would provide various benefits to IMSS. Although a few decentralised entities have a market research unit, they often lack capacity, while others view this step as an administrative exercise.

The fact-finding mission conducted as part of this study found that communication between the market research unit at the central level and the other IMSS entities is rather weak, which prevents them from drawing on the expertise developed at central level. The central market research unit could help officials undertaking market research tasks at the delegations and UMAE's level by sharing best practices and sound methodologies, as well as helping them with complex procurement activities. In addition, although several regional entities procure similar goods, they do not share market research, which could result in duplication and inefficiencies. As already discussed, better communication channels among the various regional entities could also increase the strategic use of market analysis.

The Ministry of Public Administration (*Secretaria de la Función Publica*, SFP) could also support the greater use of procurement information in designing future tenders by defining formats which allow information to be processed and re-used. Currently, contracting authorities can use information available in CompraNet for market analysis. This offers a rich source of information for public entities, including tender documentation, reports from clarification meetings and procurement decisions. However, the information is uploaded in a non-reusable format (pdf). When searching for information, public officials cannot extract the information needed directly; they have to go through the whole document, some of which are more than 100 pages. This is inefficient and prevents market analysis from playing a more strategic role in tender design. SFP could assist IMSS in its efforts to enhance market research activities by defining a policy to require contracting authorities to upload reusable documents to CompraNet.

Demonstrating the added value and impact of procurement strategies

Structured data would support the development of indicators allowing IMSS to assess the performance of its procurement system

In a context where countries are seeking to make public service delivery more efficient and cost-effective – largely because of budgetary constraints, but also to respond to growing citizen demands – it is essential to undertake an in-depth assessment of the procurement system. The OECD Recommendation on Public Procurement calls on countries and entities to drive performance improvements by evaluating the effectiveness of the public procurement system from individual procurements to the system as a whole (OECD, 2015[3]). Countries and entities should therefore assess periodically and consistently the results of procurement processes and develop indicators to measure performance, effectiveness and savings for benchmarking and to support strategic policy making on public procurement.

This assessment is usually undertaken using various indicators, and plays a pivotal role in tailoring specific strategies and taking appropriate decisions. However, the development of these indicators requires the right kind of data, as well as the possibility to reuse them.

The digitalisation of the procurement process promises greater efficiency and productivity. However, to reap all its benefits, the system should not only stock data, but also collect data in a structured and reusable way. Therefore, when developing their platforms or IT tools, governments and entities need to think about the type of reporting and data needed (OECD, 2016[18]). The previous OECD review already highlighted how the lack of sufficient and credible procurement data within IMSS limits its capacity to make fully informed strategic decisions and optimise the efficiency of its procurement function (OECD, 2013[19]). Discussions during the fact-finding mission for this report also confirmed the persistence of this issue and the extent to which it is impeding further analysis. For instance, when the review team analysed purchase orders, several inconsistencies and issues were identified. Purchase orders should have a unique identifier comprised of 9 digits. However, when analysing data from 2013 to 2016, some identifiers are assigned to two different purchase orders and 2.3% of purchase orders do not have the required number of digits. In addition, the name of the delegation or UMAE is not consistent across the different purchase orders and IMSS data. These data quality issues make it difficult to conduct a sound analysis to support decisions.

The CCA is developing a dashboard of procurement activities called the Executive Information System (*Sistema Ejecutivo de Información* - SEI), which will include information from the delegations and UMAEs' Internal Procurement System databases. The Directorate of Innovation and Technological Development (*Dirección de Innovación y Desarrollo Tecnológico - DIDT*) will be in charge of developing the SEI. The aim is for it to be the only database including all information on procurement activities, and the only source of information for developing indicators to manage and plan procurement activities and to inform decisions. Creating this dashboard will require extracting data from multiple sources – in turn this will require a common structured format to be defined so that it can support IMSS's strategic orientations.

In addition to internal tools, CompraNet is a useful source of information for internal and external stakeholders when documents are correctly uploaded and information is consistently inputted. However, our analysis of data from CompraNet as part of this assessment found so many errors it was difficult to evaluate and use the data. Procurement procedures are classified in CompraNet by the contracting authority's name and code, the procedure code, a description of the procurement procedure and the type of procurement activity (services, goods, public works, leasing). When undertaking a procurement procedure through CompraNet, IMSS entities do not always use the right codes or the right sequencing of numbers, making the use of data difficult and often impossible. This seems to be mainly due to the absence of shared guidelines for all IMSS entities on how to structure information in CompraNet. IMSS and SFP could benefit from building the capacity of officials in charge of uploading information on external platforms in data entry to enhance the quality of data for internal and external stakeholders.

The development of a structured set of data will lay the foundations for the definition and implementation of indicators that can demonstrate IMMS's procurement performance and identify areas for improvement. These indicators are usually referred to as Key Performance Indicators (KPIs) and should be adapted to the institution's setting.

The performance of public procurement systems can be assessed at three distinct levels (Figure 3.7): contract management/micro level, contracting authority/macro level and national/meta level. Those levels are closely linked, since the performance at the procedure or contract level has an impact on the performance of the entity, which has an impact on the performance of the procurement system at the national level.

Figure 3.7. Three levels for assessing the performance of public procurement

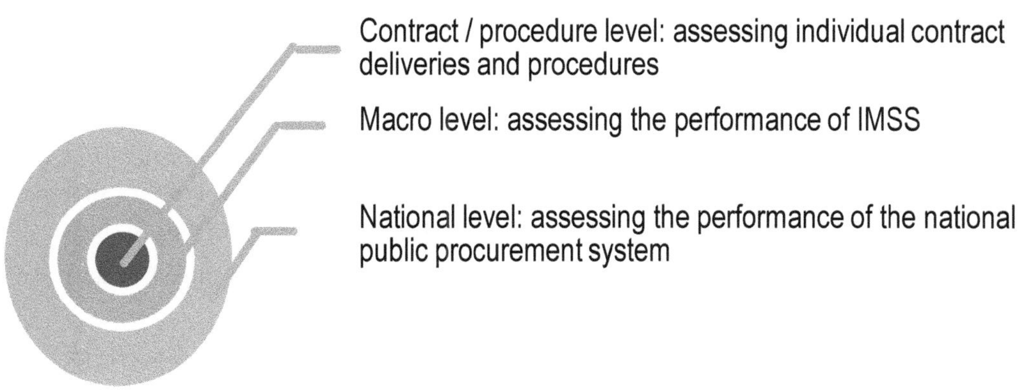

Applied to IMSS, these levels could correspond to individual contracts, decentralised entities and the whole institution. Indicators should be developed to reflect the strategies and policies developed at the entity or national level. Box 3.4 describes the key aspects to take into account when developing KPIs. In addition, it might be relevant to set specific targets that will serve as a goal for the entity. When measured, those indicators will help to identify gaps, bottlenecks and thus to continuously improve the system by undertaking relevant actions and/or tailoring specific strategies. Finally, not all the indicators have to be monitored with the same frequency. The majority could potentially be assessed monthly, and some others only quarterly or even annually.

Box 3.4. Establishing good key performance indicators (KPIs)

Good KPIs must possess some fundamental qualities to fully benefit an organisation and its suppliers. They should be:

- **Relevant**, i.e. linked to key objectives of the organisation (critical outcomes or risks to be avoided), rather than on process.
- **Clear**, i.e. spelled-out in the contractual document and as simple as possible to ensure common understanding by the buying organisation and the supplier.
- **Measurable** and objective, i.e. expressed on pre-determined measures and formulas, and based on simple data that can be gathered objectively and in a cost-effective manner.
- **Achievable**, i.e. realistic and within the control of the supplier.
- **Limited**, i.e. as few as required achieving the objectives while minimising their disadvantages (costs, efforts and risk of dispute) to both entities. To the extent possible, the use of information and documentation already available under the contract management process should be promoted rather than requiring the collection of additional data or documentation.
- **Timed**, i.e. include specific timeframes for completion.

Source: (OECD, 2013[1])

The next section describes how these indicators could be developed.

IMSS could build on its recent efforts and transform activity indicators into performance indicators

IMSS already holds information which could be used to develop indicators to monitor its procurement system. Although the PREI/SAI system is not a reporting tool, each area in IMSS has an application for extracting information. The Coordination of supply Control Area (CCA) already generates some indicators to monitor the national system, such as the share of products and services not awarded, non-compliance indicators and savings.

The dashboard of procurement activities currently being developed (the SEI) will enable IMSS to issue reports against the following indicators:

- Procurement procedures: Which procurement procedures are used by IMSS ?
- Contracts: How was the contract formalised?
- Products and services procured
- Date, year and period of procurement activities (When was it procured?)
- Quantities procured
- Procurement amounts
- Contract years
- Replenishment orders
- Inventories
- Prescription of drugs provided
- Investment levels
- Drug consumption
- Costs

- Number of products and services not awarded
- Supply orders

While providing IMSS with increased visibility on procurement spending and allowing senior management a snapshot of progress, these indicators are mostly activity indicators rather than performance indicators. Currently only two indicators measure the performance of the system: the non-compliance indicator and the savings indicator.

The performance of the procurement system depends on the performance of suppliers. Poor performance can have several explanations, such as the supplier's lack of capacity, or tender documentation which is not aligned with market capacity. To measure the performance of its suppliers, IMSS has developed a non-compliance indicator which can track orders that were delivered only partially and/or late. IMSS's procurement website provides information on "non-compliant suppliers", but only for drugs and healing, radiological and laboratory material. IMSS meets with suppliers who have a high non-compliance rate to reach an agreement or come up with alternative solutions to ensure supply (Chapter 4).

During the fact-finding mission, the pharmaceutical industry shared concerns regarding the fact that IMSS does not always take into account manufacturer's production lead-time which can impact on the effective delivery of medical devices and drugs. Besides on-going measurement of level of compliance, his indicator could be further exploited to revisit the procurement strategy for upcoming tenders (e.g. by looking at average level of compliance by months, by delivery timeframes, etc…). Decisions based on this analysis could range from implementing a stricter qualification mechanism or setting delivery timeframes that are aligned with market capabilities.

Given today's financial and budgetary constraints, a demonstration of value for money should guide procurement strategies. The performance of the procurement system is often measured through savings made, and IMSS is no exception. There are two ways to measure procurement savings: budgetary savings or performance savings. Calculating budgetary savings involves measuring how much the contracting authority is saving in terms of spent budget from one year to the next. Calculating performance savings looks at the efficiency of procurement while taking into account all financial aspects. One of the main challenges identified in the OECD survey on Centralised Framework Agreements (2015b) was the methodology for calculating this indicator. Indeed, a broad range of calculation methods are applied across OECD countries depending on the nature of contracting mechanisms or the perspective adopted (OECD, 2017[20]). Box 3.5 describes the various methodologies implemented in OECD countries.

Box 3.5. Common methodologies to measure procurement savings in the OECD

- Comparison between historical prices or reference price based on market analysis and final price proposed by the awarded supplier.
- Assessment of the total cost of ownership of products or services procured, and comparison with reference prices.
- Comparison between the price list proposed by the awarded suppliers in the first competition stage, or the average historical price paid by contracting authorities, and the discounted price obtained after second stage competition.
- Comparison between historical processing or labour costs and new processing or labour costs.

Source: (OECD, 2015[17])

IMSS has developed a methodology to calculate performance savings based either on historical prices of recurrent purchases or on reference prices gathered through the market analysis for new products or services. This methodology is similar to the first approach described in Box 3.5 which is common in other countries, yet it doesn't capture additional dimensions such as indirect costs and thus also potential savings. Indeed the evaluation of the cost of a product requires taking into account more than initial price agreed in the contract. For instance, for medical devices, in addition to the price, the analysis could take into account the costs involved throughout the life of the product: maintenance costs, training costs, insurance, as well as indirect costs such as the impact on beds and patients' length of stay and the time needed by medical professionals to use the product or to take care of patients (See Box 2.3). As discussed in Chapter 6, integrating these components into the calculations could provide IMSS with new avenues for generating savings.

Another argument for IMSS to review its methodology for calculating savings is that communication on savings is a powerful tool to reassure stakeholders (employers, the government and taxpayers) of the soundness of IMSS's procurement strategy and to ensure they adhere to it. IMSS has undertaken a significant communication campaign regarding the savings resulting from consolidated tenders. For instance, one webpage is dedicated to this topic. Table 3.3 describes the savings resulting from IMSS consolidated tenders from 2014 to 2017.

Table 3.3. Savings resulting from IMSS consolidated tenders, 2014 to 2017

Participants	Savings per year				Total savings	
	2014	2015	2016	2017	Millions USD	%
IMSS	-7%	-9%	-5%	-7%	-467	-8%
ISSSTE[1]	-12%	-12%	-8%	-8%	-181	-11%
PEMEX[2]	-8%	-11%	-9%	-8%	-19	-10%
SEDENA[3]	-7%	-10%	-5%	-9%	-12	-9%
SEMAR[4]	-35%	-6%	-2%	-3%	0	-7%
Total Dependencies	-10%	-8%	-6%	-7%	-679	-8%
Total entities	-19%	-42%	-8%	-5%	-104	-17%
Total institutes	-8%	-28%	-12%	-9%	-4	-20%
Total general	-12%	19%	-6%	-7%	-787	-9%

Notes:
1. ISSSTE: The State's Employees' Social Security and Social Services Institute
2. PEMEX: Petróleos Mexicanos
3. SEDENA: The Ministry of Defence (*Secretaria de la Defensa Nacional-SEDENA*)
4. SEMAR: The Ministry of Navy (*Secretaria de Marina-SEMAR*)
Source: (IMSS, 2016[21])

In addition to measuring price and cost savings, savings can also be demonstrated in relation to administrative costs. Procurement tools such as e-procurement, centralised procurement and consolidated procurement can save entities significant amounts in process and productivity costs. However, countries find it challenging to measure the savings and more generally the efficiencies derived from these instruments (Figure 3.8).

Figure 3.8. Who is measuring the efficiencies generated by the use of e-procurement systems?

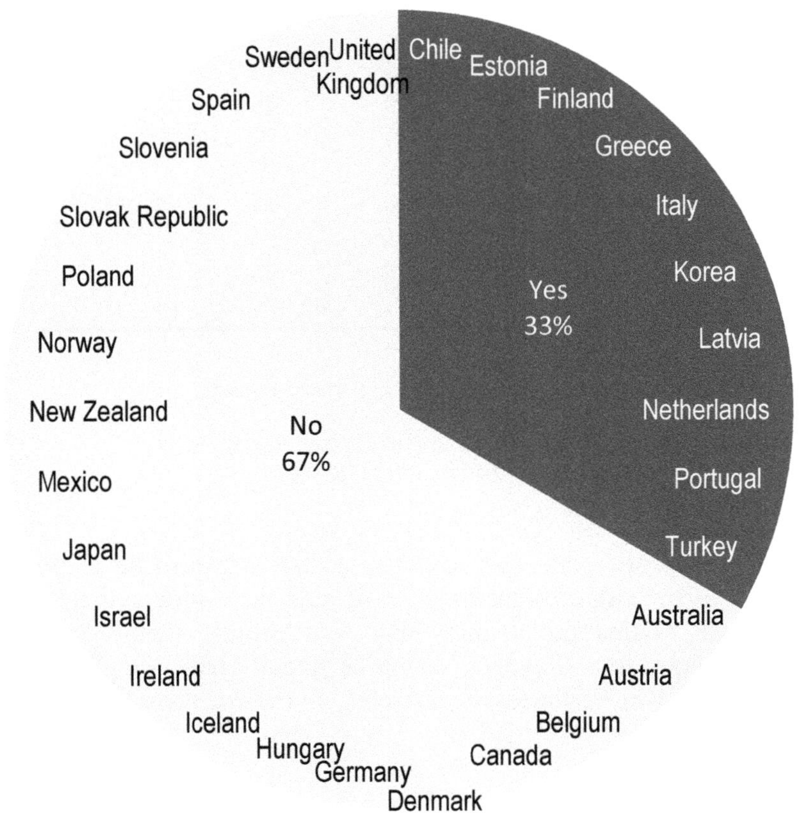

Note: Data for the Czech Republic, France, Luxembourg, Switzerland and the United States are not available.
Disclaimer: http://oe.cd/disclaimer
Source: (OECD, 2017[22])

Assessing this type of performance requires information on direct procurement process costs (i.e. procurement officials' salaries and standardised timeframes for each type of procurement procedure). It also requires a harmonised mapping exercise of roles and responsibilities within contracting authorities to ensure that indirect costs, such as hierarchical approvals or budgetary validations, are taken into account.

There is no single methodology for measuring the process costs of procurement tools. As one example though, Chile calculates the savings generated by framework agreements by estimating the difference between the costs of issuing a purchase order under a framework agreement, and the costs of issuing an individual public tender or direct award procedure.

IMSS could also develop other indicators to capture various dimensions of procurement performance. For example, the efficiency of the system could be measured by the number or share of unsuccessful tenders or the number of products and services not awarded. These indicators could signal procurement categories in need of capacity building amongst the public procurement workforce or the need for better engagement with the private sector. According to SFP, in 2015 around 10% of IMSS's open tenders and 12.7% of its restricted invitations were unsuccessful (Figure 3.9). The latter statistic signals a particular need for corrective action since restricted invitations target suppliers based on their assessed capacity.

Figure 3.9. Share of unsuccessful tenders and share of products and services not awarded, 2013-2016

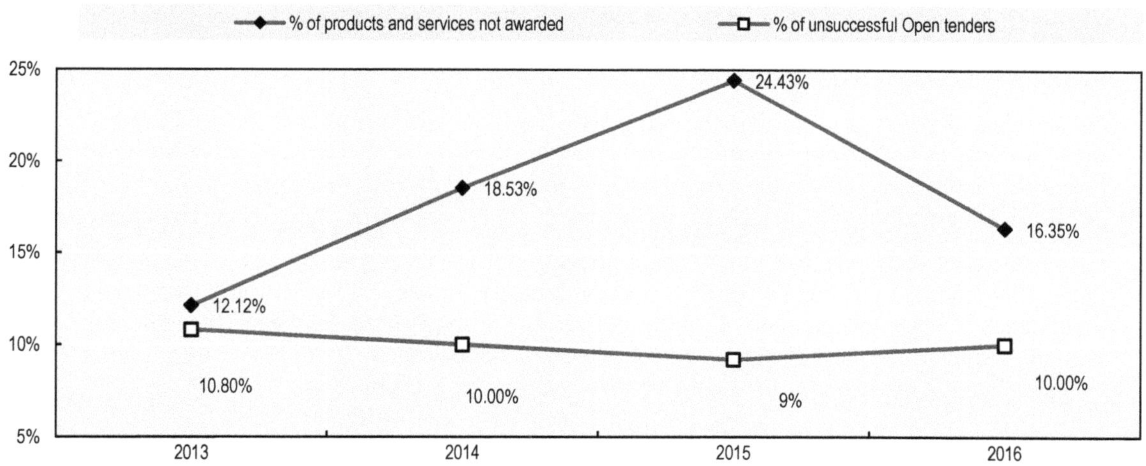

Source: Data provided by IMSS and SFP

The share of products not awarded could also signal deficiencies in specific product categories that are ultimately preventing some patients from receiving the medicines they need. Among the reasons for which products or services were not awarded in the 2017 round of consolidated tenders, 55.6% were because no offers had been submitted and 39.4% were for technical reasons (Institute of Research and Pharmaceutical Innovation, 2017[23]). This suggests the need for greater understanding of market capacities.

IMSS could also develop an indicator to assess suppliers' level of compliance. IMSS holds information on the effective delivery date of goods and provision of services, as well as the expected delivery date. This information could be used to develop a specific indicator on the relevance of delivery timeframes for each product category, region or supplier. It would help IMSS to optimise its stock management, an aspect which has been identified as a clear area for making savings (Chapter 4). Box 3.6 provides an example from the United Kingdom's National Health Service (NHS), which uses stocks strategically.

Box 3.6. Strategic stock management by the UK's National Health Service

The National Health Service- NHS operates the public health services in the United Kingdom. However, each country – England, Scotland, Wales and Northern Ireland – manages its own healthcare arrangements. NHS England is expected to deliver efficiencies of 2-3% per year, effectively setting a 10-15% real terms cost reduction target for achievement by April 2021. To achieve those targets, efforts need to be devoted to several areas including the optimisation of clinical and non-clinical resources.

For instance, some trusts- entities managing NHS hospital care in England- have developed more efficient centralised arrangements and some are working with pharmacy wholesalers to consolidate buying and reduce the number of daily medicine deliveries to hospitals.

Working more closely with manufacturers and pharmacy wholesalers should lead to consolidation of the medicines supply chain, making full use of e-ordering and invoicing and aggregating and rationalising deliveries – preferably ready for use and to the ward. This would significantly reduce the numbers of daily deliveries to hospitals to less than five, thereby reducing stock holding (a reduction to 15 days would generate a GBP 50 million one-off saving to the NHS per year), as well as reducing pharmacy staff supply chain costs.

Source: (Naylor et al., 2016[24]) and (OECD, 2016[25])

Currently, except for vaccines, all drugs have the same delivery terms. However, analysis suggests that different product categories have diverse effective delivery timeframes and some have clear potential to optimise their delivery timeframes (Figures 3.10 and 3.11). For example, as shown in the figures below, products categories including hospital clothing (product category 210) or mattresses (product category 220) experience a recurrent trend of being delivered well ahead of contractual deadlines. A closer alignment of contractual delivery deadlines with recurring practices could further incentivise supplier performance and benefit IMSS stock management.

Figure 3.10. Early delivery in days per product category

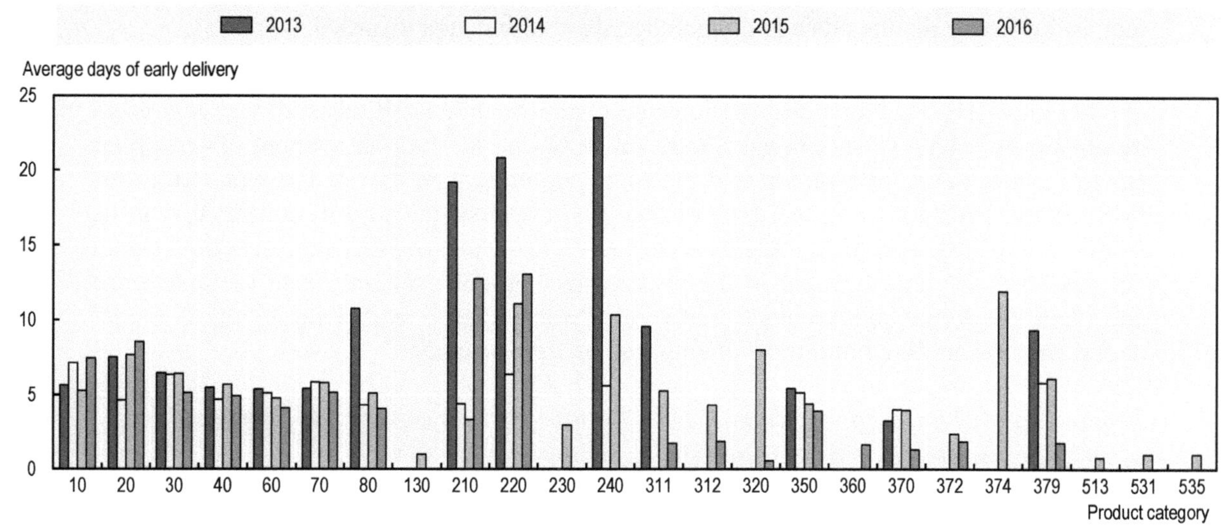

Note: In this calculation, only purchase orders delivered on time were taken into consideration.
Source: Based on data provided by IMSS

Figure 3.11. Advance days for on-time deliveries for product categories 210 and 220 (2016)

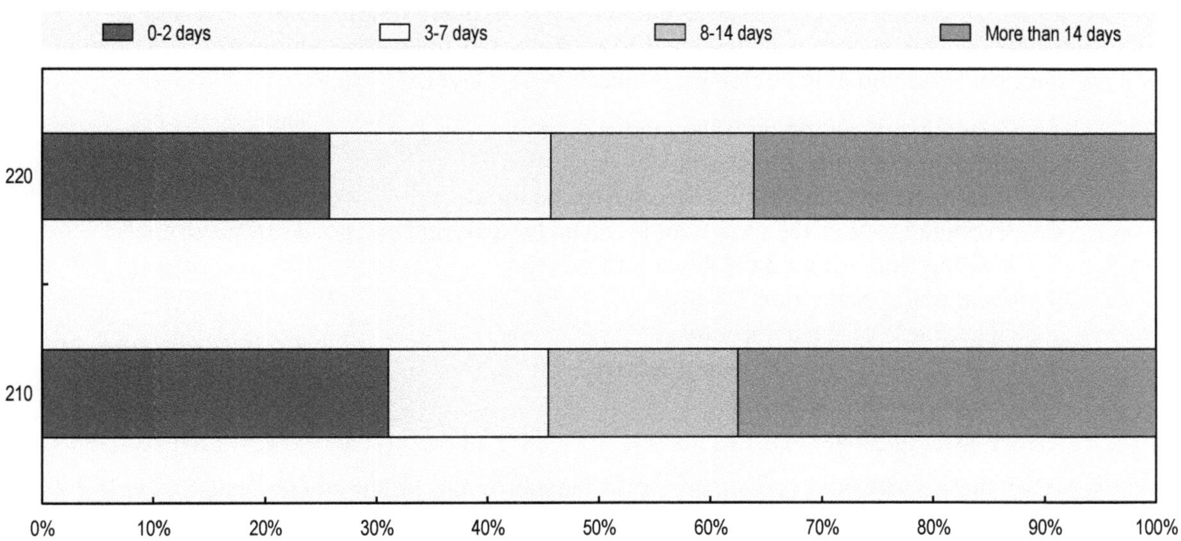

Note: The composition only refers to the deliveries that were made on time. Thus, non-compliant deliveries were not taken into account in the calculation
Source: Based on data provided by IMSS

The performance of a procurement system can also be measured by how easy it is for suppliers to access procurement opportunities. The ideal performance indicator on facilitating access would be the number of bids measured against the number of economic operators in the respective market. Although this exercise might prove challenging because it will require the identification of all potential suppliers at the national level but also at the international level, IMSS could still measure the level of effective competition or possible barriers to competition by excessive specifications by measuring several indicators such as the number of qualified bids, the number of suppliers downloading or requesting tender documents and the number/share of bids not awarded.

For instance, in a tender for pharmaceutical and medical goods (LA-019GYR047) divided into 12 lots, 22 suppliers participated in clarification meetings and were interested in submitting a bid; 13 suppliers actually submitted a bid, with an average of 3 supplier per lot; 2 lots were not awarded and the same suppliers won half of the remaining lots. IMSS could consider using this type of analysis to assess the level of competition in its tenders and design specific strategies accordingly. For example, this analysis could signal various areas for improvement in the procurement process, ranging from the coherence and stability of the procurement framework to the clarity and complexity of tender documentation and the limitations of single source procurement.

Impacting on healthcare delivery, IMSS could further assess the performance of its procurement system against broader objectives

Given that IMSS is such a major actor in the health system, it could also assess its procurement performance against national objectives. Communicating the results could further reinforce its strategic position. IMSS has developed two sets of indicators which can be used to measure the efficiency of the procurement process directly or indirectly: (1) indicators on the quality of services provided by IMSS; and (2) prescription indicators. Since 2009, IMSS has run a National Satisfaction Survey to gather information on the perceptions of the quality of services provided by IMSS to its affiliated beneficiaries. The most recent survey took place in April 2017 and had 24 757 respondents. This survey was designed to measure ten indicators which are developed at the national level and at the delegations and UMAEs level:

1. General satisfaction with the medical care
2. Provision of drugs to patients
3. Treatment received during the visit in the unit
4. Average score of the treatment received by different categories of personnel
5. Waiting time for medical consultation
6. Cleanliness of the unit
7. Cleanliness of the bathrooms
8. Evaluation of the emergency service
9. Hospitalization services
10. Surgery services

Some of these indicators reflect the performance of the procurement system. Table 3.4 provides examples of possible links between the indicators and IMSS procurement performance. IMSS could consider using these indicators to tailor specific procurement strategies further so as to enhance the satisfaction of IMSS affiliates.

Table 3.4. Examples of links between satisfaction indicators and procurement performance

Satisfaction indicators	Possible impact of procurement
Provision of drugs to patients	Supply disruption of drugs Lack of effectiveness of drugs prescribed
Cleanliness of the bathrooms/cleanliness of the unit	Bad quality cleaning products procured by IMSS (cleaning services are provided by IMSS personal
Evaluation of the emergency service	Supply disruption of drugs Lack of medical consumables and devices

In addition, IMSS uses another indicator related to medicine prescriptions. As needed, doctors prescribe medicines to patients following a consultation. These drugs should be provided by IMSS pharmacies. The prescription indicator aims to measure the percentage of prescriptions for drugs that have been totally or partially provided to patients. Tracking this indicator shows a clear drop in performance at the same time each year (December-January; Figure 3.12). This might be explained by the procurement planning calendar, in which all contracts should in principle be awarded before the end of the year, as well as the relatively high share of products and services not awarded. This indicates that products and services like drugs are often not being made available on time. IMSS should develop a specific strategy to overcome this issue.

Figure 3.12. Share of drug prescriptions that are fulfilled, 2012-2017

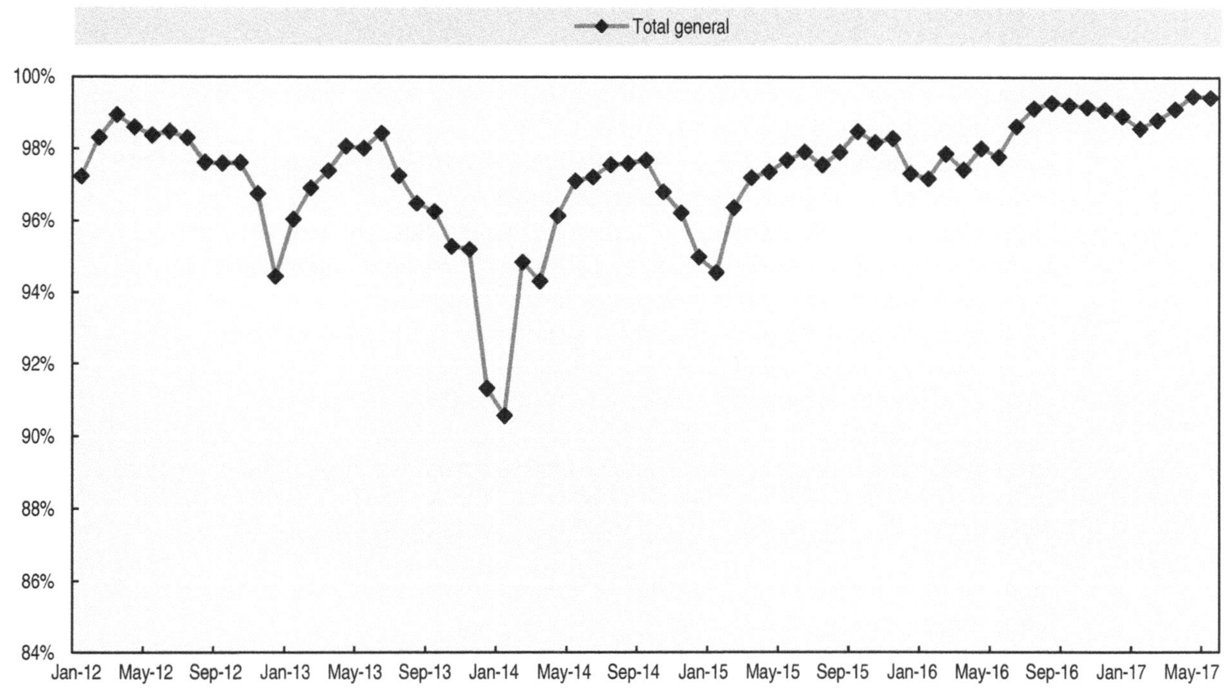

Source: data provided by IMSS

Proposals for action

IMSS plays a pivotal role in the national health system. As a health provider, the entity needs to procure goods and services which could impact the quality of health service provided by the entity. Therefore the entity needs to rely on comprehensive information to inform its procurement decisions. Building on efforts made by IMSS since the last review, the institute could further improve the use of its information systems and develop data collection methodologies supporting the definition of future procurement strategies. To this end the OECD is providing IMSS with recommendations covering three main areas: the digitalisation of the procurement system through internal and external platforms, the use of market intelligence and the demonstration of the added value and impact of procurement strategies.

Digitalise procurement to increase efficiency

- Use existing information systems to further streamline procurement operations:
  - introduce e-submission in all IMSS procurement procedures to enhance data quality and inform public procurement decisions
  - bring IMSS's information system in line with the legal framework
  - add notifications into IMSS's IT system for relevant stakeholders involved in the procurement process
- Assess periodically the alignment of IMSS's IT systems with its procurement strategies
- Develop mechanisms and a platform to share information among procurement officials.

Use procurement intelligence to help IMSS implement its strategies

- Reinforcing the methodologies to capture decentralised needs supporting the design of centralised procurement strategies by considering demand analysis as a strategic task and not as an administrative task.
- Review the methodology for consolidated tenders to find synergies among IMSS entities and promote joint procurement activities.
- Improving the understanding of market capabilities to reduce information asymmetry and increase the outreach of IMSS procurement opportunities by:
  - establishing more regular dialogue with the private sector
  - improving the methodology and the organisation of market analysis
  - increasing the publication of draft tender documents
  - improving the information for suppliers on the IMSS its website
- Support decentralised pre-tendering activities and shared market research to ensure coherent approaches and communication across the various IMSS entities.

Demonstrate the added value and impact of procurement strategies

- Improve data structure and quality to generate structured and useful data for informing procurement decisions
- Enhance officials' capacity in entering data on external platforms to improve the quality of data for internal and external stakeholders.
- Develop procurement performance indicators from existing data and by improving the methodology to calculate savings.

- Assess the performance of IMSS's procurement system against broader objectives by using health performance indicators, and tailor specific procurement strategies accordingly.

Note

[1] At an exchange rate of MXN 18.07 to USD 1.

References

Australian Government((n.d.)), *Strategic guide to e-Procurement*, http://www.finance.gov.au/publications/strategic-guide-to-e-procurement/fmis-erp.html (accessed on 23 October 2017). [7]

Burns, L. and J. Lee (2008), "Hospital purchasing alliances: utilization, services, and performance", *Health Care Management Review*, Vol. 33/3, pp. 203-215, http://dx.doi.org/10.1097/01.HMR.0000324906.04025.33. [10]

COFECE (2016), "Recomendaciones para promover la competencia y libre concurrencia en la contratación pública", http://www.cofece.mx/cofece/attachments/article/38/RecomendacionesContratacionPublica-v2.pdf (accessed on 14 November 2017). [14]

EBRD (2015), *Are you ready for e-procurement*, http://www.ebrd.com/documents/legal-reform/guide-to-eprocurement-reform.pdf. [5]

European Commission (2016), *EU Public Procurement reform: Less bureaucracy, higher efficiency*, http://ec.europa.eu/DocsRoom/documents/16412. [2]

European Commission, E.((n.d.)), *Life cycle costing*, http://ec.europa.eu/environment/gpp/lcc.htm (updated 08/06/2016) (accessed on 14 November 2017). [15]

González Anaya, J. and R. García Cuéllar (2015), "The Transformation of the Mexican Social Security Institute (IMSS): Progress and Challenges", http://dx.doi.org/10.1080/23288604.2015.1061096. [16]

IMSS (2016), *Documentacion Compra Consolidada 2016-2017*, http://www.imss.gob.mx/compraconsolidada/2016 (accessed on 09 November 2017). [21]

Institute of Research and Pharmaceutical Innovation (2017), *Presentation: Information on the Procurement of health in the public sector*. [23]

Internet World Stats (2016), *Internet usage and population in Central America*, http://www.internetworldstats.com/stats12.htm (accessed on 14 November 2017). [6]

Naylor, R. et al. (2016), "Operational productivity and performance in English NHS acute hospitals: Unwarranted variations", https://www.gov.uk/government/uploads/system/uploads/attachment_data/file/499229/Operational_productivity_A.pdf (accessed on 14 November 2017). [24]

New Zealand Government Procurement((n.d.)), *Meet the buyer*, http://www.procurement.govt.nz/procurement/for-suppliers/meet-the-buyer (accessed on 26 October 2017). [13]

Nollet, J. and M. Beaulieu (2005), "Should an organisation join a purchasing group?", *Supply Chain Management: An International Journal*, Vol. 10/110, https://doi.org/10.1108/13598540510578333 (accessed on 15 November 2017), pp. 11-17. [11]

OECD (2013), *Public Procurement Review of the Mexican Institute of Social Security: Enhancing Efficiency and Integrity for Better Health Care*, OECD Public Governance Reviews, OECD Publishing, Paris, http://dx.doi.org/10.1787/9789264197480-en. [19]

OECD (2013), *Public Procurement Review of the State's Employees' Social Security and Social Services Institute in Mexico*, OECD Public Governance Reviews, OECD Publishing, Paris, http://dx.doi.org/10.1787/9789264197305-en. [1]

OECD (2015), *Survey on Centralised Framework Agreements.* [17]

OECD (2015), *OECD Recommendation of the Council on Public Procurement*, http://www.oecd.org/gov/ethics/OECD-Recommendation-on-Public-Procurement.pdf. [3]

OECD (2016), *Improving ISSSTE's Public Procurement for Better Results*, OECD Public Governance Reviews, OECD Publishing, Paris, http://dx.doi.org/10.1787/9789264249899-en. [25]

OECD (2016), "Checklist for Supporting the Implementation of the OECD Recommendation of the Council on Public Procurement", http://www.oecd.org/governance/procurement/toolbox/search/checklist-implementation-oecd-recommendation.pdf (accessed on 15 November 2017). [18]

OECD (2017), *Government at a Glance 2017*, OECD Publishing, Paris, http://dx.doi.org/10.1787/gov_glance-2017-en. [4]

OECD (2017), "E-procurement", in *Government at a Glance 2017*, OECD Publishing, Paris, http://dx.doi.org/10.1787/gov_glance-2017-61-en. [22]

OECD (2017), *Public Procurement in Chile: Policy Options for Efficient and Inclusive Framework Agreements*, OECD Public Governance Reviews, OECD Publishing, Paris, http://dx.doi.org/10.1787/9789264275188-en. [12]

OECD (2017), *Public Procurement in Chile: Policy Options for Efficient and Inclusive Framework Agreements*, OECD Public Governance Reviews, OECD Publishing, Paris, http://dx.doi.org/10.1787/9789264275188-en. [20]

OECD (2017), *Training material on tender design.* [9]

Resah (2016), "Rapport d'Activité 2016", http://www.resah.fr/RESAH_INTERNET/Ressources/FCK/files/Resah-RA2016.pdf. [8]

Chapter 4. Shifting IMSS contract management from supplier compliance to performance

The satisfactory delivery of some of the most critical health services such as the provision of medicines largely depend on the capacity of suppliers to provide to the buying organisation the required products and services in a timely and effective manner. Yet, beyond the strict compliance with contractual commitments, performing suppliers could also impact more broadly the provision of health services and participate to the achievement of IMSS' objectives. This Chapter discusses the recent efforts carried out by the Institute to ensure greater compliance of suppliers with their contractual commitments. It also suggests means to revisit the Institute's relationship with its suppliers by developing a sound and comprehensive contract management framework.

Alongside thorough procurement strategies and complex assessment mechanisms to evaluate bids, effective contract management is a decisive factor in ensuring suppliers contribute to IMSS's high-quality health services. In addition, optimising co-operation, co-ordination, and communication – particularly with regard to the supplier base – has been found to have a profound impact on cost reductions while improving service delivery (Rajagopal, 2009[1]).

The previous OECD review identified several inefficiencies in IMSS's procurement management system (OECD, 2013[2]). This chapter assesses IMSS's progress since then in managing its pool of suppliers. It discusses suppliers' compliance with contractual terms and conditions, and sheds light on potential avenues for improving suppliers' performance further.

The OECD Recommendation on Public Procurement highlights the importance of adequate resources and expertise in contract management for ensuring efficiency throughout the public procurement cycle Box 4.1. It also insists on the benefits of a comprehensive evaluation of procurement operations to inform future procurement decisions.

Box 4.1. Principles of the OECD Recommendation relating to performance management

The OECD Council notably:

VII. RECOMMENDS that Adherents develop processes to drive Efficiency throughout the public procurement cycle in satisfying the needs of the government and its citizens.

To this end, Adherents should:

i) Streamline the public procurement system and its institutional frameworks. Adherents should evaluate existing processes and institutions to identify functional overlap, inefficient silos and other causes of waste. Where possible, a more service-oriented public procurement system should then be built around efficient and effective procurement processes and workflows to reduce administrative red tape and costs, for example through shared services.

ii) Implement sound technical processes to satisfy customer needs efficiently. Adherents should take steps to ensure that procurement outcomes meet the needs of customers, for instance by developing appropriate technical specifications, identifying appropriate award criteria, ensuring adequate technical expertise among proposal evaluators, and ensuring adequate resources and expertise are available for contract management following the award of a contract.

iii) Develop and use tools to improve procurement procedures, reduce duplication and achieve greater value for money, including centralised purchasing, framework agreements, e-catalogues, dynamic purchasing, e-auctions, joint procurements and contracts with options. Application of such tools across sub-national levels of government, where appropriate and feasible, could further drive efficiency.

X. RECOMMENDS that Adherents drive performance improvements through Evaluation of the effectiveness of the public procurement system from individual procurements to the system as a whole, at all levels of government where feasible and appropriate.

To this end, Adherents should:

i) Assess periodically and consistently the results of the procurement process. Public procurement systems should collect consistent, up-to-date and reliable information and use data on prior procurements, particularly regarding price and overall costs, in structuring new needs assessments, as they provide a valuable source of insight and could guide future procurement decisions.

ii) Develop indicators to measure performance, effectiveness and savings of the public procurement system for benchmarking and to support strategic policy making on public procurement.

Source: (OECD, 2015[3]).

Reinforcing accountability to ensure well-executed contracts

IMSS has welcome flexibility in developing contract management principles that are adapted to its structure and procurement strategies. Aside from legal provisions and the normative framework, the assessment of contract execution is largely left to IMSS's discretionary policies. This section discusses efforts by IMSS to ensure suppliers' compliance with contractual terms.

Overarching principles for contract management in the Mexican public procurement system are defined in the legislative and regulatory provisions of the Public Procurement Law for Goods, Leases and Services (*Ley de Adquisiciones, Arrendamientos y Servicios del Sector Público*, LAASP) and the Public Procurement Law for Public Works and Associated Services (*Ley de Obras Publicas y servicios relaciando con la misma*, LOPSRM).

While the LOPSRM dedicates a whole chapter to contract execution, the LAASP provides far less information. It merely includes provisions on payments to suppliers, penalties applied in case of unsatisfactory performance or delays, and options for terminating contracts. Neither do bylaws (*Reglamento de la Ley de Adquisiciones, Arrendamientos y Servicios del Sector Público* - RLAASSP and *Reglamento de la Ley de Obras Publicas y servicios relaciando con la misma* – ROPSRM) provide a more complete framework of what a structured contract management process should look like.

While the Procurement Manual (*Manual Administrativo de Aplicación General en Materia de Adquisiciones, Arrendamientos y Servicios del Sector Público*, MAAGMAASSP) includes a specific section on contract execution, it mostly deals with the administrative steps, such as verification and inspection, which trigger payments to suppliers. All these normative provisions remain silent on how IMSS should structure its relationships with its suppliers, leaving the institute with the discretionary power to develop its own contract management framework.

Reducing the default rate: an effective sanction mechanism led to MXN 250 million of cost avoidance in 2016, yet, IMSS could ensure that its strategic objectives are not hindered by the share of defaults.

The Policies and Guidelines for the Procurement of Goods, Leases and Services (*Políticas, bases y lineamientos en materia de adquisiciones, arrendamientos y servicios*) list the steps for controlling and inspecting the goods and services procured. They also define the termination of contracts and the main sanctions applicable in case of unsatisfactory performance:

- Conventional penalties: in the case of delays in delivering goods or services, IMSS can apply the penalties agreed in the contract. IMSS's internal guidelines set daily penalties at 2.5% of the value of the good or services, up to a maximum of 10%. This ceiling corresponds to the performance bond required from the winning bidder upon signature of the contract. Penalties can be raised to up to 20% of the total value of the good or services if the winning bidder has been exempted from providing this performance bond.
- Pre-established deductions for specific types of non-compliance with obligations in the contract.

Internal manuals identify who is responsible for the administrative management of contracts:

- The Technical Co-ordination of Planning and Contracts, through its Contracts Division, is in charge of contract management at the central level.
- The co-ordinator of supplies and equipment in the delegations.
- The co-ordinator of supplies in the highly specialised medical units (UMAEs).

The public servants designated as contract administrators are responsible for applying penalties and deducting payments. However, the previous OECD review found that the sanction mechanisms foreseen in the law and detailed in IMSS guidelines were inconsistently applied, if applied at all. It recommended that they should be applied systematically. This issue has also been regularly stressed by the Mexican Supreme Audit Institution (*Auditoria Superior de la Federación*, ASF) in audit reports (ASF, 2013[4]).

Greater enforcement of penalties for unsatisfactory performance by suppliers could discourage them from habitual non-compliance. As noted in the previous review, suppliers, especially those of medicines to remote regions, found it financially more advantageous to pay the conventional penalties under centralised contracts than to meet all the requirements, since deliveries to remote regions often involve low quantities and high delivery costs.

Analysis of trends in IMSS's application of sanction mechanisms provides different but complementary conclusions. Figure 4.1 shows that since the OECD recommendations to strengthen its sanctions mechanisms, IMSS has enforced cases of contractual breaches by suppliers more consistently. Following the previous review, the number of incompliances and penalties dramatically increased in 2013 and 2014 while stabilising in 2015 and 2016 at levels still illustrating a greater enforcement of sanctions mechanisms. This has allowed it to avoid incurring costs for the unsatisfactory execution of contracts. As an example, in 2016 it avoided more than MXN 251 million in costs, representing a 275% increase over 2010 and a large reduction in the waste of public money.

Figure 4.1. Evolution of incompliances and penalties, 2010-2016

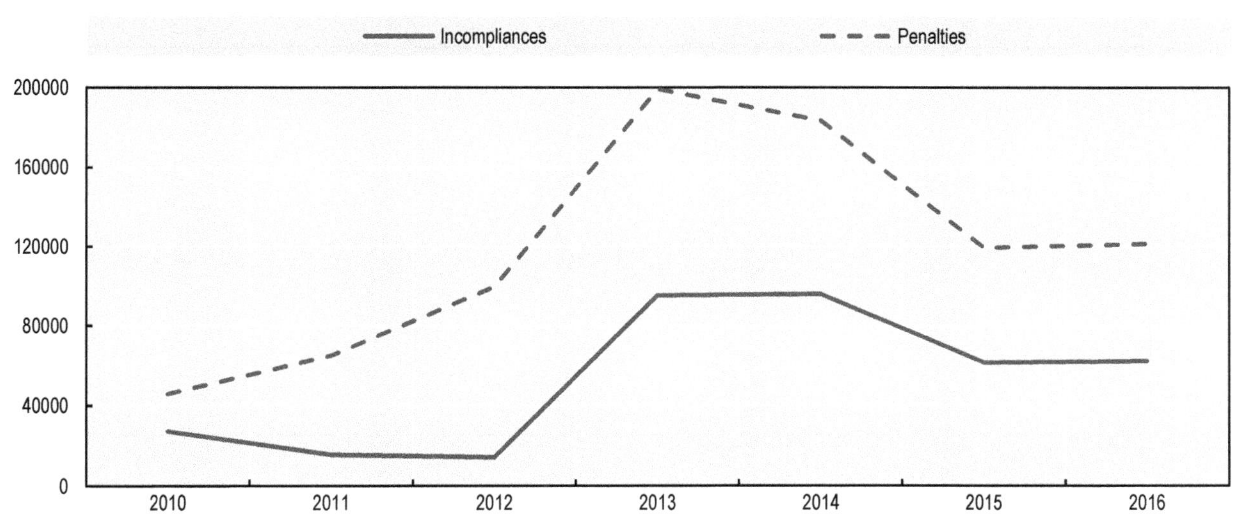

Note: the right axis represents the number of incompliances and penalties reported in a given year
Source: OECD calculations based on data provided by IMSS

While enforcing sanctions is allowing IMSS to avoid incurring costs for the unsatisfactory execution of contracts, the share of non-compliant contracts is still high, which could also harm the efficiency of the system. In 2016, 17% of orders were sub-optimal either because of delays, or partial or non-execution of contractual obligations.

Efficient contract execution is of major importance in all procurement systems. At the time of contract award, the commitments put forward by the successful bidder are hypotheses only – these need to be delivered during the execution phase. Choosing suppliers with the capacities to execute the contract according to the agreed terms and conditions is therefore central in the market analysis supporting the choice of a procurement strategy (see later sections in this chapter).

This exercise is also instrumental in ensuring that awarded suppliers in consolidated tenders are able to meet large-scale nationwide delivery of medicines or medical devices. The 2014 annual audit report on public accounts of the Mexican Supreme Audit Institution highlighted that failure to execute a contract could severely impede the benefits attained in this type of tender process (ASF, 2014[5]). For example, in a sample of audited consolidated tenders, the report found that 123 references in three contracts were meant to produce savings of more than MXN 221 million. However, these savings were not realised due to non-compliance by suppliers, which represented 77.4% of the total awarded amount and forced delegations to use alternative, more expensive, providers outside the consolidated tender.

Figure 4.2 suggests that specific product categories, such as "medical devices" and "non-medicine products and services", are more prone to non-compliance than others. For these categories the share of non-compliant purchase orders can reach levels as high as almost 20% of the total number of products ordered. A cautious review of the underlying reasons for non-compliance could therefore be carried out to assess whether the requirements put to tenders need to be revisited.

Figure 4.2. Share of compliant suppliers by year and product types, 2013-2016

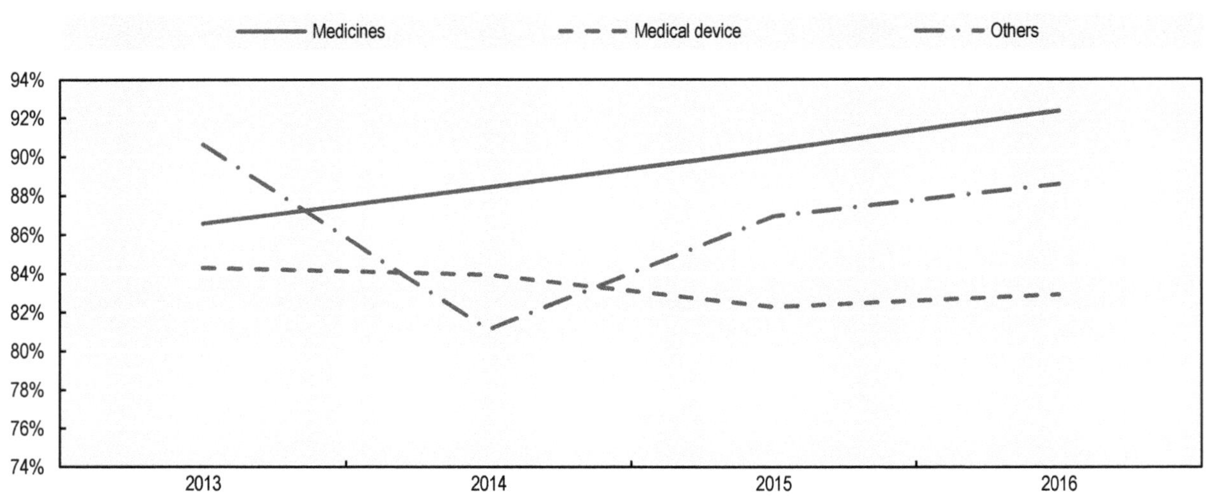

Source: OECD calculations based on IMSS data

Identifying mechanisms and strategies which ensure that suppliers abide by their initial commitments and value propositions is therefore crucial to secure the benefits that were promised in the tendering phase.

Making suppliers accountable not only for inputs, but also for procurement outcomes: IMSS could assess their past performance according to previously agreed and objectively defined criteria

The large share of purchase orders being subject to sanctions calls for tools and strategies which could help to decrease the share of defaulting suppliers. The previous review recommended, among other strategies, grouping the smallest purchase orders which would not otherwise provide sufficient financial interest to suppliers facing fixed transportation and logistics costs. It also recommended assessing the relevance of using past performance evaluation in tender processes.

By comprehensively monitoring and documenting suppliers' performance, public officials can require corrective actions when performance fails to meet the contract requirements. Performance monitoring can also inform future procurement strategies and the selection of suppliers, when their past performance is assessed for award of contracts (OECD, 2016[6]).

As shown in Figure 4.3, repeated non-compliance by suppliers with contractual terms might indeed encourage IMSS to consider assessing their past performance before deciding to award a contract.

Figure 4.3. Share of suppliers that are less than 75% compliant (in terms of number of orders)

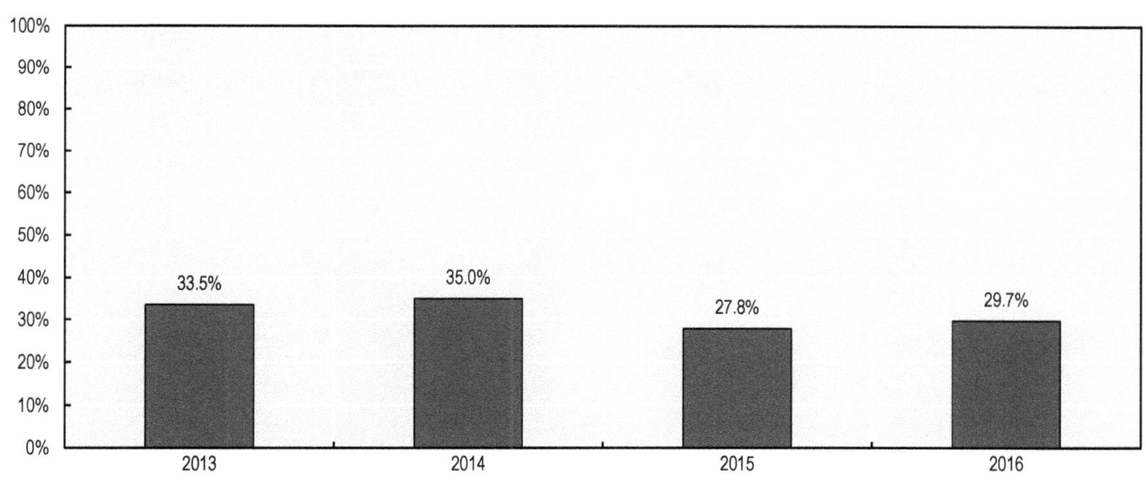

Source: Based on data provided by IMSS

Articles 54 to 61 of the LAASP allow for sanctioning suppliers in case of serious and repeated contractual breaches. The list of sanctioned suppliers is co-ordinated by the SFP and accessible online. It provides contracting entities with the opportunity to verify whether participating bidders have been sanctioned in the past (OECD, 2017[7]).

Sanctions range from a simple fine to a temporary exclusion from future tender processes up to a maximum of five years. While the Mexican normative framework introduces a sort of temporary debarment procedure for suppliers whose performance is repeatedly unsatisfactory, IMSS has not developed a more systemic and structured system to factor in the assessment of bidders the question of past performance.

Other OECD countries take into account suppliers' past performance in tenders in two different ways. The first mechanism is somewhat similar to Mexico's debarment mechanism and integrates this component at the selection stage. In other procurement systems, such as Korea's, past performance is used as a selection criterion (OECD, 2016[6]). To be part of Multiple Award Schedules (Korean framework agreements), suppliers must prove that at least three previous contracts were executed satisfactorily. With the introduction of the EU Directives in 2014 reforming public procurement, past performance, when it relates to the subject matter of the contract, is being introduced in EU countries as a mechanism to screen bidders and exclude those whose past performance has been poor.

The US takes a different approach (Box 4.2). It imposes the use of past performance as an award criterion in tenders exceeding a certain amount. The fundamental difference with this approach is that past performance becomes a component of the relative merits of the bids, rather than a factor excluding suppliers from competing. In this way, suppliers' past performance is taken into account in the comprehensive assessment of their offers.

Box 4.2. Past performance as an award criterion in the US

Federal law generally requires agencies to evaluate and document contractor performance on contracts or orders whose value exceeds the simplified acquisition threshold (generally USD 150 000). The evaluation must generally address the quality of the product or service supplied by the contractor, its efforts to control costs, its timeliness and compliance with schedules, its conduct of management or business relations, its performance in subcontracting with small businesses, and other applicable factors (e.g., tax delinquency). The evaluation and any contractor response comprise the past performance information that is stored in government databases (e.g., Past Performance Information Retrieval System and the Federal Awardee Performance and Integrity Information System), and may be used in future source selection decisions.

Federal law also generally requires agencies to consider contractors' past performance when making source selection decisions in negotiated procurements whose value exceeds the simplified acquisition threshold. In a negotiated procurement, the contract is awarded to the bidder whose proposal represents the "best value" for the government based on various factors identified in the solicitation. These factors typically must include price and past performance. However, other factors may be considered, and procuring agencies determine the weight given to various factors.

Additionally, agencies are required by law to consider whether the contractor has a "satisfactory performance record" when determining whether the contractor is sufficiently "responsible" to be awarded a federal contract. Agencies generally cannot award a contract without determining that the contractor is "responsible." While agencies are generally prohibited from repeatedly finding a contractor non-responsible based upon the same deficient past performance, they may debar or suspend contractors for wilful failure to perform under a contract or contracts, or for a history of failure to perform or of unsatisfactory performance of a contract or contracts.

Source: Adapted from (Manuel, 2015[8]).

Using past performance as a selection or evaluation tool in procurement process sparks debate worldwide, notably over the objectivity of performance assessment, barriers to entry for new suppliers and whether it prevents companies from correcting deficient relationships with the public sector.

However, research assessing the outcomes of recurrent tenders in a specific setting demonstrated that evaluating suppliers' past performance could have positive effects on their future performance. Based on an experiment carried out by an Italian public utility company that introduced a new rating system, the research found that reputational incentives could be a powerful mechanism for improving supplier performance (Decarolis, Pacini and Spagnolo, 2016[9]). The analysis showed that across the 136 parameters scored to assess the satisfactory execution of contracts by suppliers, overall compliance increased from 25% to 80% without a major impact on prices. As critics feared that this evaluation mechanism could create a potential barrier to new entrants, the contracting authority assigned the average ranking to new suppliers by default. This would then be reviewed according to future contract performance.

Besides informing procurement decisions, these efforts can help to define a broader performance assessment framework which could also reshape the relationship between IMSS and its suppliers.

Taking into account its centre-led procurement structure, IMSS could maximise the use of information to monitor suppliers' performance

Being the primary users of procured goods or services, decentralised units can feed suppliers' performance back into defining their next procurement strategy. However, to do so, the central unit should identify those aspects of contract execution on which information should be reported to assess suppliers' performance. As an example, in the case of the procurement of medicines, supplier performance will not only depend on timely delivery, but also on the quality of the product delivered, its traceability or its expiry date.

Decentralised entities provide the central procurement unit with weekly updates of suppliers' non-compliance in terms of instances where breaches have been reported. However, reporting is limited to the identification of a breach and, in case of delays, the amount of undelivered medicines and the number of days the supplier has been subject to penalties.

While providing information on sanctions imposed on suppliers is a first step to assess contractors' compliance, the reported information cannot in itself capture all dimensions of suppliers' performance.

The IT systems in which this information is entered also include the effective dates on which goods or services have been delivered. This information could be used to analyse late delivery, which is one dimension of supplier performance. It could also provide IMSS with further insights into delivery trends for specific product categories and could help to define future delivery timeframes.

As Figure 4.4 shows, an analysis of the average delays in purchase orders subject to penalties suggest an increased tendency for delivery delays to increase on average. While this could be explained by a number of factors specific to some product categories or some delegations, this could also imply weaknesses in the current penalty scheme, as penalties are limited to a maximum of four days of delays.

Figure 4.4. Average delivery delay for IMSS procured products, 2013-2016

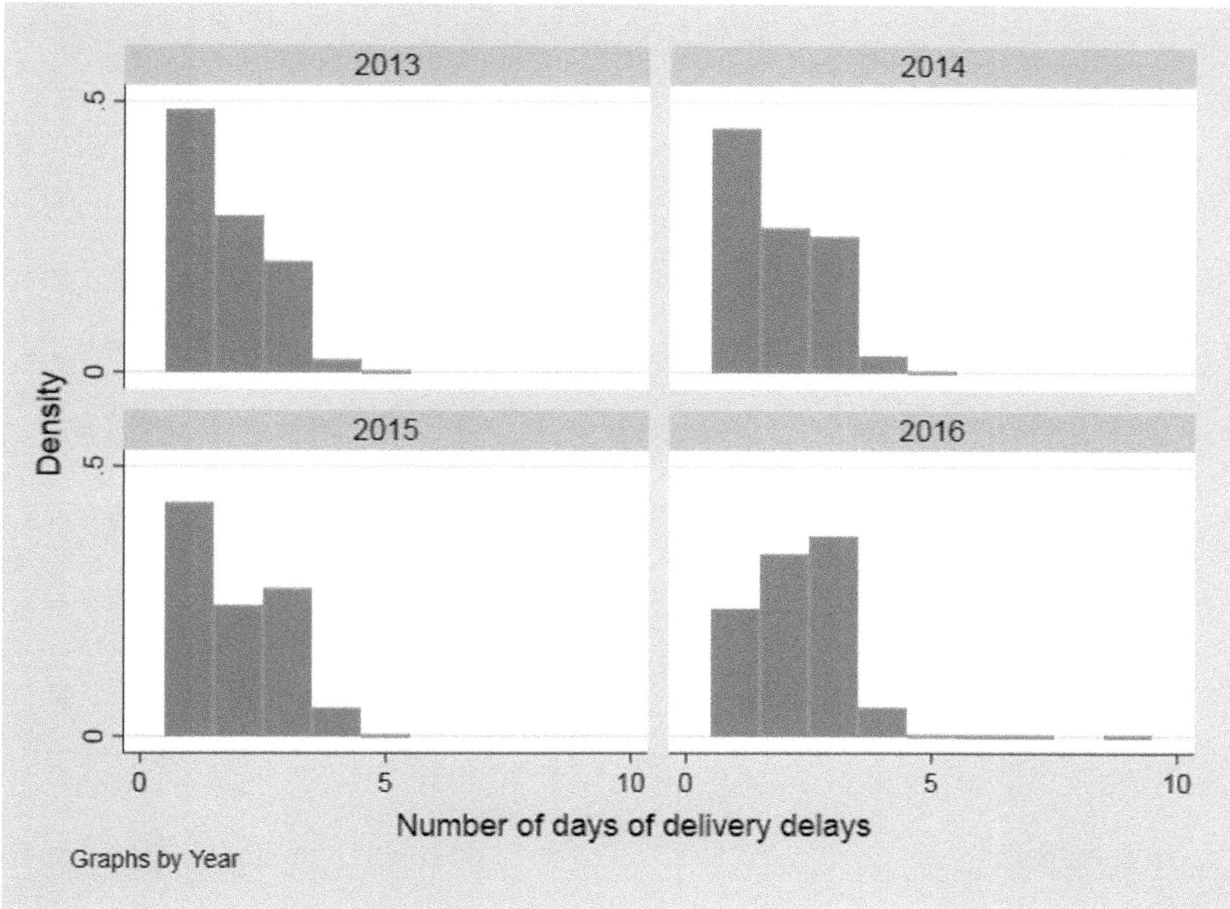

Source: OECD calculations based on data provided by IMSS.

In addition, although IMSS monitors the share of non-compliant products by suppliers, by product references or by delegations both for central and decentralised procurement, this analysis could usefully be complemented by an analysis of the number of non-compliant purchase orders using the same parameters. While the total number of non-compliant products provides an initial overview of overall suppliers' adherence to contractual terms and conditions, it only partially captures the economic impact of these defaults.

Assessing the share of purchase orders that suffers from contractual breaches could provide additional evidence of suppliers' performance and be used as a proxy for the indirect costs linked to these defaults (see Figure 4.5 for an example).

Figure 4.5. Share of non-compliant purchase orders, 2013-2016

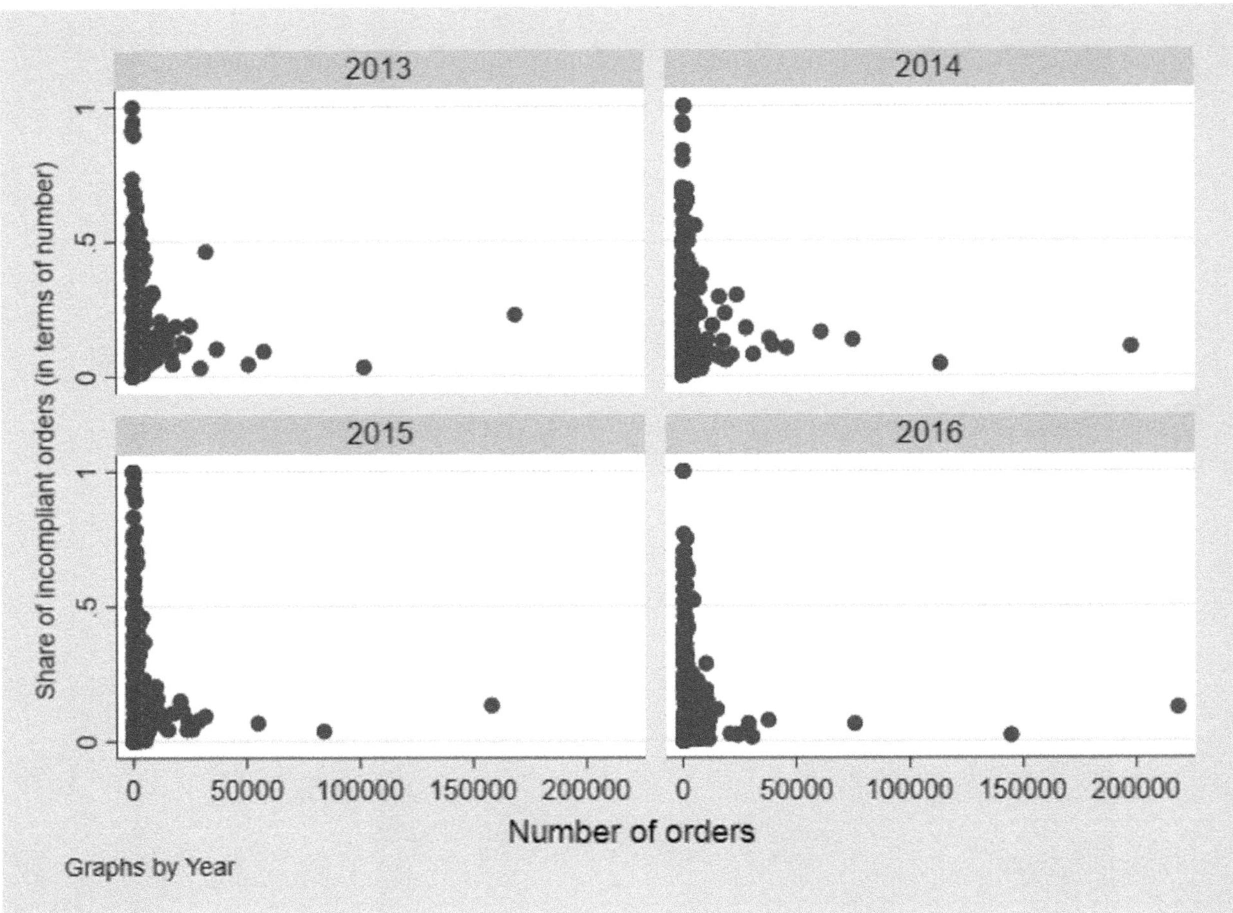

Source: OECD calculations based on data provided by IMSS

Figure 4.5 shows that non-compliance rates for purchase orders are increasing among suppliers receiving few purchase orders. On the other hand, the largest suppliers, those receiving more than 25 000 purchase orders per year as shown in the figure above, have low rates of non-compliance, suggesting that contract management for those suppliers could focus on other aspects of contract execution.

The strategies adopted in certain tenders also provide opportunities to increase the scope for gathering information on contract execution. In specific procurement strategies such as consolidated tenders, this feedback mechanism could be extended to collect information from the contract managers of the other entities participating to those tenders. IMSS can already benefit from additional quantitative and qualitative information gathered through contract management processes developed by other institutions, such as PEMEX, the Mexican state-owned oil company (Box 4.3).

Box 4.3. Contract management processes in PEMEX

The PEMEX directorate which defines the company's procurement methodologies and sourcing strategies has a sub-directorate responsible for relations with suppliers and contractors (*Subdirección de Desarrollo y Relación con Proveedores y Contratistas*, SDRPC).

The centre-led procurement function poses some challenges in objectively assessing suppliers' performance. SDRPC is responsible for the overall oversight of suppliers, and liaises with business units to collect information on suppliers' performance. It uses several IT systems to gather information from the following sources:

- Suppliers registration system: as well as being used to reference bidders and contractors, this tool is also used to implement commercial and financial risk assessments of bidders. Depending on the strategic importance or risk profile of the company, and the amount of contracts they hold with PEMEX, suppliers and contractors may be invited to subscribe to an extended registration. In this case, they are asked to provide additional information and documentation on a wide range of business aspects, including financial, product and service quality certifications, health and safety, and corporate social responsibility policies.
- Transactional information: This information is gathered from PEMEX Enterprise Resource Planning System. This tool, coupled with the system for electronic invoicing, is central to contract administration and includes information which can provide insights into suppliers' performance. An approval workflow tracks the submission of invoices, their validation by business units, and corresponding payments processed by the Finance Corporate Directorate. However, this transactional information only partially and indirectly depicts suppliers' performance on contracts signed with PEMEX.
- Surveys: To address the above information gap and considering PEMEX's centre-led procurement function, additional information is gathered from project managers through periodic surveys. These ask them for feedback on suppliers in the following areas:
  - Understanding the business and client service
  - Innovation and technology
  - Quality
  - Contract management and compliance
  - Human resources
  - Security and social responsibility

Source: Adapted from (OECD, 2017[10])

While these additional analyses could maximise the use of existing information to monitor suppliers' performance, developing a stronger contract management framework will require additional efforts, such as categorising the supplier base against their relative roles in contributing to the delivery of high quality healthcare services. For example, information reported to the central procurement unit does not capture certain perspectives that are essential for implementing strategic contract management such as the quality of after-sales services provided by suppliers or their capacities to develop client relationships.

Re-engineering the relationship between IMSS and its suppliers

While efforts by IMSS to enforce contract terms and conditions have led to greater supplier compliance with their contractual commitments, the high rate of defaults – along with the absence of a comprehensive performance assessment – pose questions about the efficiency of the existing contract management framework. As well as an effective contract management framework, IMSS's commitments to abide by its own obligations also have an impact on its relationships with suppliers.

IMSS's existing guidelines and processes set out similar general contract management principles to those found in other Mexican public institutions. However, the provision of health services puts a greater emphasis on the satisfactory execution of contracts by suppliers.

The direct link between the quality of inputs provided by suppliers such as medicines and equipment, and the output delivered by the public institution responsible for health services, reinforces the centrality of contract execution in health-related procurement. Health providers need to be able to rely not only on compliant, but also well-performing, suppliers.

Supplier relationship management is an approach to managing an organisation's interactions with the companies that supply it with products and services. It can help to reduce costs and enhance the quality of service delivery (Mettler and Rohner, 2008[11]). Going beyond contractual compliance, it defines the processes and relationships for developing an environment conducive to good performance.

A successful contract management strategy can achieve positive results by:

- managing the organisation's own responsibilities during the contract
- ensuring the supplier meets the minimum performance criteria, such as compliance
- allowing supplier performance to improve, both in the short and long term, by developing effective supplier relationships.

While compliance has already been discussed above, the other two points are the subject of the rest of this chapter.

Strengthening supplier performance

Managing the organisation's own responsibilities during the contract: IMSS should consider using not only sticks but also carrots, such as timely payments, to incentivise suppliers' performance

Aside from penalties and additional sanctions, a contract management system that provides suppliers with stable and fair contractual frameworks can improve their performance. Failure to do so not only generates breaches and failures, it also increases the likelihood that premiums will be added to unit prices, thus harming the overall value for money of bidders' financial conditions.

For example, a study of Brazilian pooled procurement experience in the pharmaceutical sector found that failures by some members of the pool to abide by their contractual obligations – notably timely payment – adversely affected the financial conditions granted by suppliers in subsequent tenders (Barbosa and Fiuza, 2011[12]).

Similarly, the previous OECD review found that suppliers' understanding of IMSS procurement strategies could lead to undesirable effects and produce harmful consequences during contract execution. For example, discussions with suppliers clearly revealed that procurement strategies such as subsequent reverse auctions led them to believe that IMSS's overarching objective is to procure specific items at the lowest possible price (OECD, 2013[2]). Indeed in this procurement strategy, bidders are asked to lower their initial proposed price throughout negotiation rounds, and the bidder proposing the lowest price is awarded the contract. This procurement strategy entails that bidders are being asked to compete on price only and to further reduce their margins which could have ultimately an impact on or the willingness of suppliers to abide later in contract execution by costly obligations, such as delivery to remote locations.

IMSS's main obligation to its suppliers, as for all public entities subject to public procurement laws, is to pay promptly for goods and services delivered effectively. Aside from the fact that late payment might be factored in by suppliers in their financial proposal and generate a premium in addition to unit prices offered, payments on time can act as a positive incentive for suppliers to abide by their contractual obligations.

Regular surveys carried out by SFP show that suppliers' perceptions of the timeliness of IMSS's payment – and more generally on the management of payments processes – rank the lowest across Mexican federal public administrations (Figure 4.6).

Figure 4.6. Supplier satisfaction index for management of payments by Federal public entities

Source: Information provided by SFP

According to the public procurement law (art. 51), payment terms should not exceed 20 days following the receipt of the invoice. However, IMSS recognises that in practice payment significantly exceeds this timeframe, either because of the absence of validation by the technical area or because of material errors on the invoices. As shown in

Figure 4.7, significant payment delays occur at both central and local levels, with the average payment timeframe almost amounting to 10 months.

Figure 4.7. Average IMSS payment timeframe for procurement of medicines (2016)

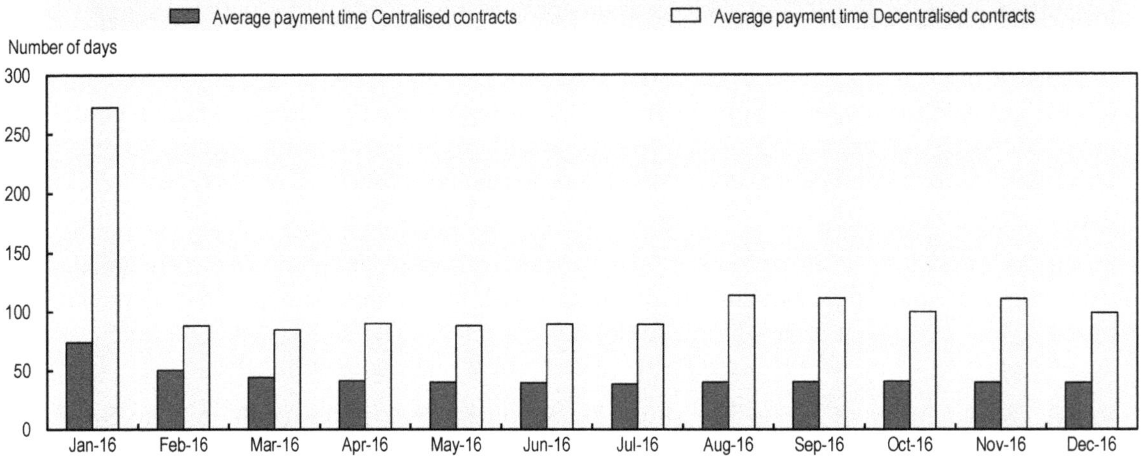

Source: Data provided by IMSS

While this harms suppliers of all sizes and their relationships with IMSS, international experiences suggest that late payments by the public sector affect small and medium-sized enterprises significantly, harming their ability or willingness to participate in public tenders.

However, this issue is not exclusive to IMSS – it is widespread in the Mexican public sector. According to the Ministry of Finance and Public Credit (*Secretaria de Hacienda y Crédito Publico*, SHCP), the amount owed by all the public entities in Mexican states to their suppliers and contractors equalled MXN 49 billion at the end of 2016 (Valdelamar, 2016[13]).

Payment delays not only affect the buyer-supplier relationship, they also increase IMSS's liabilities. Article 51 of the RAASP mentions that unpaid pecuniary amounts can generate interest. Therefore, in contracts which are satisfactorily executed the initial estimated savings are put at risk by delayed payments and potential claims from suppliers. By improving payment timeframes IMSS would therefore not only encourage suppliers to fulfil their contractual obligations, but also protect itself better against future financial liabilities.

Building alignment between IMSS and its suppliers: IMSS could ground suppliers' performance in procurement strategies and selection process

A number of studies stress the benefits of a strategic alignment between buyers and suppliers (see for example (Barratt, 2004[14])). Better supply chain integration can indeed be a strong lever to improve organisational performance. Across different industries, the notion of integration is generally discussed with reference to aligning general corporate strategies and priorities among different organisations within a supply chain. Measures of success include enhanced profitability and customer satisfaction.

Building alignment between IMSS and its suppliers needs to start early in the procurement process, as shown in Figure 4.8. It cannot be achieved after procurement strategies have been implemented and suppliers selected. It requires early communication between IMSS and its suppliers, and the tender process needs to be able to identify companies that are best aligned with its priorities.

Figure 4.8. Development of contract management strategies

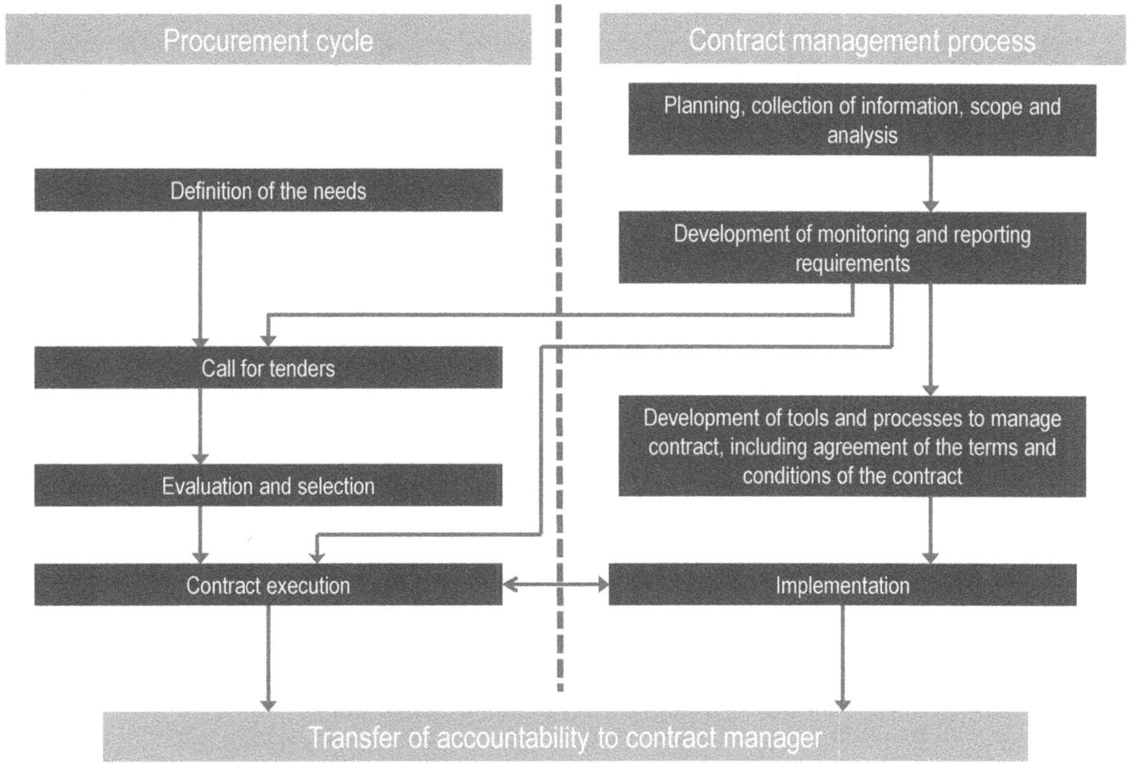

Source: Produced by OECD Secretariat

One crucial feature of contract management in IMSS is medicine procurement, which represents almost 60% of IMSS's total procurement expenditures. Medicines have to be delivered across the country, and sometimes to remote locations. This process is highly dependent on suppliers' ability to respond to emerging needs, such as unpredictable levels of demand, which cannot always be anticipated. The importance of a responsive supply chain has been acknowledged for a long time in the literature as a means of responding quickly to unpredictable demand; and to minimise stock outs, forced markdowns and obsolete inventory (Fisher, 1997[15]).

The previous OECD review identified weaknesses in the management of medicine stocks by the decentralised entities, mostly delegations (OECD, 2013[2]). In response, IMSS defined a process to measure average medicine consumption and to issue replenishment orders as soon as levels dropped below optimal. IMSS also developed processes whereby delegations in the vicinity could provide needed medicines to other locations in an emergency. This process has had the benefit of limiting emergency purchase orders.

Other contracting relationships exist which can respond to the specificities of medicine procurement. For example, on-demand consumption or just-in-time delivery are delivery mechanisms which could provide several advantages to buying organisations, such as limiting stock management costs. Imported from procurement practices in the manufacturing and automotive industries, these approaches require suppliers with extended delivery capacity in order to effectively perform their obligations. IMSS has decided to develop a consumption-on-demand strategy for a selected number of low-cost medicines that are purchased in large volumes. Through this strategy, levels of stocks are monitored and replenishment orders are issued to suppliers as soon as stocks in pharmacies reach a minimum threshold. Applied to 25 drug references, this strategy provides IMSS pharmacies with greater stock flexibility. According to the terms and conditions of the corresponding tenders, bidders are requested to provide the pharmacies directly with the selected medicines within three calendar days of stocks falling below the minimum levels. This specific delivery scheme therefore calls for a thorough assessment of suppliers' capabilities. In addition, under these operating conditions, relations with the supplier should be built on a high degree of mutual trust and openness to increase operational efficiency. When entering into this type of more responsive relationship, it is important that the buyer selects suppliers that have consistently exhibited high levels of quality and delivery reliability.

Tailoring the contract management framework to IMSS's decentralised structure and suppliers' portfolio

To maximise the effectiveness of its contract management framework, IMSS could tailor it against its procurement organisation and allocation of responsibilities

Another element to take into consideration for effective and comprehensive contract management is IMSS's organisational structure. While procurement strategies are designed at the central level, most of the follow-up activities during contract execution are left to decentralised units in the delegations and the highly specialised medical units. As it is these entities which are handling the management of stocks and the receipt of goods and services, they are best-placed to bear this responsibility.

Across OECD countries, almost 85% of centralised purchasing bodies are defining and implementing collaborative procurement instruments, such as framework agreements, to delegate contract management activities linked to purchase orders (OECD, 2017[16]). This relationship resembles the organisational features of IMSS.

To ensure consistent monitoring of contract execution, central purchasing bodies (CPBs) often disseminate to decentralised contract managers best-practice guidelines for sound and robust contract management (GOV U.K. Crown Commercial Service, 2014[17]). The CPB of New Zealand, for example, has developed a framework to ensure that significant contracts managed by contracting entities are consistently assessed and that reported benefits are harmonised (Box 4.4).

Box 4.4. Implementing strategic contract management in New Zealand

New Zealand's Ministry of Business, Innovation and Employment has recently been directed by ministers to establish a framework for the management of government's significant service contracts with third-party providers. The purpose of the framework is to provide confidence to government and the public that important services are being effectively delivered in New Zealand.

The framework includes agency and system-wide visibility, standardised management, oversight and accountability of agencies' significant service contracts. Through the implementation of the framework, agencies will have visibility of their significant service contracts, be positioned to respond to changes, mitigate risks and have assurance that their significant service contracts achieve their intended outcomes.

The framework for managing significant contracts helps agencies outlines a strategic alignment between the agency's objectives and suppliers' execution of the contracts. To do so, it reinforces the following dimensions:

- Visibility on procurement spend by assessing the criticality of the contracts signed with suppliers to achieve the objectives of the agency
- Clarity on expectations by identifying the critical factors which drive effective management of contracts
- Accountability by understanding how contracts are performing and how this performance contributes to the achievement of the agency's objectives
- Building evidence by assessing the agency's performance against pre-defined standards
- Improved capability in agencies and across the government by developing tools and systems to drive best practice

Agencies are required to report back on their significant service contracts every six months, with a first report due in March 2017.

Source: (MBIE, 2017[18]).

To delegate these responsibilities effectively and ensure consistent practices, IMSS could define a standardised minimum contract management framework which would be applied to all delegations and UMAEs. Although guidelines have been developed to define requirements for the inspection process for the delivery of therapeutic and non-therapeutic goods, these do not integrate a structured mechanism for identifying products to be inspected. Neither do they indicate how often the evaluation should be conducted.

Some delegations reported during the fact-finding mission that they inspect all medicines received from suppliers. But since delegations receive on average more than 1 600 medicines per purchase order, a comprehensive inspection of all items received does not seem feasible. This therefore suggests that uneven practices are taking place in delegations and UMAEs, thus questioning the comprehensiveness of the breaches reported besides delays in deliveries. Defining the general principles to be applied in contract management activities would provide IMSS with the assurance that reported activities provide a reliable picture of contract execution.

To strategically allocate resources, IMSS could adapt contract management activities to the criticality of the goods or services procured.

While implementing standardised and robust contract management principles is a prerequisite to ensure that suppliers will deliver the expected value for money promised in their bids, contract management success or failure are also highly dependent on additional factors, such as buyer capabilities and the robustness of IMSS's procurement (NAO, 2016[19]).

A comprehensive and effective contract management framework typically includes the following items (OECD, 2017[10]):

- Planning, information collection and analysis, providing a clear understanding of the contract's surrounding environment (regulatory, commercial, etc…) and allowing for the identification of project risks, mitigation measures and potential effects.
- Contract administration which defines roles and responsibilities in managing the contract, allows for responsiveness in mitigating risks, and ensures objectives are achieved.
- Effective performance reporting and monitoring, providing relevant standardised information on which controls could be based and to support informed decisions.
- Efficient relationship management, creating a long-term relationship of mutual benefit between the parties and enabling them to more effectively anticipate risk before it occurs.
- Governance and integrity mechanisms providing an appropriate setting for interactions with suppliers.
- Effective knowledge sharing and information management ensuring that information on the project can be easily retrieved and accessed, and enabling the parties to comply with obligations on information retention, disclosure and protection.
- Change management which ensures that change events are managed smoothly without creating unnecessary risk or the unintended acceptance of risk.
- Contingency plans allowing for prompt and appropriate reactions to unplanned events.
- Ongoing review of the contract management framework and adapting the framework to changes in strategic business orientations.

IMSS's efforts to implement the various areas listed above would depend on the relative importance of the supplier in the execution of IMSS public service delivery. A review of IMSS's procurement portfolio reveals a great heterogeneity of products and services procured under different strategies and at different levels. For example, consolidated tenders reveal considerable market concentration (Figure 4.9).

Figure 4.9. Market concentration in consolidated tenders for medicines and healing materials, 2017

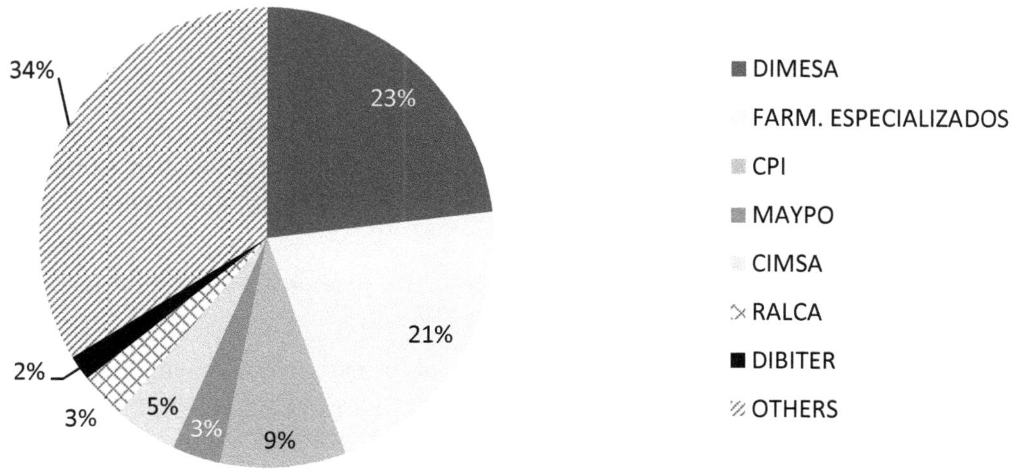

Note: Vaccines and patent/single-source drugs not included
Source: (Investigación Farmacéutica, 2017[20]).

As IMSS's supply base is so diverse, reflecting the types of goods and services it provides, to maximise the value added by suppliers, contract management activities should be tailored to the main characteristics of the suppliers and to the features of their relationship with IMSS.

The example from New Zealand above (Box 4.4) also highlights the relevance of adapting contract management activities to the nature and the importance of the contract to the buying organisation. This builds on the longstanding literature on product segmentation and notably on the seminal work done by Krajlic (Kraljic, 1983[21]) on the classification of products or services based on their supply risk and profit impact. Building upon this exercise, IMSS could tailor its contract management strategies to the criticality of the goods or services procured.

In Australia, Health Purchasing Victoria (HPV), an organisation responsible to the Minister of Health, works with public hospitals and health services in the state to support their procurement operations. It has developed a policy framework, known as the HPV Health Purchasing Policies, to cover the health service's internal procurement practices. HPV has designed these policies to ensure consistency and probity in procurement practice within public hospitals and health services. To implement these policies, a contract management strategy aligned with product categorisation has been developed to indicate to individual entities that the extent and nature of contract management activities depends on the nature of the goods or services procured (Annex 4.A). IMSS could build on this example to develop a contract management strategy tailored to its procurement portfolio.

Proposals for action

To increase the efficiency of the post-award phase and to ensure that the objectives agreed during the bidding stage actually materialise, IMSS should support its suppliers in transitioning from compliance to performance through the following measures:

Strengthen accountability in IMSS's relations with its suppliers

- Ensure that contractual breaches are enforced, but also kept to a level which would not adversely affect the benefits promised in the tendering phase.
- Decrease significantly the average timeframe for paying suppliers; long delays harm the IMSS/supplier relationship and are likely to lead to bidders adding premiums to their proposed prices.
- Make suppliers accountable for procurement outcomes by assessing their past performance according to previously agreed and objectively defined criteria.
- Use existing information in the IT system to capture additional perspectives of contract execution and gain a better understanding of the impact of suppliers' performance on IMSS.

Revisit IMSS's relationship with suppliers to promote better performance and ultimately better healthcare services

- Define contract management strategies at the early procurement stages and embed related requirements into procurement strategies and the selection of suppliers.
- Design a contract management framework adapted to how IMSS organises procurement, i.e. with decentralised units with diverse experience and heterogeneous needs being responsible for the day-to-day management of contracts.
- Tailor contract management activities according to the relative importance of the products and services procured so that resources are efficiently allocated across IMSS's procurement portfolio.

Annex 4.A. Contract management strategy in Monash Health (Health Purchasing Victoria)

Annex Table 4.A.1. Contract management strategy tool

Complexity Quadrant	Value for Money (VFM)	Risk Management and Contingency Planning	Capability and Responsibility	Performance Monitoring	Continuous Improvement
	1. What are essential set of controls (systems and processes) the organisation needs to have in place to ensure value for money outcomes are achieved?	**2. What are the minimum controls the organisation requires to determine if the supply is at risk and what back up arrangements could be required to ensure continuity of service?**	**3. What are the minimum actions the organisation can take to determine the appropriate capability exists to undertake contract management?**	**4. What does the organisation need to do to know if suppliers are fulfilling their contract obligations and if expected commitments are being realised?**	**5. What can the organisation do to improve procurement practice to drive value for money?**
Transactional Low value/low risk, low volume/low frequency of use. Generic or commoditised items	Pricing is relative to industry standards Analysis of TCO in limited circumstances i.e. low initial costs but high ongoing costs	Understanding of market in order to identify other supply points if required By Sourcing Team (buyers) on demand	Level 1 procurement skills	Formal Contract Management Plan Not required / use simple form Delivery In Full, On Time measured by Supply Team Annual review of pricing agreement	Monitor spend by key categories to identify opportunities for aggregation of demand, HPV collective agreements or prequalification arrangements Focus on business improvement via process optimisation

Leveraged High volume / frequency / spread of use. Typically many suppliers	When developing contracts, consider pricing mechanisms such as volume based discounts to enhance VFM Communication and training plan for new contracts to create internal awareness and ensure compliance Develop financial benefits checklist Consider inclusion of non-performance penalties in contract development Aggregation of suppliers considered Assessment of TCO recommended	Use short-form risk assessment and supplier segmentation to understand potential risks Based on market analysis, determine if business continuity plan is required where competitive market does not exist Clear escalation path for issues established and tracking mechanism for all issues Consider Probity Plan. Engage Probity Advisor if indicated (may be internal or external)	Level 1 procurement skills Articulate roles and responsibilities and appoint relationship manager and service delivery manager	Performance management built into contract management framework Implement standard supplier scorecard template and ensure regular benchmark of supplier performance on scorecard Generate standard procurement KPI reporting for management on a regular basis Annual review of pricing agreement and performance against service / delivery KPIs	Processes are in place to monitor variations and extensions of contracts against supplier Implement a supplier relationship management plan, including feedback from supplier and staff performance Engage with contract users to identify opportunities for improvements Establish framework for review of performance and the application of non-performance penalties as required Review financial benefits to monitor achievement of VFM Participate in HPV reference groups

Focused Limited suppliers &alternatives, Limited volume/frequency/spread of use, potential high risk to operations Higher level of customisation, scope for innovation, high switching costs	When developing contracts, consider pricing mechanisms such as alliance, penalties/incentives/risk share arrangements, and other pricing models to enhance value Ensure total cost of ownership has been calculated and accounted for including all ongoing service requirements Build service performance KPIs into contract Develop tailored financial benefits checklist to drive VFM Consider inclusion of non-performance penalties in contract development	Undertake long-form risk assessment and supplier segmentation to understand potential risks Require suppliers to submit business continuity plans Detailed contingency planning is undertaken and regularly reviewed Establish a clear escalation path and tracking mechanism for all issues Complete Probity Plan. Engage Probity Advisor if indicated (may be internal or external)	Level 3 procurement skills Articulate roles and responsibilities and appoint a relationship manager and service delivery manager Consider level of involvement required by technical / subject matter expert	Develop KPIs tailored to contract and project outcomes. Ensure these can be efficiently and consistently measured with minimal effort KPIs are included in the ITS Ensure supplier buy-in for performance management program in order to develop the framework of a relationship that works for all parties involved Implement a tailored supplier scorecard (using the template) and ensure regular benchmark of supplier performance on scorecard Reviews conducted quarterly for 1st 12 months, thereafter 6-12 monthly for the term	Processes are in place to monitor variations and extensions of contract against suppliers Implement a supplier relationship management plan, including feedback from both suppliers and staff on contract performance Establish framework for review of performance and the application of non-performance penalties as required Review financial benefits to monitor achievement of VFM and identify areas of improvement Evaluate tender & contract administration performance

Strategic High value Competitive market High visibility, affects most areas of business Critically affects operations	When developing contracts, consider pricing mechanisms such as alliance, penalties/incentives/risk share arrangements to enhance value Ensure total cost of ownership has been calculated and accounted for including all ongoing service requirements Build service performance indicators into contract Develop tailored financial benefits checklist to drive VFM Consider inclusion of non-performance penalties in contract development Communication and training plan for new contracts Seek to drive value beyond price	Undertake long-form risk assessment and supplier segmentation to understand potential risks Require suppliers to submit business continuity plan Detailed contingency planning is undertaken and regularly reviewed Establish a clear escalation path and tracking mechanism for all issues Complete Probity Plan Engage Probity Advisor if indicated (may be internal or external)	Level 4 procurement skills Articulate roles and responsibilities, appointing relationship managers and service delivery managers, ensuring a clear escalation path for all issues Consider establishment of project Steering Committee to oversee procurement process and ensure probity and VFM outcomes throughout process Consider level of involvement required by technical/subject matter expert where the good or service being procured is highly technical	Develop KPIs tailored to contract and project outcomes. Ensure these can be efficiently and consistently measured Ensure supplier buy-in to performance management program Implement a tailored supplier scorecard template and ensure regular benchmark of supplier performance on scorecard Establish feedback forums to identify performance issues or improvement opportunities Establish regular stakeholder meetings as part of the performance monitoring process to identify and quickly raise any performance issues Reviews conducted quarterly for 1st 12 months, thereafter 6-12 monthly for the term of the contract	Processes are in place to monitor variations and extensions of contract against supplier Regular reviews by senior management of performance reporting Establish framework, including relevant stakeholders, for review of performance and the application of non-performance penalties as required Non-performance penalties are enforced i.e. a case by case basis considering the degree of loss or disruption and/or the availability of alternatives Review financial benefits to monitor performance Identify areas of improvement, and opportunities for innovation (one initiative annually)Evaluate tender & contract administration performance

Source: (Monash Health, 2015[22]).

References

ASF (2013), "Financial audit with a focus on performance", http://www.asf.gob.mx/Trans/Informes/IR2013i/Documentos/Auditorias/2013_0195_a.pdf (accessed on 21 November 2017). [4]

ASF (2014), "Financial audit with a focus on performance, (in Spanish) Auditoria Superior de la Federación", https://www.asf.gob.mx/Trans/Informes/IR2014i/Documentos/Auditorias/2014_0163_a.pdf. [5]

Barbosa, K. and E. Fiuza (2011), "Demand Aggregation and Credit Risk Effects in Pooled Procurement:Evidence from the Brazilian Public Purchases of Pharmaceuticals and Medical Supplies", No. 299, Sâo Paulo School of Economics, Sâo Paulo, http://bibliotecadigital.fgv.br/dspace/bitstream/handle/10438/10009/TD%20299%20-%20C-Micro%2014%20-%20Klenio%20Barbosa%20e%20EduardoFiuza.pdf;sequence=1. [12]

Barratt, M. (2004), "Understanding the meaning of collaboration in the supply chain", *Supply Chain Management: An International Journal*, Vol. 9/1, pp. 30-42, http://dx.doi.org/10.1108/13598540410517566. [14]

Decarolis, F., R. Pacini and G. Spagnolo (2016), "Contractors' Past Performance and Procurement Outcomes: A Firm-level Experiment", *Stanford Institute for Economic Policy Research Discussion Paper*, No. 16-036, Stanford Institute for Economic Policy ResearcH, Stanford, https://siepr.stanford.edu/sites/default/files/publications/16-036.pdf (accessed on 21 November 2017). [9]

Fisher, M. (1997), "What Is the Right Supply Chain for Your Product?", *Harvard Business Review 75*, https://hbr.org/1997/03/what-is-the-right-supply-chain-for-your-product. [15]

GOV U.K. Crown Commercial Service (2014), *Commercial capability: contract management standards*, https://www.gov.uk/government/publications/commercial-capability-contract-management-standards (accessed on 21 November 2017). [17]

Investigación Farmacéutica (2017), *Major results of the consolidated tenders 2017, (Principales Resultados de los Fallos de CC 2017)*. [20]

Kraljic, P. (1983), "Purchasing Must Become Supply Management", *Harvard Business Review*, https://hbr.org/1983/09/purchasing-must-become-supply-management (accessed on 21 November 2017). [21]

Manuel, K. (2015), "Evaluating the "Past Performance" of Federal Contractors: Legal Requirements and Issues", https://fas.org/sgp/crs/misc/R41562.pdf (accessed on 21 November 2017). [8]

MBIE (2017), *Significant Service Contracts Framework*, http://www.procurement.govt.nz/procurement/for-agencies/key-guidance-for-agencies/significant-service-contracts-framework (accessed on 10 July 2017). [18]

Mettler, T. and P. Rohner (2008), "Supplier Relationship Management im Krankenhaus", *HMD Praxis der Wirtschaftsinformatik*, Vol. 45/1, pp. 87-95, http://dx.doi.org/10.1007/BF03341177. [11]

Monash Health (2015), *Contract management strategy tool*, http://www.monashhealth.org/page/Suppliers (accessed on 21 November 2017). [22]

NAO (2016), *Good practice contract management framework*, https://www.nao.org.uk/wp-content/uploads/2016/12/Good_practice_contract_management_framework.pdf (accessed on 21 November 2017). [19]

OECD (2013), *Public Procurement Review of the State's Employees' Social Security and Social Services Institute in Mexico*, OECD Public Governance Reviews, OECD Publishing, Paris, http://dx.doi.org/10.1787/9789264197305-en. [2]

OECD (2015), *OECD Recommendation of the Council on Public Procurement*, http://www.oecd.org/gov/ethics/OECD-Recommendation-on-Public-Procurement.pdf. [3]

OECD (2016), *The Korean Public Procurement Service: Innovating for Effectiveness*, OECD Public Governance Reviews, OECD Publishing, Paris, http://dx.doi.org/10.1787/9789264249431-en. [6]

OECD (2017), *OECD Integrity Review of Mexico: Taking a Stronger Stance Against Corruption*, OECD Public Governance Reviews, OECD Publishing, Paris, http://dx.doi.org/10.1787/9789264273207-en. [7]

OECD (2017), *Public Procurement Review of Mexico's PEMEX: Adapting to Change in the Oil Industry*, OECD Public Governance Reviews, OECD Publishing, Paris, http://dx.doi.org/10.1787/9789264268555-en. [10]

OECD (2017), *Government at a Glance 2017*, OECD Publishing, Paris, http://dx.doi.org/10.1787/gov_glance-2017-en. [16]

Rajagopal, A. (2009), "Buyer–supplier relationship and operational dynamics", *Journal of the Operational Research Society*, Vol. 60/3, pp. 313-320, http://dx.doi.org/10.1057/palgrave.jors.2602560. [1]

Valdelamar, J. (2016), "Gobiernos estatales deben 49 mil mdp a proveedores", *El Financiero*, http://www.elfinanciero.com.mx/economia/gobiernos-estatales-deben-49-mil-mdp-a-proveedores.html (accessed on 22 November 2017). [13]

Part II. The way forward to procurement excellence

Chapter 5. Fostering stakeholder engagement in the procurement of health services at IMSS

Openness should be a critical feature of public procurement for reducing waste, preventing corruption and restoring trust. It should not only be required in laws and regulations, but should also be part of the culture of integrity and the accountability practices of public organisations. This chapter discusses the steps taken by IMSS to ensure transparency and stakeholder participation in public procurement within the framework of Mexico's transparency regulations. These steps include improving consultation processes when amending procurement regulations; initiatives to enhance supplier engagement so as to upgrade competition and transparency in tenders; and mechanisms to facilitate citizen participation in public procurement activities, for example as social witnesses and observers. The chapter concludes with recommendations for IMSS to strengthen still further its mechanisms for stakeholder engagement and to take transparency to a stage where citizens can benefit from systematised and consistent information.

Stakeholder engagement and transparency in procurement procedures help to create a level playing field for suppliers and achieve value for money. In addition, they can be critical for fostering competition in public procurement and opening channels for civil society participation. Indeed, scrutiny by civil society organisations, the media, and the wider public of procurement operations creates positive incentives for public officials and complements government accountability and control mechanisms.

The Recommendation of the OECD Council on Public Procurement outlines specific principles when dealing with transparency and stakeholder participation (Box 5.1). Since the publication of the previous OECD public procurement review of IMSS (OECD, 2013[1]), the institution has made continuous efforts to reach out to the main stakeholders of its procurement activities. These initiatives are reviewed and assessed throughout this chapter.

Public procurement carries a high risk of integrity failures. This is so not only because of the interaction between the public and the private sectors in procurement operations, but also because of the amounts involved. In fact, the OECD *Foreign Bribery Report* (OECD, 2014[2]) found that 57% of cases of foreign bribery were related to obtaining public procurement contracts, based on data from the 427 foreign bribery cases that have been concluded since the entry into force of the OECD Anti-Bribery Convention in 1999.[1]

Furthermore, openness should be a critical feature of public procurement in the pursuit of reducing waste, preventing corruption and restoring trust. Openness should not only be required in laws and regulations, but should also be part of the culture of integrity and the accountability practices of public organisations (Box 5.2; and see Chapter 7).

This chapter reviews the legal requirements for transparency in procurement, as well as the provisions for involving stakeholders in defining procurement regulations, and involving suppliers in the procurement system. The chapter concludes with recommendations for further improving transparency and access to information policies, for improving consultation surrounding procurement regulations, and for strengthening the role of social witnesses and observers.

Box 5.1. Principles for transparency and stakeholder participation in the Recommendation of the OECD Council on Public Procurement

Adherents are recommended to ensure an adequate degree of transparency of the public procurement system in all stages of the procurement cycle. To this end, Adherents should:

i) Promote fair and equitable treatment for potential suppliers by providing an adequate and timely degree of transparency in each phase of the public procurement cycle, while taking into account the legitimate needs for protection of trade secrets and proprietary information and other privacy concerns, as well as the need to avoid information that can be used by interested suppliers to distort competition in the procurement process. Additionally, suppliers should be required to provide appropriate transparency in subcontracting relationships;

ii) Allow free access, through an online portal, for all stakeholders, including potential domestic and foreign suppliers, civil society and the general public, to public procurement information notably related to the public procurement system (e.g. institutional frameworks, laws and regulations), the specific procurements (e.g. procurement forecasts, calls for tender, award announcements), and the performance of the public procurement system (e.g. benchmarks, monitoring results). Published data should be meaningful for stakeholder uses; and

iii) Ensure visibility of the flow of public funds, from the beginning of the budgeting process throughout the public procurement cycle to allow (a) stakeholders to understand government priorities and spending, and (b) policy makers to organise procurement strategically.

Adherents are recommended to foster transparent and effective stakeholder participation. To this end, Adherents should:

i) Develop and follow a standard process when formulating changes to the public procurement system. Such standard process should promote public consultations, invite the comments of the private sector and civil society, ensure the publication of the results of the consultation phase and explain the options chosen, all in a transparent manner;

ii) Engage in transparent and regular dialogues with suppliers and business associations to present public procurement objectives and to assure a correct understanding of markets. Effective communication should be conducted to provide potential vendors with a better understanding of the country's needs, and government buyers with information to develop more realistic and effective tender specifications by better understanding market capabilities. Such interactions should be subject to due fairness, transparency and integrity safeguards, which vary depending on whether an active procurement process is ongoing. Such interactions should also be adapted to ensure that foreign companies participating in tenders receive transparent and effective information; and

iii) Provide opportunities for direct involvement of relevant external stakeholders in the procurement system with a view to increase transparency and integrity while assuring an adequate level of scrutiny, provided that confidentiality, equal treatment and other legal obligations in the procurement process are maintained.

Source: (OECD, 2015[3]).

Box 5.2. Principles for transparency and stakeholder engagement in the OECD Recommendation on Public Integrity

Adherents are recommended to encourage transparency and stakeholders' engagement at all stages of the political process and policy cycle to promote accountability and the public interest, in particular through:

a) promoting transparency and an open government, including ensuring access to information and open data, along with timely responses to requests for information;

b) granting all stakeholders – including the private sector, civil society and individuals – access in the development and implementation of public policies;

c) averting the capture of public policies by narrow interest groups through managing conflict of interest situations, and instilling transparency in lobbying activities and in the financing of political parties and election campaigns; and

d) encouraging a society that includes "watchdog" organisations, citizens groups, labour unions and independent media.

Source: (OECD, 2016[4]).

Meeting transparency and access-to-information requirements for public procurement

IMSS should consider establishing a centralised quality control function for the information disclosed in different sources, while implementing the Open Contracting Data Standard format. This would reduce the potential for inconsistencies among different platforms.

IMSS is required by law to proactively disclose relevant procurement-related information. Mexico has about two decades of experience in working on freedom of information regulations. The 2002 Federal Law on Transparency and Access to Government Public Information *(Ley Federal de Transparencia y Acceso a la Información Pública Gubernamental*) was the first to establish the duty of public entities of the federal government to disclose information proactively and upon request by individuals. This initiative was reinforced in 2007 when access to information became a constitutional right in Mexico.

More recently, in May 2015, Congress issued the General Law on Transparency and Access to Public Information (*Ley General de Transparencia y Acceso a la Información Pública*, LGTAIP), which requires even more information items to be disclosed proactively, many of them having to do with public procurement. Indeed, the LGTAIP is explicit about the procurement-related information that should be disclosed. This includes the outcome of procedures of direct awards, restricted invitations and public tenders, including the public versions of the files and the awarded contracts containing the information described in Table 5.1.

Table 5.1. The information to be proactively disclosed regarding procurement contracts

Direct awards	Restricted invitation or public tender
Bid proposal submitted by the participant	Call for tender and its legal basis
The legal basis to carry out the process	Name of the participants or invitees
Authorisation for the direct award	The awarded bidder and justification
If applicable, the quotes considered, specifying the suppliers and the prices	Invitations issued
The name of the company or individual awarded the contract	The award decision
The requiring and the purchasing units	The contract and its annexes, if applicable
Number and amount of the contract, date, and time for delivery or execution	Surveillance and oversight mechanisms
Surveillance and oversight mechanisms	Budget code
Progress reports (physical and financial) of the works or services awarded	Origin of the resources
Completion agreement	Contractual modifications, including objective and date
Payment	Progress reports (physical and financial) of the works or services awarded
	Completion agreement
	Payment

Source: (Government of Mexico, 2015[5]).

This freedom of information regime is applicable to IMSS. In fact, as detailed in Table 5.2, during the period October 2015-September 2016, IMSS was the institution whose information was the most consulted in the Transparency Duties Portal (*Portal de Obligaciones de Transparencia*, POT).[2] Although the information consulted is not necessarily procurement-related, data show that 15.3% of the cases throughout the federal public administration were looking for information on contracts (INAI, 2016[6]).

Table 5.2. Ministries and entities whose information was most consulted in the Transparency Duties Portal

October 2015-September 2016

Ministry/Entity	Times consulted	% of total
IMSS	1 806 271	5
Revenue Service (SAT)	1 598 166	4.5
Ministry for the Environment and Natural Resources (SEMARNAT)	1 105 191	3.1
Ministry for Transport and Communications (SCT)	1 040 926	2.9
Ministry of Finance and Public Credit	1 029 705	2.9

Source: (INAI, 2016[6]).

The LGTAIP empowers citizens to request specific information that has not been proactively disclosed. Data across Mexico's Public Administration illustrate that the number of requests for information has increased substantially in the past four years (from 109 406 in 2013 to 202 365 in the period encompassing the fourth quarter of 2015 and the third quarter of 2016).

The response to a citizen's request can be either positive (e.g. information is disclosed and provided to the requester) or negative (e.g. information is not disclosed, either because it was non-existent, reserved, or confidential). When disclosed, the information can be provided by electronic means or on paper. During 2016, citizens filed 33 038 information requests; in 89% of the cases, IMSS provided the information that was requested. In 11% of the cases, information was not provided.

Besides the POT and the duty to answer individual information requests, entities in the federal public administration, including IMSS, have to disclose procurement-related information on several other platforms, including the e-procurement portal CompraNet and in SIPOT, a new portal being developed by the National Institute for Transparency, Freedom of Information, and Personal Data Protection (*Instituto Nacional de Transparencia, Acceso a la Información y Protección de Datos Personales*, INAI) to facilitate compliance with the expanded requirements of the LGTAIP. On top of that, IMSS publishes information on the Mexican Government's Open Data portal (datos.gob.mx) and on its own websites.

CompraNet provides free information and no previous registration is required to consult it. It includes information on tender procedures, contract awards history, and challenges (*inconformidades*) filed with the procuring entity's Internal Control body. These items of information refer to ongoing and completed tenders. All the consolidated tenders are, in fact, managed through CompraNet, which also includes information on the procurement process (e.g. annual procurement programmes on acquisitions, leases and services, calls for tender and its amendments, minutes of the clarification meetings, and the reports of social witnesses).

In 2011, IMSS created the Procurement Portal (*Portal de Compras del IMSS*, http://compras.imss.gob.mx). The portal was created with the intention of enhancing transparency and improving the understanding of IMSS expenditures. It presents IMSS procurement activities in a user-friendly manner, and provides a full picture of how, on what and why IMSS spends its resources, as well as the benefits achieved through these activities. It also includes information on what was procured by delegations and highly specialised medical units (*Unidades Médicas de Alta Especialidad*, UMAEs).[3]

The portal contains information directed to suppliers and potential suppliers and the wider public. For example, some of the useful information for suppliers includes the most purchased goods by IMSS, the annual procurement plan, frequently asked questions, and suppliers who sold the most to IMSS. Potential suppliers can benefit from information on how IMSS procures, how to sell to IMSS, and how to register in the IMSS suppliers' catalogue. Likewise, the general public can find the reports by social witnesses who observe tender procedures (described later in this chapter), and the regulations applicable to IMSS procurement. There are also various categories of general statistics regarding IMSS procurement. To increase transparency further, IMSS could include additional information, such as contract modifications and a list of contracts awarded to each supplier.

In addition to providing important information to suppliers and the general public, the portal functions as a knowledge tool for IMSS's various purchasing units, including the decentralised ones (i.e., the delegations and UMAEs).[4] For example, the Procurement Portal has a section on suppliers who have failed to comply with contracts. This information could be used by the purchasing units to assess the risks of working with specific suppliers.

While IMSS is required by law to proactively disclose relevant procurement-related information, there is a risk of inconsistency between the different platforms (i.e., CompraNet, SIPOT, IMSS Procurement Portal, datos.gob.mx). Although this is not a problem exclusive to IMSS, different transparency requirements impose a heavy burden on the public officials who have to process and upload information in the various platforms and under different formats. There is also a risk of inconsistency in the information disclosed, creating confusion and distrust among stakeholders. An initiative led by the Ministry of Public Administration (*Secretaría de la Función Pública*, SFP) aims to standardise these requirements by following the Open Contracting Data Standard (OCDS). In fact, the Mexican Government launched its Open Contracting Portal in November 2017. By starting to work under this standard now, IMSS will be prepared for when it becomes a formal requirement. In the meantime, IMSS could set up a team in the Transparency Unit to control the quality of information and verify consistency among different platforms. Indeed, the implementation of the OCDS and quality control could be parallel efforts to make the best use of human resources.

Improving consultation processes to amend public procurement regulations

As a measure of good practice, create an internal policy to subject IMSS's procurement-related rules to the regulatory quality requirements and controls established in the Federal Law of Administrative Procedure (LFPA), but which are currently not necessarily applicable to IMSS.

IMSS has been a reference for procurement reform, making sustained efforts to improve procurement practices. As such it would benefit from institutionalising a policy allowing stakeholders to comment on draft regulations on procurement. Early regulatory consultation would be in line with consultations carried out for the actual procurement processes (held before even the publication of draft calls for tender). This policy would be consistent with wider transparency and openness practices, beyond those required by law, and would support other strategies for creating trust among suppliers and other stakeholders.

In Mexico, regulatory consultation (i.e. consulting stakeholders on the contents of draft regulations) is strongly influenced by the requirements formally established in two separate pieces of legislation. First, the Federal Law of Administrative Procedure (*Ley Federal de Procedimiento Administrativo*, LFPA) sets out specific public consultation requirements as an integral part of the Regulatory Impact Assessment (RIA) process applicable to draft primary and secondary regulations.[5] Second, transparency legislation has established more general consultation requirements that are independent of the RIA process. In particular, this law requires all regulatory proposals to be published on the website of the relevant ministry or regulatory agency.

The RIA process provides important public consultation opportunities, as well as relevant safeguards to ensure that adequate account is taken of comments received from stakeholders. In particular, the Federal Commission for Regulatory Improvement (*Comisión Federal de Mejora Regulatoria*, COFEMER) publishes all draft RIA as soon as they are received, as well as its own comments on the draft RIA and all inputs received from stakeholders. This generalised publication of a wide range of RIA-related documentation is good practice among OECD countries. Importantly, publication of COFEMER's response to the draft RIA provides stakeholders with additional information that can potentially allow them to participate more effectively in the process. For example, by highlighting weaknesses in the analysis, this material may assist stakeholders to identify data or other materials they possess which could be fed into the analysis to enhance its quality. More generally, the publication of all stakeholder comments on the proposal provides the basis for a more detailed dialogue on its merits among interested parties (OECD, 2014[7]).

The draft RIA is required to be open to consultation for at least 20 working days; in practice, however, much longer consultation periods appear to be the norm. This reflects, in part, the need for COFEMER to undertake its initial analysis of the RIA document and publish its response. Consequently, the process provides extensive opportunities for stakeholder input.

It is always a possibility that procurement-related regulations only impose compliance costs for government institutions, but not for private individuals. In such a case, an exception may be requested. For example, COFEMER exempted the State Employees' Social Security and Social Services Institute (*Instituto de Seguridad y Servicios Sociales de los Trabajadores del Estado*, ISSSTE) Procurement Guidelines (also known as POBALINES) from the RIA process in October 2011 on this basis.[6]

In light of the possibility of exceptions to the regulatory quality controls, it would be convenient for IMSS to establish an internal protocol to subject itself systematically to the regulatory impact process when developing new procurement rules, even in cases where there are no compliance costs beyond those to be managed internally by the institute. By doing so, IMSS would not only subject itself to the control and the expertise provided by COFEMER, but it would also benefit from the wide open and sophisticated consultation RIA process, allowing stakeholders to access more information on the draft procurement regulations IMSS wants to advance and hence facilitating their more effective engagement.

Institutionalise early regulatory consultation (pre-RIA) for the reform or development of procurement rules

Consultation can play different roles at the various stages of the regulatory process. Extended post-RIA consultation, while of substantial value in its own right, is not a complete substitute for pre-RIA consultation. The OECD has previously noted an evolving tendency in member countries to adopt different forms of consultation in combination, to improve its overall performance. This reflects growing understanding of the strengths and weaknesses of different consultation strategies and of the fact that they are suited to specific circumstances and to different stages in the consultative process. As consultation is tending to begin much earlier in the policy-making process, it is increasingly common for it to be conducted in several stages, with different mechanisms employed at different times. In the Mexican context, it has been noted that post-RIA consultation is often very much oriented towards technical issues. This is a result of the fact that a proposed regulation is well advanced in its development by the time the draft RIA has been published. Hence, there might not be much room to modify a draft regulatory proposal once it reaches COFEMER (OECD, 2014[7]).

COFEMER does support effective consultation by actively distributing the draft RIA to key stakeholders and soliciting their inputs in many cases. However, while consultation on the draft RIA is extensive, and is one of the strengths of Mexico's impact assessment process, there is no formal requirement for consultation to be conducted prior to its publication. While the adoption of transparency regulations appears to have significantly expanded the amount of consultation undertaken by public entities overall, there are also wide divergences in practice. While some entities undertake substantial pre-RIA consultation, others do not, preferring to use the RIA process as their main consultation vehicle.

In order to realise the benefits of early consultation, including measuring the potential acceptance of reforms or new rules and identifying undesired potential outcomes, IMSS would benefit from establishing pre-RIA consultation as a standard practice.

Engaging suppliers in the procurement system

Start the supplier engagement process earlier and make it more systematic, even involving the other institutions participating in the consolidated tenders. This would allow suppliers' suggestions to have a real impact on tender processes and procurement strategies.

Good governance of public procurement entails inclusiveness and participation. Consultation and dialogue with relevant stakeholders can help identify opportunities for improvement, bottlenecks in processes, and risks (including integrity risks). Allowing the participation of stakeholders in the procurement system not only helps to improve processes, but also adds a layer of scrutiny to safeguard integrity and advance transparency. Furthermore, wide opportunities for dialogue may help spot collusion risks and improve tender design to maximise competition.

During 2016, IMSS organised several meetings with business chambers. These meetings allowed the chambers to express their concerns before launching the annual consolidated tender. The meetings took place every week and allowed the chambers to raise issues in the contractual relationships stemming from the consolidated tender. These comments led to adjustments in the calls for tender and delivery conditions. Furthermore, feedback received from suppliers led IMSS to move the consolidated tender for 2017 forward by one month, an improvement that was praised by the industry.

Monthly meetings with business associations also take place during the bidding period and every two months once contracts have been awarded. Participants include the following business organisations:

- Industry Chambers Confederation (*Confederación de Cámaras Industriales*, CONCAMIN)
- Mexico's Exployers Confederation (*Confederación Patronal de la República Mexicana*, COPARMEX)
- Business Co-ordination Council (*Consejo Coordinador Empresarial*, CCE)
- National Chamber of the Pharmaceutical Industry (*Cámara Nacional de la Industria Farmaceútica*, CANIFARMA)
- National Association of Medical Supplies Distributors (*Asociación Nacional de Distribuidores de Insumos para la Salud*, ANDIS)
- Confederation of National Chambers of Commerce, Services, and Tourism (*Confederación de Cámaras Nacionales de Comercio, Servicios y Turismo*, CONCANACO-SERVYTUR).

Formal dialogue between IMSS and potential suppliers also takes place through the clarification meetings as part of the bidding process. Clarification meetings can either be physical meetings or held on line. All tenders should include at least one clarification meeting, but there can be more. The minutes of the clarification meetings are public and displayed on paper in the IMSS offices and electronically on CompraNet.

On 20 July 2017, IMSS launched the Strategy to Advance Competition in Public Tenders, which aims to facilitate participation by the largest number of bidders in the market and to upgrade procurement conditions in terms of price and quality for IMSS. The strategy is based on two pillars:

1. Strengthening the tender processes carried out by IMSS (to be described in the next section).
2. Protocol for carrying out priority tenders.

The protocol establishes higher standards than those required by law for tenders that have been classified as a priority using the following criteria:

- Social impact: tenders with a high impact due to the type of good or service to be purchased.
- Adjustments in the call for tender: tenders whose terms have been adjusted relative to previous processes in order to increase participation.
- Size: tenders exceeding MXN 500 million.

The protocol starts by identifying those tender processes at risk of being subject to external pressures. The whole process of these tenders is public and involves stakeholders at every stage. As of July 2017, IMSS had identified eight priority processes for goods and services and five for works which will be subject to the protocol during 2017. The implementation of the protocol consists of the following steps (see Figure 5.1):

- A meeting is organised with external stakeholders, including business chambers and civil society organisations, two weeks before the publication of the call for tender. During these meetings, IMSS staff explain the tender process and, if it differs from previous processes, explain the reasons why.
- The call for tender is published on CompraNet for ten working days.
- A press conference is held the day of the publication of the call for tender and the day of the award of the contract. These press conferences involve external stakeholders, such as business chambers and civil society organisations.
- Clarification meetings, opening of bids, and the award event are broadcasted on several platforms (IMSS's own platform, Twitter, and Facebook).

Figure 5.1. IMSS's protocol for carrying out priority tenders

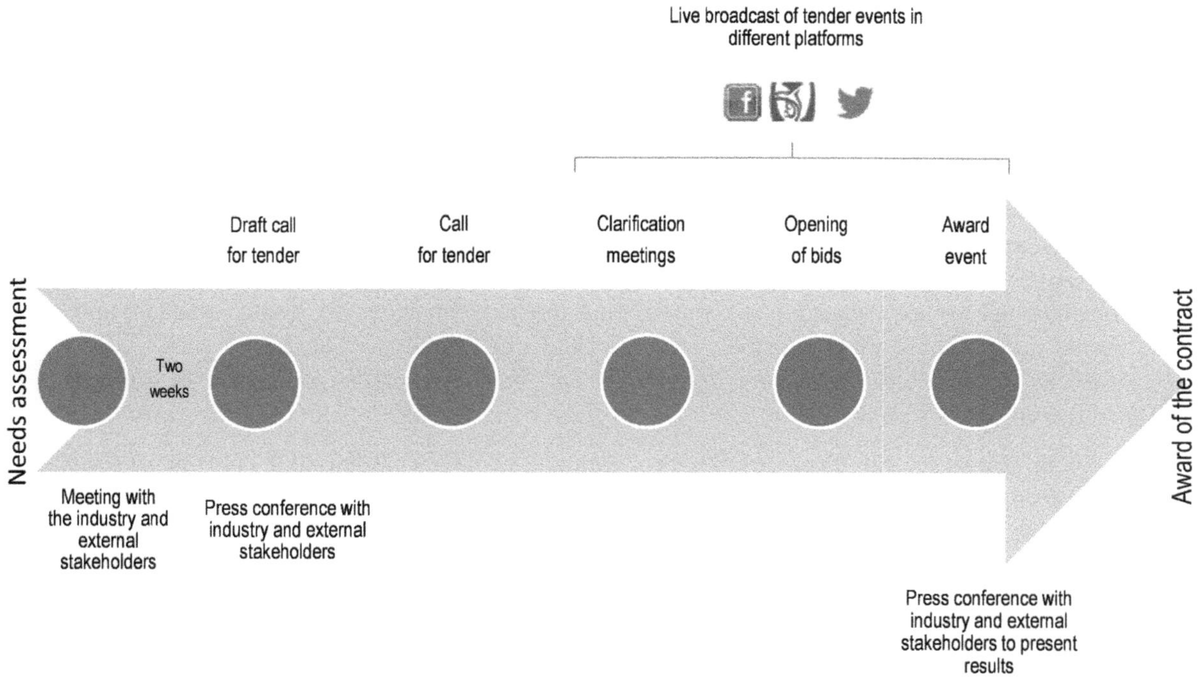

Source: Information provided by IMSS.

While the business community has praised the dialogue established with IMSS, it has also indicated some shortcomings. For example, it has asked IMSS to reconsider the design of the meetings envisioned in the protocol, as they are mainly informative and take place at the very end of the pre-tender stage, which reduces opportunities for IMSS to improve the process and the capacity of the business chambers to influence positively the tender strategies, establish technical conditions for the national market, or participate in the market research carried out by IMSS.

In this sense, IMSS could further systematise these meetings, for example by providing a calendar and timely notification of each meeting and by recording the agreements reached on a control board, where their fulfilment can be monitored and tracked. This would address industry concerns over the follow up of the issues identified by the business community. Briefing meetings aimed at the supplier community could take place earlier, even during the needs assessment stage. In this way, IMSS would help suppliers and business chambers engage more effectively and would keep them motivated to participate.

In addition, in the specific case of consolidated tenders, IMSS could involve the other procuring institutions in the discussions with suppliers (i.e., ISSSTE; PEMEX; the ministries of health and defence; the Navy; the institutes of health; and the federal states), particularly when there are problems linked to their own purchases. For example, the industry complains about delayed payments by some of these institutions and, while IMSS has offered to mediate and even excluded some federal states from participating in the 2017 consolidated tender due to their lack of commitment to addressing the problem, it would be helpful to have these institutions at the table to address and prevent future issues.

IMSS could improve integrity by starting every meeting with the business community and civil society organisations by providing information on the anti-corruption sanctions applicable to businesses in the National Anti-corruption System (NACS) and the requirements of the Protocol for Procurement Officials' Behaviour.

Mexico's newly established National Anti-corruption System (NACS), signed into law on 18 July 2016, consists of a package of laws – eight in total – marking a turning point in Mexico's approach to anti-corruption policies. One of the declared objectives of the NACS, and particularly of the General Law on Administrative Responsibilities (*Ley General de Responsabilidades Administrativas*, LGRA) is to strengthen enforcement mechanisms for investigating and sanctioning integrity breaches by public officials and firms under both administrative and criminal jurisdictions. Therefore, the LGRA establishes sanctions for private individuals and businesses who participate in corrupt behaviour (Box 5.3).

In a similar vein, the Protocol for Procurement Officials' Behaviour[7] (*Protocolo de actuación en materia de contrataciones públicas, otorgamiento y prórroga de licencias, permisos, autorizaciones y concesiones*) establishes rules for contact between business agents and public officials in charge of procurement activities, as well as those responsible for issuing licenses, permits, and concessions. Likewise, the Protocol establishes the mechanism for business agents to declare links or relationships with senior public officials or those in charge of procurement activities.

As a preventive measure, IMSS could use the meetings envisioned in the IMSS protocol for priority tenders to inform the business community and potential suppliers about the sanctions established in the LGRA for businesses who participate in corrupt behaviour and the rules to follow when in contact with procurement officials. In addition, IMSS could also inform these audiences about other regulations, such as those applicable to conflicts of interest and gifts, as well as the channels for reporting wrongdoing. Finally, IMSS could help to disseminate the Agreement for Transparency and Ethical Principles for Suppliers[8] in these meetings, as it has been signed by the main business chambers who work with IMSS (CONCAMIN, COPARMEX, ANDIS, CANIFARMA, CONCANACO-SERVYTUR, and CCE).

Box 5.3. Managing corrupt behaviour by private individuals, businesses and procurement officials

Article 81 of the General Law on Administrative Responsibilities establishes the administrative sanctions to be applied to private individuals and businesses for participating in corrupt behaviour.

Sanctions for private individuals can range from:

- economic sanctions, which could double the benefits realised
- temporary exclusion from tender processes for goods, leasing, services, or public works, for a period between three months and eight years
- the need to pay compensation for damages to the public entities.

Sanctions for businesses include:

- economic sanctions, which could double the benefits realised.
- temporary exclusion from tender processes for goods, leasing, services, or public works, for a period of between three months and 10 years
- suspension of business activities for a period of between three months and three years
- closure of the business entity
- the need to pay compensation for damages to the public entities.

Source: (Government of Mexico, 2016[8]) (Government of Mexico, 2017[9]).

Encourage greater feedback in the post-award stage through new communication channels, such as debriefings for suppliers and opinion surveys.

Unsuccessful tenderers may want to know why their bids failed. The OECD recognises that verbal debriefing after a contract has been awarded is good practice, and is commonly used in many member countries to engage with the market and expand the supply base. Adequate debriefings with suppliers provide a valuable opportunity for both parties to benefit from the process. Verbal debriefings can improve the relationship with suppliers and the quality of their offers while providing IMSS with valuable insights (Box 5.4). However, verbal debriefings must be used judiciously and be guided by a clear framework in order to reduce any associated risks (i.e. integrity risks) and costs. A debriefing can also be made available to the successful bidder as a first step in establishing a sound working relationship and setting a precedent for constructive feedback.

When IMSS awards a contract, a public meeting is organised in the case of paper-based or mixed tenders. Bidders can participate in this meeting, during which a minute is drafted. The award is also published on CompraNet the same day it is issued. Those bidders who do not participate in this meeting are sent the award statement. However, IMSS has no regulatory framework for debriefing unsuccessful bidders. Indeed, such debriefings are not a common practice in Mexico's public administration, as it is not required by the acquisitions or the public works laws. There are also no procedures for debriefing meetings with suppliers, although businesses may approach IMSS officials and ask about issues or request feedback (OECD, 2017[10]).

In order to increase the benefits of debriefings, while mitigating any potential risks, IMSS should develop guidelines to establish a clear framework to guide them. The amount of information that can be conveyed will vary according to the circumstances of the particular contract, but IMSS could give a broad indication of the reasons for the decision (e.g. either related to financial or technical aspects) and provide information on where bidders ranked in the tender list.

Box 5.4. The benefits of debriefing

Debriefing is beneficial to bidders by:

- helping them to rethink their approach in order to make future bids more successful
- offering targeted guidance to new or smaller companies to improve their chances of doing business in the public sector
- providing reassurance about the process and their contribution or role
- providing a better understanding of what differentiates public sector procurement from private procurement.

That dialogue can also assist IMSS by:

- identifying ways to improve subsequent solicitation processes, including the associated communication
- making sure best practice and guidance are updated to reflect any relevant issues that have been highlighted
- encouraging better bids from suppliers in the future
- getting a better understanding of how that segment of the market thinks, enhancing market intelligence
- helping establish a reputation as a fair, open, and ethical buyer with whom suppliers will want to do business in the future
- potentially reducing the number of challenges (*inconformidades*).

Source: (OECD, 2017[10]).

As well as debriefing meetings, IMSS could use surveys to solicit the opinions of suppliers once tender processes are over. In fact, as discussed in Chapter 4, although the Ministry of Public Administration (*Secretaria de la Función Publica*, SFP) runs surveys to assess the performance of procurement procedures and the status of payments to suppliers, these are applied throughout the public administration, not only in IMSS. While IMSS could use the data from these surveys as a benchmark for the public administration, it could also develop a more focused survey for its own needs, as occurs for example in PEMEX (see Chapter 4).

Ensuring citizen participation in the procurement system

Make the participation of social witnesses more effective, by making it an internal rule to respond to social witnesses' reports and provide feedback to SFP on previous witnesses and experiences, while also suggesting measures to address the weaknesses identified by the OECD.

Citizen participation is defined as a citizen action that influences or seeks to influence policy decisions, or as an action that incorporates the demands and values of citizens into public administration services. Given the integrity risks present in procurement operations, it is considered good practice for governments to involve representatives of civil society, academics or end-users in scrutinising the integrity of the procurement process. Direct social control mechanisms encourage their involvement as external observers of the entire procurement process or of key decision-making points.

The *Strategy to Advance Competition in Public Tenders*, and particularly its first pillar (strengthening the tender processes carried out by IMSS, see above), includes several measures to facilitate citizen participation in public procurement:

- Strengthening the monitoring mechanisms for procurement: this consists of greater transparency over the prices achieved in tender processes. The aim is to allow IMSS officials and the Internal Control Body (*Órgano Interno de Control*, OIC) to carry out a permanent comparison and detect deviations. It also aims to provide enough information to motivate participation and competition in tender processes. It includes the participation of social witnesses (described below).
- Implementation of 10 good practices for procurement at the central and delegation levels: this consists of implementing good practice beyond what is required by law. These include a Strategy to Advance Transparency in Procurement in Delegations and Highly Specialised Medical Units (*Unidades Médicas de Alta Especialidad*, UMAEs). These good practices include widening the scope of market research, electronic reporting of all procurement operations, and live broadcast of tender events on IMSS platforms, Facebook and YouTube.
- Permanent participation of external stakeholders to advance transparency: this consists of creating networks of public and private stakeholders to observe IMSS's tender processes. SFP, the OECD, and the United Nations Office on Drugs and Crime (UNODC) are permanently invited to participate. Furthermore, IMSS is working with Mexican Transparency (*Transparencia Mexicana*) so that it not only observes priority tenders, but also some other tenders chosen randomly.

Social witnesses are non-government organisations and individuals identified by SFP through a public selection process. SFP keeps a registry of approved social witnesses and evaluates their performance – unsatisfactory performance potentially results in their removal from the registry. When a federal entity requires the involvement of a social witness, it informs SFP, who designates one from the registry.

Social witnesses' functions include proposing strategies to improve transparency, impartiality and compliance with the legal framework, as well as reporting any illegal acts they may find. Their participation is required by law in public tenders whose value exceed five million days, the minimum wage applied in Mexico City[9], as well as in other cases where SFP deems it appropriate. Indeed, IMSS could involve social witnesses even for tenders that are below the threshold when purchasing critical items or where risks are high (e.g. based on previous experience, the composition of the market, or even in a random selection, etc.). They participate from the stages of the draft call for tender right up to the signing of the contract.

As of 16 August 2017, SFP had registered 45 social witnesses in CompraNet for public procurement projects (up from 5 in 2005): 7 civil society organisations[10] and 38 individuals.[11] SFP notes that the monitoring of the most relevant procurement processes of the federal government by social witnesses has so improved procurement procedures through their contributions and experience that they have become a strategic element for ensuring the transparency and credibility of the procurement system. An OECD-World Bank Institute study (2006, cited in (OECD, 2017[10])) found that the participation of social witnesses in the procurement processes of the Federal Electricity Commission (*Comisión Federal de Electricidad*, CFE) created savings of approximately USD 26 million in 2006 and increased the number of bidders by over 50% (OECD, 2017[10]).

The use of social witnesses by IMSS increased sharply between 2008 and 2009 (Figure 5.2). Between 2008 and 2016, IMSS used social witnesses in 188 tender procedures.[12]

Figure 5.2. Number of IMSS tender procedures involving social witnesses, 2008-2016

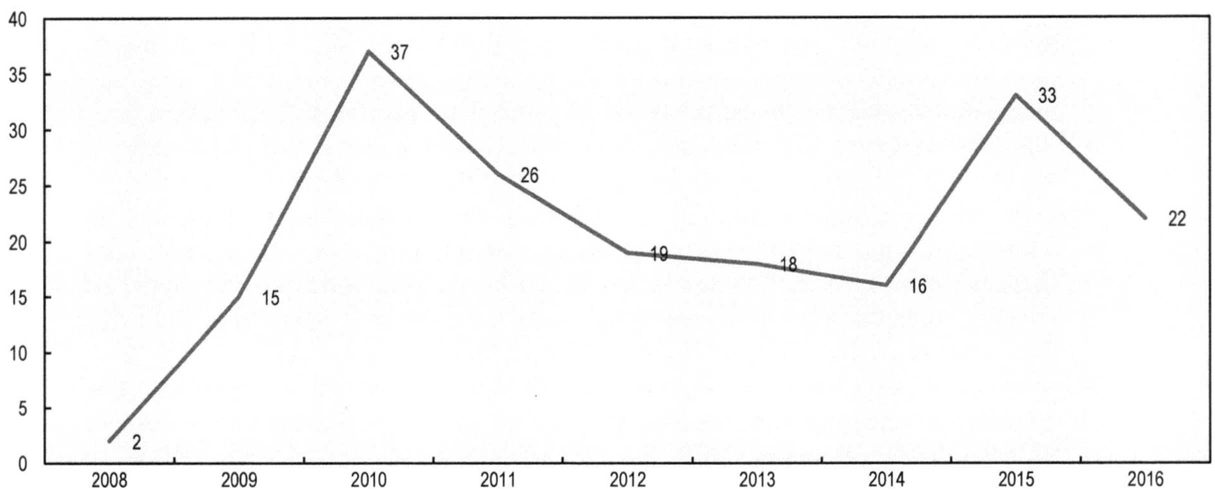

Source: IMSS Procurement platform, http://compras.imss.gob.mx/?P=tsociales, accessed 16 August 2017.

At the end of a procurement process, the social witness issues a report containing his comments and recommendations. These reports are published on both CompraNet and IMSS's Procurement Portal. However, social witnesses do not have the authority to stop a procurement process or revoke a decision. They may express opinions, but do not have any influence or right to make decisions. When a social witness raises concerns over a possible corrupt action during a procurement process, their opinions and concerns are recorded in the report.

Despite the fact that social witnesses' reports are public and easily accessible, there is no evidence that IMSS provides any kind of response to these reports. Indeed, the OECD team could not find any responses either on CompraNet or on the IMSS Procurement Portal. IMSS could increase the effectiveness of the social witnesses' reports by committing to provide public answers to them. This could be done by establishing such commitments in IMSS' internal procurement regulations and would create more incentives for IMSS officials to manage procurement processes with integrity.

In previous reviews of Mexico's institutions (i.e., PEMEX (OECD, 2017[10]), ISSSTE (OECD, 2013[11]; OECD, 2016[12])) the OECD recognised the value of social witnesses, but also pointed to some potential weaknesses. For example, in interviews with some of the witnesses, it became evident that while they were experts in a relevant field (i.e., works engineering, accounting, law, etc.), they were not necessarily specialists in integrity risks. Hence, IMSS could partner with SFP and provide it with feedback to increase the expertise of social witnesses and assess their performance.

In addition, it was observed that the same social witness may participate in several processes involving the same procuring institution, creating the risk of familiarity with procurement officials and business agents. IMSS should work with SFP to rotate social witnesses so as to avoid this familiarity, which may lead to conflicts of interest.

Consider strengthening the role of observers by implementing a feedback mechanism for them, for example a survey or a debriefing session at the end of the event in which they participated.

In addition to social witnesses, any individual interested in witnessing a tender event may participate as an observer. This participation is allowed to advance transparency, compliance with legal requirements, impartiality and integrity. However, the role of observers is more ad hoc and is not formally regulated. Furthermore, observers do not produce any feedback for IMSS. Hence, their impact is close to impossible to measure.

IMSS could institutionalise the role of observers by providing a clear role for their engagement. Specifically, IMSS could implement mechanisms to receive their feedback, for example, via a survey or a debriefing meeting after a tender event. Such tools could also be applied to individuals who follow the tender events through social media, so that the effectiveness of this practice can be better assessed.

Proposals for action

IMSS has advanced in establishing communication and engagement channels for suppliers and the wider public in its procurement policies and activities. This chapter has explored ways in which IMSS could increase still further the effectiveness of this engagement. The first set of recommendations focus on transparency and access to information policies, followed by other recommendations to improve consultation surrounding procurement regulations. The final section concentrates on the role of social witnesses and observers:

Meeting transparency and access-to-information requirements for public procurement

- Establish a centralised quality control function for the information disclosed in different sources, while implementing the OCDS format. This will reduce the potential for inconsistencies between different platforms.
- As a measure of good practice, create an internal policy to subject IMSS procurement-related rules to the regulatory quality requirements and controls established in the LFPA and which are currently not necessarily applicable to IMSS.

- Institutionalise early regulatory consultation practices (pre-RIA) for the reform or development of procurement rules.

Engaging suppliers in the procurement system

- While the Strategy to Advance Competition in Public Tenders is a solid step forward for supplier engagement, IMSS could start the engagement process earlier and make it more systematic, even involving the other institutions participating in the consolidated tenders. In this way suppliers' suggestions could really have an impact on tender processes and procurement strategies.
- Enhance integrity by starting every meeting with the business community and civil society organisations by providing information on the anti-corruption sanctions applicable to businesses in the National Anti-corruption System (NACS) and the requirements of the Protocol for Procurement Officials' Behaviour.
- Encourage greater feedback in the post-award stage through new communication channels, such as debriefings for suppliers and opinion surveys.

Encourage citizen participation in the procurement system

- Make the participation of social witnesses more effective, by making it an internal rule to respond to social witnesses' reports and provide feedback to SFP on previous witnesses and experiences, while also suggesting measures to address the weaknesses identified by OECD
- Strengthen the role of observers by implementing a feedback mechanism for them, for example a survey or a debriefing session at the end of the event in which they participated.

Notes

[1] Based on data from the 427 foreign bribery cases that have been concluded since the entry into force of the OECD Anti-Bribery Convention in 1999.

[2] The POT is a web-based portal where the federal ministries and agencies publish the information that is required to be proactively disclosed by law. It is available at portaltransparencia.gob.mx, accessed 9 August 2017.

[3] Even though the Annual Procurement Plan also includes information by delegation, it is coded and hard to identify what each delegation is planning to buy.

[4] IMSS currently has 35 delegations and 25 UMAEs.

[5] However, in the case of primary regulations, draft bills are not subject to the regulatory quality requirements (including consultation) set out by the LFPA when they are introduced in Congress by legislators themselves or by State assemblies, only when introduced by the Federal Executive.

[6] IMSS's POBALINES could not be found in COFEMER's website, so they were probably not even submitted for COFEMER review.

[7] Published on 20 August 2015 and amended on 19 February 2016 and 28 February 2017.

[8] The main objective of the agreement is to establish self-regulatory commitments to improve competition in the procurement of medicines and facilitate responsible business practices in the market.

[9] In 2017, these thresholds are MXN 400.2 million (approximately EUR 18.6 million) for goods, leasing, and services and MXN 800.4 million (approximately EUR 37.2 million) for public works and related services.

[10] Mexico's Public Procurement Academy, Engineering Academy, Mexico's Academy for Comprehensive Performance Audit, Alternative: Your possible future, Mexican Institute of Technical Audit, Citizen Control for Accountability, and Mexican Transparency.

[11] CompraNet website, available at www.funcionpublica.gob.mx/unaopspf/tsocial/tsocial.htm, accessed 16 August 2017.

[12] Based on the number of social witnesses' reports published in the IMSS Procurement Platform, http://compras.imss.gob.mx/?P=tsociales, accessed 16 August 2017.

References

Government of Mexico (2015), *Ley General de Transparencia y Acceso a la Información Pública*, http://www.diputados.gob.mx/LeyesBiblio/pdf/LGTAIP.pdf (accessed on 09 August 2017). [5]

Government of Mexico (2016), "Ley General de Responsabilidades Administrativas", https://www.gob.mx/cms/uploads/attachment/file/145712/2016_07_18_VES_Decreto_por_el_que_se_expiden_la_LGSNA__la_LGRA_y_la_LOTFJA.pdf (accessed on 14 August 2017). [8]

Government of Mexico (2017), *Protocolo de Actuación en Materia de Contrataciones Públicas, Otorgamiento y Prórroga de Licencias, Permisos, Autorizaciones y Concesiones*, https://www.gob.mx/sfp/documentos/protocolo-de-actuacion-en-materia-de-contrataciones-publicas-otorgamiento-y-prorroga-de-licencias-permisos-autorizaciones-y-concesiones-97983 (accessed on 20 November 2017). [9]

INAI (2016), *Informe de Labores 2016*, http://inicio.ifai.org.mx/Informes%202016/Informe%20de%20labores%202016.pdf (accessed on 09 August 2017). [6]

OECD (2013), *Public Procurement Review of the Mexican Institute of Social Security: Enhancing Efficiency and Integrity for Better Health Care*, OECD Public Governance Reviews, OECD Publishing, Paris, http://dx.doi.org/10.1787/9789264197480-en. [1]

OECD (2013), *Public Procurement Review of the State's Employees' Social Security and Social Services Institute in Mexico*, OECD Public Governance Reviews, OECD Publishing, Paris, http://dx.doi.org/10.1787/9789264197305-en. [11]

OECD (2014), *OECD Foreign Bribery Report: An Analysis of the Crime of Bribery of Foreign Public Officials*, OECD Publishing, Paris, http://dx.doi.org/10.1787/9789264226616-en. [2]

OECD (2014), *Regulatory Policy in Mexico: Towards a Whole-of-Government Perspective to Regulatory Improvement*, OECD Reviews of Regulatory Reform, OECD Publishing, Paris, http://dx.doi.org/10.1787/9789264203389-en. [7]

OECD (2015), *OECD Recommendation of the Council on Public Procurement*, http://www.oecd.org/gov/ethics/OECD-Recommendation-on-Public-Procurement.pdf, consulted on 9 August 2017. [3]

OECD (2016), "OECD Recommendation of the Council on Public Integrity", http://www.oecd.org/gov/ethics/Recommendation-Public-Integrity.pdf, consulted on 9 August 2017. [4]

OECD (2016), *Improving ISSSTE's Public Procurement for Better Results*, OECD Public Governance Reviews, OECD Publishing, Paris, http://dx.doi.org/10.1787/9789264249899-en. [12]

OECD (2017), *Public Procurement Review of Mexico's PEMEX: Adapting to Change in the Oil Industry*, OECD Public Governance Reviews, OECD Publishing, Paris, http://dx.doi.org/10.1787/9789264268555-en. [10]

Chapter 6. Rethinking IMSS procurement strategies to maximise efficiency and sustainability

Ensuring that IMSS procurement maximises its potential for better healthcare requires the institute to strive continuously to improve. This chapter discusses the impact of IMSS's past procurement strategies on competition, value for money and efficiency. It also identifies possible risks which could undermine the sustainability of their benefits. It provides recommendations for mitigating those risks and to secure benefits from procurement for the institute and its beneficiaries in the long term.

Over the past ten years, IMSS has reached a number of milestones along the road to achieving full procurement efficiency and strong competition in the markets in which it operates. These milestones include leading the largest consolidated procurement scheme in the Mexican public sector. Continuing along this fruitful path, however, requires continuous rethinking of how IMSS's procurement policies and practices can provide better healthcare services by boosting their efficiency and ensure their long-term sustainability. Considering that one-third of public procurement expenditures across most of OECD countries is dedicated to health care, this exercise is essential for any healthcare system wishing to optimise the use of its resources and to provide the best possible care to contributors (OECD, 2017[1]). Further opportunities are available for IMSS to increase efficiencies and maximise competition. This chapter explores some of them, which include opportunities for making savings, eliminating inefficiencies, ensuring a level playing field for suppliers and aligning procurement strategies with national healthcare objectives.

How can procurement strategies maximise value for money in the long term?

Implementing longer term assessments of the financial impact of its procurement strategies would provide IMSS with the opportunity to reassess their effectiveness

By monitoring the financial impact of procurement strategies over time, IMSS can extract valuable lessons on which components are effective and others whose impact is diminishing, thus laying the foundations for further improvements in the institute's procurement policies and practices.

That healthy competition can lead to savings is widely acknowledged and has led IMSS to develop specific procurement strategies to foster competition. Among others, aggregating needs is often seen as a strategy that can support greater competition (Albano and Nicholas, 2016[2]). Yet competition, and the efficiencies it entails, also has a temporal dimension: competition today can have an impact on competition tomorrow; this is particularly the case in the context of recurrent purchasing activities in consolidated tenders for medicines. The fact that a certain measure increases competition in the short term does not mean that it will always produce the same effect. The effects of a measure on competition must thus be considered in a long-term context.

In 2013, IMSS led the largest consolidated procurement scheme in the Mexican public sector. Since then, approximately 43 consolidated procurement procedures have taken place, covering a number of high-rotation goods, such as medicines, vaccines, medical equipment, radiological material and laboratory material. The 2017 procurement operation resulted in savings of nearly MXN 3 352 million in comparison to the previous year's costs. The average price of products purchased outside of the consolidated procurement scheme has been calculated to be 1.98% higher than the price of the same goods purchased by means of a consolidated procedure (Investigación Farmacéutica, 2017[3]).

The Coordinating Commission for the Negotiation of Medicines Prices and other Health Products (Comisión Coordinadora para la Negociación de Precios de Medicamentos y otros Insumos para la Salud, CCNPMIS) estimates that the accumulated savings achieved since 2013 through the consolidated purchase of patented drugs alone amount to MXN 2 340 million. The competitive prices for drugs and therapeutic goods achieved through consolidated procurement operations mean they are currently used as a reference by institutions in the Mexican public health sector seeking to purchase similar goods.

Savings totalling MXN 14 215 million were achieved between 2013 and 2016 by all the dependencies, entities and institutes participating in consolidated purchases (Figure 6.1). IMSS benefited from almost 60% of these savings (MXN 8 432 million).

Figure 6.1. IMSS accumulated savings in consolidated tenders, 2013-2016

MXN millions (left axis); % savings (right axis)

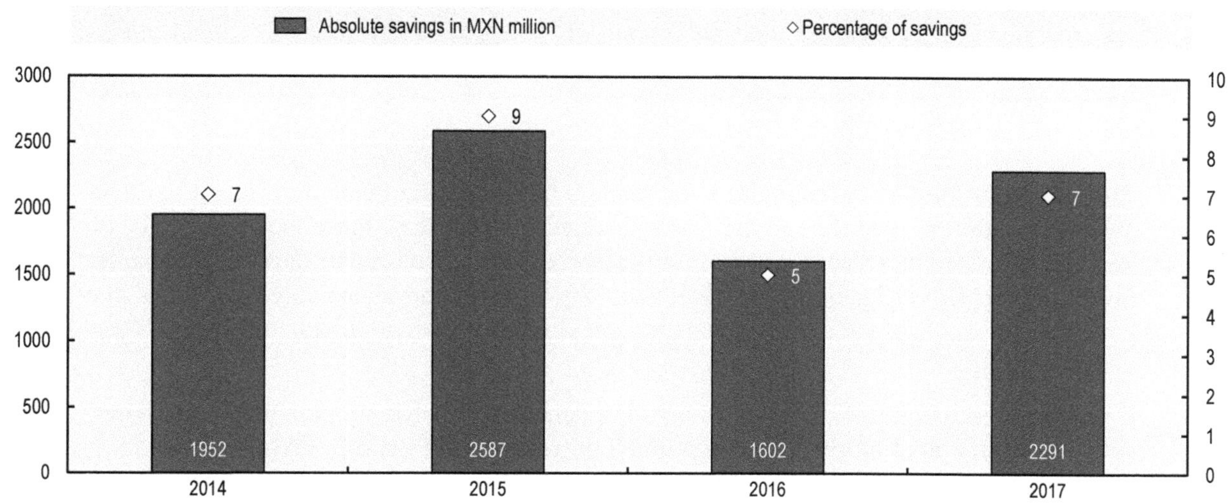

Source: Information provided by IMSS

However, there are indications that some of the advantages of consolidated purchases may be losing their initial lustre over time. Aggregating needs may increase competition in the short term by attracting large firms that had not previously been interested in participating in non-consolidated procurement procedures. But when a significant share of public contracts for a specific product is awarded to a reduced number of winning firms, it is likely that some firms may be pushed out of the market or become weaker competitors (through loss of experience or learning) in the medium term. This could weaken competition in future competitive procedures if no additional measures were taken to ensure their participation.

Similarly, excluding companies from participating in future procurement procedures because of contractual breaches may be a procompetitive measure in certain contexts by encouraging companies to execute their contractual obligations satisfactorily. Yet it could also affect competition in the long run, particularly in concentrated markets with high entry barriers. Achieving savings by aggregating needs in the short term may therefore result in inefficiencies and weakened competition in the long term if the risks of this procurement strategy are not thoroughly monitored and mitigated.

That these impacts of IMSS's consolidated procurement strategies are occurring is suggested by a decrease in the rate at which the savings achieved have been falling, as well as by signs that competition may have become weaker. Indeed a number of consolidated procurement procedures have been declared partially void for specific items because of the absence of competition (Table 6.1). Between 2013 and 2016, consolidated procedures were declared void for an average of 17.6% of product references, mainly medicines. Six product references have been continuously declared void since 2014 (Investigación Farmacéutica, 2017[3]), questioning the effectiveness of aggregating those specific needs into consolidated tenders.

Table 6.1. Void references in consolidated tenders, 2013-2016

Number of product references for which consolidated procedures have been declared void			
Year	No. of product references included in the call for tender	No. of product references for which the procedure was declared void	% of void references
2013	1,890	229	12%
2014	1,905	353	18.5%
2015	1,760	430	24%
2016	1,651	270	16%

Source: Data provided by IMSS

This has led to the IMSS having to issue tenders for individual items or to resort to direct award procedures, even though the price obtained by the use of these mechanisms is, on average, 105% higher than the maximum reference price determined through the market investigation (Investigación Farmacéutica, 2017[3]). Comprehensively assessing the potential for savings of consolidated tenders therefore also requires integrating these indirect costs.

Besides general strategies, IMSS has also implemented specific procurement techniques, such as reverse auction mechanisms, aimed at generating financial savings. Under this mechanism, participants are able to offer additional discounts on their initial prices once these are made public (the Mexican Federal Law on Acquisitions, Leasing and Services, or LAASSP, specifies that no maximum reference prices shall be used). Aspects of the offer other than price cannot be modified. This method brings prices down as competitors underbid each other. The consolidated purchase procedures currently carried out by IMSS frequently feature reverse auctions (also known as subsequent discount offer or SDO schemes). Figure 6.2 provides an overview of the savings to IMSS linked to the use of SDOs between 2014 and 2017.

Figure 6.2. Savings to IMSS in subsequent discount offers, 2013-2017

MXN millions (left axis); % savings (right axis)

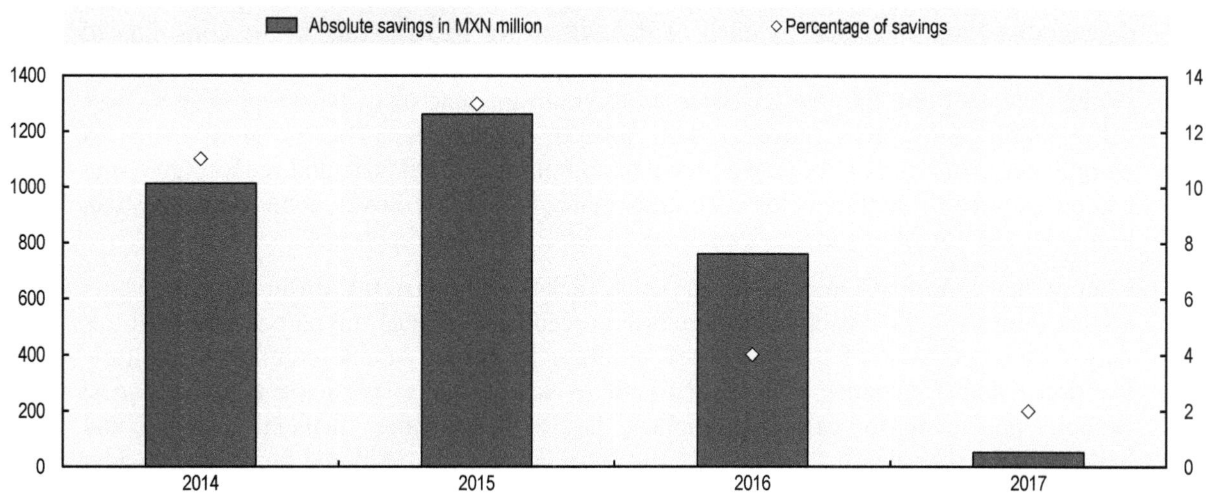

Source: Data provided by IMSS

As Figure 6.2 illustrates, the savings achieved by SDOs have been sharply decreasing over the past two years. This suggests there could be a limit to the price reductions that competitors can offer, beyond which further discounts would make their commercial activity inviable – which could explain this reduction in savings. Moreover, SMEs can be adversely affected by the use of this mechanism because of its extensive focus on price reduction and thus reducing profit margins. This is why the LAASSP forbids SDOs whenever SMEs participate in a tender procedure.

This analysis shows that this particular procurement strategy has also lost its effectiveness over time, at least for the type of goods and services it is used for (notably medicines). Multidimensional assessments can help determine whether the mechanisms require improvements to generate more savings, or whether they have reached their peak because efficiency savings cannot grow any more. Knowing this would allow IMSS to concentrate on other elements which could have a greater impact on the efficiency of its procurement strategies.

Eliminating inefficiencies

IMSS could remedy several sources of inefficiencies in its procurement strategies, such as contract heterogeneity and short duration, hindering further savings

Although IMSS's procurement practices and policies have many virtues and have led to efficiency gains for IMSS, as well as the provision of better healthcare services supported by a more solid budget, it seems that the system still has ample room for improvement.

In addition to the issues discussed above, there are two other elements which are leading to inefficiencies. Firstly, the structure of consolidated purchases led by IMSS is extremely complex, which can give rise to problems related to contract management (discussed in Chapter 4). Although the tendering process is consolidated, each single procedure gives rise to dozens of different contracts, each with its own payment and delivery conditions. These can in turn generate inefficiencies and produce market foreclosure effects.

Contract management and monitoring, as well as the handling of payment processes, are decentralised and managed by each of the authorities participating in the consolidated procedure (Chapter 4). When the signing entities operate at state level, the contracts to which they are party may be governed by the relevant state laws, whose provisions may differ significantly from those of their federal counterparts. This situation increases compliance costs for suppliers, who have to comply with both state and federal laws, and can be a source of inefficiencies in contract management. Moreover, some states may ask to modify the conditions in the framework of the consolidated purchase.

Contractual conditions may also vary significantly amongst the different agreements issued from a single consolidated purchase procedure. Some of the participating entities may request delivery of the purchased products by means of one contract to multiple locations, including areas that are difficult to access. Other participants may request bespoke packaging for certain medicines. It also complicates financial planning and budgeting for suppliers – with the ensuing financial costs. IMSS could therefore consider ways in which the complex structure of consolidated procurement procedures could be simplified and streamlined.

Standardising contracts

Standardisation of contracts could be one way forward for consolidated tenders. It provides a number of substantial benefits – not only to suppliers, but also to contracting entities, by harmonising the balance of risks. One possible approach would be to include in the tender documentation a model contract (Box 6.1) or catalogue of general conditions containing the basic clauses and terms applicable by all the contracting authorities to the procurement of each reference code or to the procedure as a whole. It could be specified that these basic conditions would not be modifiable by any of the parties post-award.

These conditions could include price terms, delivery conditions, payment terms, provisions governing the distribution of risks, or clauses governing non-compliance procedures. Any contractual conditions not included in this document could be subsequently negotiated individually.

Box 6.1. Government model contracts in New Zealand

The New Zealand Ministry of Business, Innovation and Employment has released government model contracts, a set of standard conditions of contract for routine low-value, low-risk government purchases of common products. They are meant to become the default government contract, aimed at creating "a standard, simple, plain English set of conditions of contract for common goods and services" to be used by all public bodies, in order to:

- provide simple, plain English contracts that are easy to use for both agencies and suppliers, and simplify doing business with government
- provide a fairer balance of risk between buyer and supplier
- standardise the treatment of legal risk in low-value, low-risk contracts
- reduce the need for negotiations and legal advice in routine purchases
- promote consistent practice across government, support improved procurement practice and align with international best practices
- promote process efficiencies in high-volume, low-value transactional contracting.

Source: (New Zealand Ministry of Business Innovation and Employment (MBIE), 2017[4])

Extending the products covered by consolidated procurement

IMSS could also assess whether consolidated procurement could be extended to other goods and services not currently procured under this scheme. Consolidated purchase procedures currently only cover the acquisition of medicines and other healthcare supplies, such as vaccines and healing, radiological and laboratory materials. Although this portfolio of products includes high-rotation goods which are essential for the fulfilment of IMSS's mission, it is not as extensive as it could be. There is a very broad and varied range of products, services and work that are common necessities for most public entities, even if they are not as directly related to the provision of healthcare services as healthcare supplies. An expansion of this product portfolio could help IMSS extend the immediate savings obtained in the purchase of medicines and other healthcare supplies to the procurement of other products.

In principle, all core items and services required across various institutions could be candidates for inclusion. Some examples of these widely used goods, services and works include food products, transportation services and vehicles, stationary supplies, maintenance and cleaning services, external consultancy services, research and renovation work.

IMSS and its consolidated procurement partners could begin by compiling an inventory of the various participants' requirements in order to identify core inputs used by all or the majority of the institutions which could be delivered through consolidated procurement.

For example, with regard to the procurement of food served in hospitals, even though different hospitals across the country cater to different food preferences, in principle two categories of food items could be identified. The first category would include volume core items, such as water, that constitute an essential requirement for all hospitals across the country. The second category would include specialty local or regional foods. Whereas the former category could be procured through national consolidated procurement, the latter could preferably be the object of regional consolidation of purchases.

Using multiannual contracts to generate further savings

By extending the duration of contracts derived from consolidated tenders, IMSS will create additional opportunities for savings not solely from more competitive pricing but also from reduced internal costs and extended production lead-time.

Longer contracts may also increase efficiency, although the question as to whether longer or shorter contracts fit an optimal procurement strategy can only be answered through a market study, together with a careful analysis of the organisation's needs. For instance, long-duration contracts may have a lock-in effect, favouring incumbents and preventing entry to the market by new competitors. On the other hand, they may have many positive effects which outweigh these negative impacts. For instance, multiannual contracts may:

- give rise to economies of scale and scope that result in price savings
- open the market for larger-sized companies interested in higher-value contracts
- increase competition and foster innovation by offering firms better chances to recoup investments
- create operational efficiencies by shortening suppliers' learning curves
- guarantee continuity of supply
- facilitate the alignment of procurement practices with medium- and long-term strategic priorities
- reduce the administrative burden associated to frequently recurrent purchases
- hinder collusion by providing a tool to avoid repetitive contracting and extending the waiting period for cartel members to engage in bid rotation.

Engaging in multiannual contracting is one of the lines of action included in IMSS's Strategy to Foster Competition in Public Procurement (IMSS, 2017[5]), based on OECD recommendations.

IMSS has made use of multiannual contracts in some contexts, e.g. for the procurement of integrated services (discussed below). IMSS estimates that the use of multiannual contracts for integrated services procurement helped the institute save MXN 2,969 million in 2016 while avoiding supply delays and stock outs.

However, multiannual contracts are not used for consolidated procurement. Contracts stemming from consolidated procurement procedures can currently only be valid for a maximum period of one year. While, as noted above, it is not possible to assert that multiannual contracts are always the most appropriate option, it would appear that in this case, recurring needs, high volumes and value would warrant a thorough assessment of the possibility of implementing multiannual contractual frameworks for consolidated purchases.

The LASSP and the LSS (*Ley del Seguro Social*, or Social Security Law) do allow for multiannual contracting, setting out the conditions under which multiannual contracts may be authorised. The IMSS's Technical Council is responsible for approving multiyear contracts, which must also be reported to the Ministry of Finance and Public Credit (SHCP); moreover, the Requiring Areas must provide budgetary support for multiannual contracts. These areas could work together to explore the possibility of extending the use of multiannual contracts to consolidated procurement procedures.

This would however entail an agreement amongst participating entities on the duration of such contracts. Yet, the benefits implied by extending contract duration, such as increased spend visibility for suppliers, and additional time available to conduct market research and define tender design for contracting entities, could open the door to additional savings.

To reduce any loss in flexibility derived from the use of multiannual contracts, IMSS could include a number of safeguard clauses, such as price review mechanisms, clauses allowing for the option to update the products with any innovations developed during the contract's validity period, or penalties for suppliers suffering from stock outs (as long as this event is not due to unforeseeable circumstances or force majeure). This latter would make them responsible for any extra amounts paid to other firms for acquiring sold-out products. In general, longer contract periods would also increase IMSS's ability to include clauses fostering innovation by suppliers (for instance, clauses linking financial compensation to better patient outcomes from the purchased solutions), since a longer contract would allow firms to recoup any necessary investments in innovation (see Chapter 9). The possibility of extension could also be stipulated in multiannual contracts.

The extension of contracts for procuring drugs would also bring additional benefits for suppliers, thereby reinforcing the attractiveness of IMSS's consolidated tenders. Indeed extending the duration of contracts could have an immediate effect on the timeframe of the overall procurement process. Best practice for supply management of drugs suggests that the time between the start of the bidding process and the contract award should be at least five months (Management Sciences for Health, 2012[6]). For consolidated tenders led by IMSS this period lasts at best three months, mostly because of the short duration of the ensuing contracts.

Besides the short duration of the tendering phase, the current duration of contracts also affects the production lead time required for manufacturers to produce the drugs. This situation has two main effects. Firstly, it affects the level of replenishment of stocks in IMSS pharmacies, ultimately affecting patients in need of those specific medicines, as shown in Figure 6.3.

Figure 6.3. Level of supply of medicines

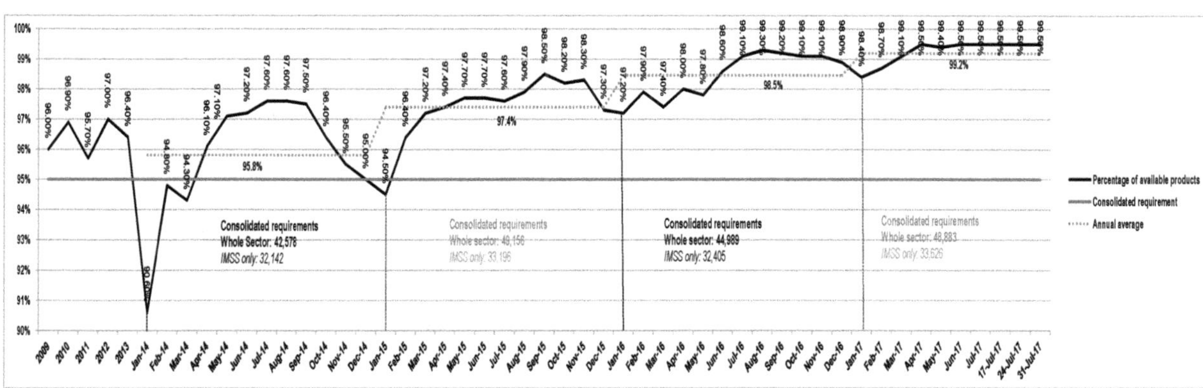

Source: Information provided by IMSS.

Indeed, one can see in the figure above that although stocks are regularly improving and are now at historically high levels, stocks are low at the beginning of each year when new contracts enter into force. Secondly, short contracts also prevent smaller manufacturers of generics from competing, thus affecting the efficiency of IMSS procurement process (See chapter 8)

Ensuring a level playing field in IMSS procurement

IMSS should ensure that its tenders are encouraging participation and supporting increased competition by federating expertise from technical and procurement areas.

Tender documents play an important role in creating efficiencies as well as in promoting competition. The OECD Recommendation on Public Procurement (OECD, 2015[7]) advises that tender opportunities be designed to encourage broad participation and that adherents ensure that procurement outcomes meet the needs of customers, for instance by developing appropriate technical specifications. Moreover, the OECD Recommendation on Fighting Bid Rigging (OECD, 2012[8]) acknowledges that the way in which tender documents are written influences the outcome of the selection process because it has an impact on the number and type of suppliers that are attracted to the tender.

Ensuring flexible tender documents

When tender documents are flexible, for instance when they include functional requirements detailing the expected outcomes without imposing technical specifications to deliver them (see Chapter 9), the number and variety of potential bidders will be higher since the process will be open to providers of a range of substitute products and services. Innovation will also be fostered, since suppliers will be given the chance to propose alternative sources of supply (see Box 9.6, Chapter 9). Moreover, allowing for innovative or alternative solutions will make collusive practices more difficult. These factors result in better value for money and stronger competition. Besides innovation, alternative definitions of the same needs would target different markets, thus broadening the playing field in IMSS procurement operations.

In fact, IMSS has already tested the benefits of providing alternatives to the traditional definition of some of its needs. In the context of the Strategy to Foster Competition in Public Procurement (IMSS, 2017[5]), it identified that leasing schemes may in some instances be more advantageous for the institute than the traditional purchasing solution. An instance of this is the substitution of IMSS's vehicle fleet with the procurement of integrated rental services in 2016, which saved MXN 101 million.

Leasing can also help IMSS increase financial flexibility. IMSS assessed the opportunity costs linked to the large initial outlay required for purchasing a fixed asset such as vehicles. These entail a decrease in the resources available to be assigned to working capital. These opportunity costs can be avoided by substituting purchasing models with leasing models, which liberates working capital resources. As well as contributing to direct and indirect savings, this procurement strategy also helped to target different type of suppliers, thus mitigating risks of market concentration and technological lock-in.

Drafting clear tender documents

When tender documents are clear, suppliers will be better able to understand the goals of the procurement procedure. Moreover, clarity reduces room for discretion, and therefore corruption, on the part of buyers. These factors will make suppliers confident in the procurement procedure, which will in turn increase participation and competition.

However, in the health sector specifications can be complex given the technical jargon necessary to describe the results expected of bidders. This is why, in most cases, technical specifications in IMSS tenders are written by subject matter experts in the requiring areas rather than procurement officials. Yet, IMSS should also ensure that procurement experts are closely involved in the design of tender documents to complement the technical skills with strategic procurement skills, a prerequisite for identifying and assessing the relative merits of various procurement strategies.

Suppliers' inputs, as experts in product characteristics as well as in market conditions, can also be helpful in ensuring that definition of needs meets market capabilities.

Using award criteria wisely

The choice of award criteria can also have an impact on the efficiency of a procurement procedure. Whenever possible, award criteria should be diverse, non-discriminatory and clearly defined. This may make the difference between choosing the solution that best fits IMSS's holistic needs and choosing a product that, while cheaper than other alternatives, will fail to provide IMSS with the most advantageous solution. As discussed in Chapter 9, economic considerations alone fail to capture the many ways in which IMSS's procurement practices can influence the results of different working areas across the institute. When objectively measurable award criteria reduce the risk of abuses of discretion, and therefore limit the likelihood of post-award challenges, while encouraging current and future participation. Moreover, the more diverse the award criteria, the harder it will be for suppliers to implement collusive schemes.

Generally speaking, the award criteria used in IMSS's procurement often seem to consist of a "binary" evaluation method: a pass or fail mechanism in which the cheapest tender that satisfies minimum technical requirements will win. This is particularly the case for medicines. Instead, IMSS's tender documents should regularly include award criteria that, in addition to price, also assess a variety of factors such as the entire life-cycle costs (including the costs of use, ownership, maintenance, and disposal), guarantees, speed of delivery, energy savings and post-sale services. Currently, these elements are not systematically considered. Doing so could allow the institute to reward cost-cutting and innovation and introduce additional dimensions on which competition takes place among bidders. Award criteria should of course be set so as not to grant individual advantages and to avoid abuses of discretion. Their description and their weight in the contract award must be appropriately specified in advance by means of the tender terms, to allow suppliers to better prepare their bids and to prevent challenges being raised by bidders at the post-adjudication stage.

IMSS's procurement framework already allows for the use of diverse award criteria, since the points and percentages award method is encouraged by the LAASSP (art. 36) and its implementing regulation, and is allowed for (if not encouraged) by the LOPSRM (art. 38).

There are currently no formally established quality systems or co-ordination mechanisms to assess the adequacy, clarity and restrictiveness of tender documents. The Contracting or Requiring Areas are in charge of drafting the technical specifications, proposing the technical evaluation method and specific criteria. However, they receive no training in performing these tasks and there is no independent or third-party review of their work in this regard.

The Co-ordination of Supply Control maintains quarterly contacts with local entities and Highly-specialised Medical Units (*Unidades Médicas de Alta Especialidad* or UMAEs) in order to gather data on their real consumption, particularly of medicines. They use these data as the basis for defining procurement requirements. However, this collaboration refers to the types and quantities of products and does not define how clearly, adequately or restrictively the specifications are to be written.

IMSS could establish an independent review mechanism or quality system (such as a review undertaken by procurement units, independent commodity experts or committees) to ensure that tender documents are drafted as clearly and understandably as possible, that they do not unnecessarily restrict entry or competition, and that they are able to extract the best value in both the long and short term for IMSS. This review mechanism could be led by a separate internal team or involve the support of external experts.

Additionally, IMSS could consider providing the Requiring and Contracting Areas with training on drafting tender documents.

Identifying and removing entry barriers

As described above, consolidated and centralised procurement may be the source of many advantages for procuring entities and suppliers alike. However, it may also create barriers to market entry that prevent potential suppliers from participating or that reduce their ability to do so.

Currently, around 51% of IMSS's total procurement expenditure is allocated to only four companies, the largest of which has a 23% market share (DIMESA, see Table 6.2). Concentration levels are higher in the context of consolidated procurement, where three bidders made up 53% of IMSS consolidated procurement expenditure in 2016-2017. As Table 6.2 also shows, the market shares of IMSS's main suppliers have been growing steadily over the past few years.

Table 6.2. Evolution of awarded contract value and share in total procurement expenditure, medicines and healing material

Value expressed in MXN million

No.	PROVIDER	AWARDED		AWARDED		AWARDED		AWARDED	
		2014	%	2015	%	2016	%	2017	%
1	DIMESA	3,656	14%	5,292	20%	6,711	24%	6,904	23%
2	FARM. ESPECIALIZADOS	4,407	17%	3,474	13%	4,853	17%	6,336	21%
3	CPI	1,619	6%	2,022	8%	2,424	9%	2,677	9%
4	MAYPO	2,155	8%	1,621	6%	1,526	5%	1,016	3%
5	CIMSA	698	3%	692	3%	1,264	5%	1,357	5%
6	VITASANITAS	658	3%	818	3%	773	3%	0	0%
7	RALCA	331	1%	463	2%	759	3%	975	3%
8	DIBITER	526	2%	-	0%	295	1%	526	2%
9	LANDSTEINER PHARMA	435	2%	875	3%	8	0%	0	0%
10	SAVI	4,201	16%	39	0%	0	0%	0	0%
	Subtotal	**18,688**	**73%**	**15,294**	**58%**	**18,613**	**67%**	**19,792**	**66%**
	OTHERS	6,779	27%	11,048	42%	9,246	33%	10,071	34%
	TOTAL	**25,467**	**100%**	**26,342**	**100%**	**27,859**	**100%**	**29,863**	**100%**

Note: The fiscal year indicated is the contract performance year. Vaccines and patent/single-source drugs not included.
Source: Information provided by IMSS

This concentration level is not on its own a fool-proof sign that market competition is weak or that IMSS procurement policies and practices are raising entry barriers to the market, but it might be an indicator, depending on the characteristics of the market.

The fact that only four companies hold the vast majority of IMSS's business is a risk factor for the creation of several lock-in effects that can exclude firms of all sizes, and which may weaken competition in the long run:

- Over time, companies that repeatedly receive similar types of contracts through IMSS procurement gain know-how and experience that place them at a significant advantage over other firms. This is particularly the case when award criteria place a heavy weight on prior experience in the performance of similar or related contracts.
- Lock-in effects can exist when specific investments, for instance in distribution or logistics networks, are required by companies to perform a certain contract. This is particularly the case when these investments constitute sunk costs, namely when they cannot be utilised for purposes other than the one for which they were made.
- The fact that IMSS and its consolidated procurement partners have become jointly dominant buyers for certain goods in the Mexican market only exacerbates these effects, as there are not many, or any, other buyers whose business could provide firms with a similar competitive advantage.

For these reasons, preventing entry barriers should be a priority for IMSS. There are strategies that IMSS can pursue in order to encourage participation, and therefore competition, by facilitating access to procurement opportunities for competitors of all sizes. Some of these strategies are described here, and can be adopted at the stage of tender design. Chapter 8 describes how IMSS can use procurement strategies to attract small and medium-sized enterprises (SMEs).

Opening procurement procedures to the participation of international bidders can be one way to stimulate competition in the market. It appears, however, that IMSS is not fully benefitting from this option. Although the purchases of some goods, such as integrated services, are open to international competition, in general national tenders are the most frequent. Currently, only 35% of suppliers in IMSS consolidated tenders are non-Mexican.

IMSS's Contracting Area determines whether open tenders can be national (open only to Mexican firms offering goods produced in Mexico with a minimum of 50% of national content); "international under treaties" (open only to Mexican firms and firms from countries that have signed a free trade treaty, including a chapter on government procurement with Mexico); or "open international" (where any firm can participate regardless of their nationality).

The IMSS Strategy to Foster Competition in Public Procurement (IMSS, 2017[5]) acknowledges the virtues of opening up IMSS procurement procedures to international competition and aims to extend the use of this practice. However, additional efforts are required to ensure that this strategy is put into practice effectively: as the charts in Figure 6.4 show, the vast majority of tender procedures carried out by IMSS over the past years have been national in scope.

Figure 6.4. Degree to which IMSS tenders are open to international bidders, 2014-2017

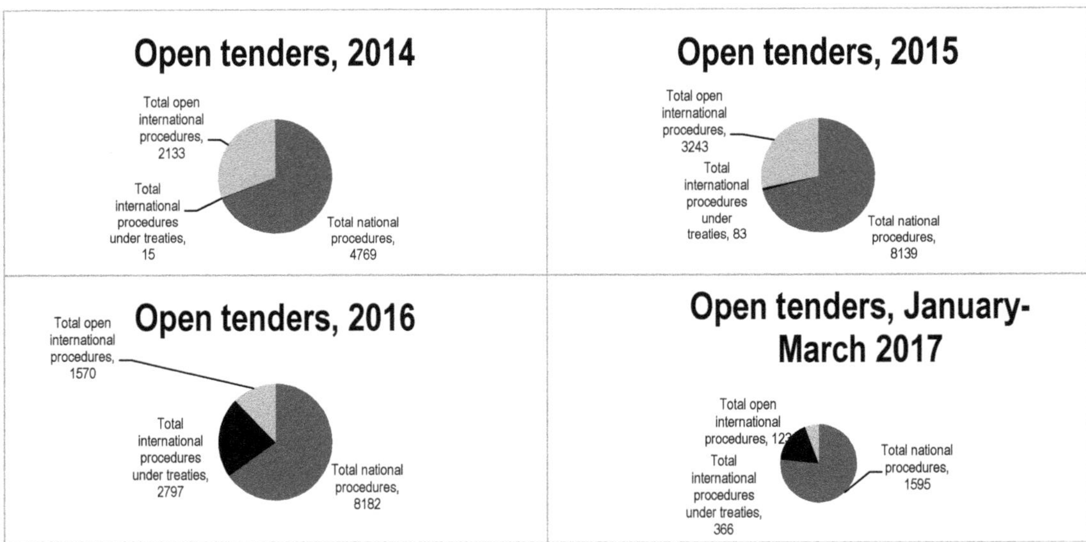

Source: Information provided by IMSS

Since 2013, IMSS has been making full use of reservation clauses[1] provided for in free trade agreements in its consolidated purchases of therapeutic goods. The aim is to protect the domestic industry. In 2016, these reservation clauses covered MXN 5 billion for medicines and MXN 2.64 billion for healing materials. This meant that a total of MXN 7.64 billion could only be awarded to national firms or firms providing goods with at least 65% of national content. However, this scheme has the side effect of limiting competition.

It would be advisable for IMSS to encourage non-local and foreign bidders to participate in its procurement procedures. Any restrictions to their participation – such as the use of reservation clauses in free trade agreements and the use of national procedures – could be limited to the strict minimum required (rather than allowed) by law. The Mixed Consultative Supply Commission, responsible for defining policies on the use of these reservations, could issue a recommendation in this regard.

IMSS could also consider publishing a summary of the call for tenders in English so that international bidders could more easily find out about opportunities for participating in IMSS's procedures.

Opening the market by splitting contracts into lots

IMSS could systematically assess, on the basis of a market investigation, whether some of the higher-value contracts tendered should be split into lots, in order to promote participation and foster competition in the long run. This assessment is particularly relevant for consolidated procurement.

As noted above, in the context of high-value procurement procedures there is a danger that some firms, particularly those smaller than their main competitors, can be forced to exit the market or lose important competitive advantages over time. However, IMSS can counteract this effect by splitting acquisitions into lots so that firms can bid on individual lots or on combinations of lots.

In this way, the institute can increase the number and the types of firms that are able to participate and compete – not only at the present time, but also in future procurement procedures. This practice may be a tool to preserve competition over time, and therefore help the procuring entities obtain better value for money in the long run. This is in line with the OECD Recommendation on Public Procurement, which advises that in order to maximise the participation of bidders, tenders should allow for bids on certain lots or objects within the contract, or on combinations thereof, rather than only on the whole contract (OECD, 2015[7]).

This approach has been successfully tested by IMSS for medical device procurement, with good outcomes and improvements in competitive conditions. However, this does not necessarily mean that large contracts should always be split into lots; the decision must be thoroughly weighed on the basis of an in-depth market study assessing the benefits and costs of different strategies. Splitting contracts into lots does not automatically guarantee a competitive result or better value for money for two reasons:

1) Splitting a contract might mean losing out on economies of scale because larger firms might be uncertain about their chances of winning enough lots to allow them to exploit the synergies available. In this situation, firms might offer a higher price for each lot than they would have offered for an entire contract, in order to make sure that they cover their costs even if they win fewer lots than anticipated.
2) A single firm may still win the tender for all the lots.

The first problem can be tackled by designing a tender that features package bidding, where bidders can present different offers for individual lots and for packages of lots. However, in practice it might be difficult to define the relevant packages of lots; for instance, if the contract is split into very heterogeneous lots in terms of value – one very high-value lot and one very low-value lot – the barriers to entry may be somewhat lowered, but not removed. Moreover, a lots-to-bidders ratio that allows for a relatively homogeneous distribution of similarly-valued lots amongst competitors may facilitate collusive schemes. Additionally, comparing a high number of different offers for individual and bundled lots can prove to be a complex exercise for the buyer. Box 6.2 shows the approach developed by the European Union to deal with this issue.

Box 6.2. Bundles of lots in the European Union Public Procurement Directive

The European Union (EU) Directive on public procurement (Directive 2014/24/EU) reflects the concern that splitting a contract into lots may lead to firms offering less value for money than they would have had the contract not been split.

The Directive allows EU member states to allow contracting authorities to specify in the tender documentation that they reserve the possibility of awarding combinations of several (or all) of the lots to the same company, specifying the lots or groups of lots that may be combined.

In this context, contracting authorities could assess the offers with a view to determining firstly, which tenders offer the most advantageous conditions for each individual lot, and then carrying out a comparative assessment of these offers against the tenders submitted by specific companies for combinations of lots.

Source: Adapated from European Union (2014), Directive 2014/24/EU of the European Parliament and of the Council of 26 February 2014 on public procurement and repealing Directive 2004/18/EC

The second problem could be addressed with the introduction of participation limits (which restrict the maximum number of lots for which individual firms can compete) or award limits (which set a maximum number of lots that can be awarded to each individual company). However, the more stringent the participation limits, the higher the chance that some lots will receive no bids.

Moreover, participation limits may reinforce the entry barriers created by a heterogeneous grouping of lots, as in the example above: if a contract is split into one high-value lot and one low-value lot, a participation limit of only one lot may have the effect of allowing small firms to only bid for the low-value lot, and vice versa. However, this strategy could be used, to pro-competitive effect, to promote new entry into highly concentrated markets. Finally, the adoption of participation limits may provide a cover for market-sharing bid-rigging schemes (particularly when firms can predict the way in which the contract will be split), which would be difficult to spot by competition authorities.

Award limits would encourage participation by weaker bidders, who would have an incentive to bid on as many lots as possible, as they may receive lots that stronger bidders could not be awarded due to the award limit (Box 6.3). However, although award limits may increase participation, they may also prevent the buyer from choosing the best-value bids for each and every lot.

Box 6.3. Award limits in the UK

Ofcom, the UK's telecommunications authority, has set rules for the mobile spectrum auction that is to take place in late 2017. The watchdog has set caps of 255 MHz for the "immediately usable" spectrum and 340 MHz for the overall amount of mobile spectrum that any one operator can hold as a result of the auction.

These limits have important consequences for the largest operators currently holding the biggest mobile-spectrum shares: EE, part of British Telecom Group, is not allowed to bid for spectrum in the 2.3GHz band and will only be able to win a maximum of 85MHz of 3.4GHz spectrum. Vodafone can only win a maximum of 160 MHz of spectrum across both bands.

With these limits, Ofcom expects to preserve long-term competition in the market.

Source: (Ofcom, 2017[9]).

To sum up, whether and how to divide a contract into lots are crucial questions that should be routinely examined when designing each procurement procedure (and especially a consolidated one). The use of these mechanisms entails both advantages and challenges, and it is up to the purchasing authority to carefully weigh them up in each individual case. Market investigations are an essential tool to allow IMSS make an informed choice about these crucial tender design aspects.

Besides divisions into lots for technical-related reasons, IMSS could consider designing lots along geographical lines. This procurement strategy could help to foster participation by regionally competitive SMEs and to create additional savings by reducing transportation costs. Market studies, notably analyses of the price structure of typical bids, would play a pivotal role in assessing the potential benefits of this procurement strategy.

For the purposes of fostering competition and obtaining efficiencies, IMSS has created a strategic regionalisation tool for specific product categories. This allows IMSS to divide the Mexican territories into homogeneous regions with procurement requirements of a similar value. The procurement procedure is then carried out at the regional level. In this way, the institute encourages entry by firms that are competitive at the regional level, but that might be less able to compete at the national level. Thanks to this approach, the 2017 open tender for security services for IMSS buildings saved MXN198 million.

It is important however to determine on a case-by-case basis the appropriateness of using this mechanism. Improperly used, regional consolidation may have the potential of excluding larger firms from the market, thereby foregoing savings for IMSS derived from efficiencies of scale and scope.

Another approach which can ensure that IMSS receives proposals offering the best value for money is to limit the use of exceptions to open tenders as much as possible. Open tenders are currently the default procurement mechanism; as they are the most competitive procurement mechanism they therefore provide IMSS with the best chances of obtaining good value for money. However, the LOPSRM and the LAASSP list a number of situations in which exceptions to the open tender procedure can be allowed. While these legal provisions do not entail an obligation not to opt for an open tender, they merely allow for the possibility to do so. Consequently, the use of exceptions to open tenders constitutes a sizeable share of IMSS procurement procedures representing 23% of total procurement expenditures from January to May 2017.

The Ministry of Public Administration is already retraining procurement officers to emphasise that the use of exceptions to open tenders is not mandatory, even if it is legally allowed. The aim is to strongly discourage their use – except in certain situations embodied in legal provisions:[2]

- where there is only one provider in the market able to sell the required good or provide the required service (as long as there are no technically reasonable substitutes)
- in the case of unforeseeable circumstances or *force majeure*
- where the procurement procedure is carried out for military purposes
- where the procurement of a product by means of an open tender represents a risk for national security or public safety
- for contracts to be concluded in the context of a prior framework agreement.

In the case of the health sector in general and IMSS in particular, the most common exception lies with the acquisition of medicines from single-source suppliers, a common practice considering the number of patented drugs dominating the market of medicines. However, a recent report from the Mexican Competition Authority found that one year after the patent expiration, the average number of competing generic versions available on the market is 2.8 (COFECE, 2017). Therefore, IMSS could systematise its use of competitive procurement methods right after the expiry of patents in order to encourage the entry of new competitors.

Ensuring procurement strategies contribute to achieving IMSS objectives and support operational excellence

So far, this chapter has discussed the opportunities for IMSS to achieve greater value for money in procurement. However, for an institution like IMSS that provides public healthcare services, other considerations are also salient. The impact of procurement on healthcare is multidimensional; therefore, an assessment that is limited to analysing direct financial performance can only offer a partial view.

IMSS's procurement strategies should therefore not only focus on identifying the best price, or only the best quality-price ratio – they should also integrate holistic considerations of the broader impact that procurement may have on the healthcare system. This is also discussed further in Chapter 8.

Improving patient experience would support IMSS mandate

People-centred healthcare was the focus of the OECD Policy Forum and Ministerial Meeting on the Future of Health held in January 2017 (OECD, 2017[1]); the performance of healthcare systems is often measured by what they do and how much they cost, but their effects on patients should also be an essential objective of their design. These effects may range from comfort and life quality, to the absence of pain or the ability to live independently (OECD, 2017[1]).

In this context, healthcare procurement has an important role to play. Procurement can affect different aspects of the quality of the care provided, bringing about improvements in patient well-being and reductions in the length of hospital stays, readmission rates, post-care complications or infection risks. Moreover, these improvements are usually associated with savings (Box 6.4).

The avoidance of nosocomial infections, i.e. originating or takin place at the hospital, is an important component of quality care. Nosocomial infection may occur, among other causes, when the safety features of medical equipment are not sufficiently effective. Ensuring the safety of medical equipment is a way in which procurement procedures can contribute to the holistic improvement of healthcare.

Box 6.4. Broadening value-for-money procurement in Norway

The Norwegian company Helseforetakenes Innkjøpsservice AS (HINAS) is owned by the four regional Norwegian health authorities and serves as a means for its owners to co-ordinate public procurement.

HINAS has set in place an innovative procurement model for certain products (IV catheters) that allows for the pre-purchase testing of products in order to measure, amongst other factors, handling safety for nursing staff, as well as ease of use and the pain levels arising from the use of the catheters as reported by patients. The award criteria include not only cost factors, but also the qualitative aspects assessed by means of these tests.

Following the two-month evaluation period established in the tender terms, HINAS realised that the cheapest product available was not the best option, since its deficiencies in flexibility and sharpness meant that clinical staff often had to go through several attempts to pierce the skin with it, occasionally having to remove and replace it, which was additionally burdensome in terms of both time and financial cost. On this basis, the contract was not awarded to the bidder that submitted the lowest-priced bid (which prompted an unsuccessful legal case against the procurement authority) (Gerecke, Clawson and Verboven, 2015[10]).

In this way, HINAS not only improved the safety conditions for clinical staff, but also improved the experience of patients and saved costs in the long run (Istad, 2016[11]).

Source: (Gerecke, Clawson and Verboven, 2015[10]); (Istad, 2016[11]).

In order to not only cut costs, but also to achieve the best patient outcomes, building trust amongst different areas in order to examine the various options available is essential. In this context, the importance of close collaboration between the Requiring Areas and the Contracting Area cannot be overstated. For instance, the Contracting Area can work with the Requiring Areas to reduce their individual preference lists or to ensure that the Contracting Area understands which products or services have been scientifically proven to ensure the best patient outcomes. The Contracting Area should therefore not limit itself to covering the requests received, but should also engage in a productive dialogue with the Requiring Areas to ensure that the needs are covered in the most efficient way possible and in a way that is also integrated with the healthcare system.

Saving hospitalisation costs: IMSS would save around 23.5% if it reduced the average length of patient stay by one day.

The average length of stay in hospitals (ALOS) is a common indicator of a healthcare system's efficiency, measuring how many days hospitalised patients stay, on average, in hospitals. Although shorter ALOS usually entail a higher average cost per day, in general they tend to reduce the total cost of care per patient. For this reason, most countries seek to reduce ALOS while maintaining or improving the quality of care provided (OECD, 2015[7]). Procurement can play a crucial role in this regard by finding solutions that can contribute to this goal (Box 6.5).

The ALOS at IMSS hospitals is currently 5.23 days (IMSS, 2017[12]), namely 1.23 days above the 2013 Mexican average (OECD, 2015[13]). Considering that a day in hospital is one of the most expensive services provided by IMSS – specifically, the seventh most expensive service out of 80 services provided (Table 6.3) – a reduction in this expenditure would represent substantial savings for the institute and could be invested in improving the quality of care provided.

Table 6.3. The top-ten most expensive services provided by IMSS to non-contributors

(out of 80 services)

Ranking	Service	Price per day (MXN)
1	One day of intensive therapy (third-level units)	34,643
2	One day of intensive therapy (second-level units)	34,509
3	Haemodynamic study/procedure (second-level units)	27,248
4	Surgical intervention (second-level units)	19,327
5	Gynaecological surgery (third-level units)	12,757
6	Gynaecological surgery (first- and second-level units)	7,638
7	One-day stay at an IMSS hospital	7,256
7	One-day stay at an incubator	7,256
8	Chemotherapy session	4,911
9	Haemodialysis session	4,736
10	Magnetic resonance studies	4,341

Source: Annex I to Agreement ACDO.AS3.HCT.220217/32.P.DF, Official Journal of 21 March 2017, Section 1, page 18.

Box 6.5. Reducing the length of patient stays through innovative procurement in France

UniHa (*Union des Hôpitaux pour les Achats*) is a co-operative procurement network that brings together 67 French public hospitals to carry out joint procurement procedures.

The union had noted that the average length of stay for patients at UniHa hospitals was too long, which entailed risks for patients (such as nosocomial infections), additional workloads for medical and nursing teams, and general extra costs for the healthcare system.

Meanwhile, medical devices and surgery techniques were available on the market that offered the chance to significantly reduce post-operative monitoring (particularly for gastrointestinal surgery). This would allow patients to benefit from the most recent laparoscopy techniques with micro-invasive medical devices; medical and nursing teams would see their workload reduced while developing new competences; and finally, hospitals would save money.

UniHa issued a tender for a framework agreement whose specifications required not only the supply of medical devices, but also the provision of assistance and training for a minimum of 18 months to the medical teams in post-operatory care for colorectal and bariatric surgery.

UniHa hospitals choosing to join the framework agreement would be signing up, in all cases, for the provision of medical devices plus the performance of an audit and supply of a diagnostic report on the hospital's practices. Apart from this, hospitals would have the option to choose, on the one hand, between a detailed action plan, including an objective average duration-of-stay target and follow-up on its implementation, and on the other hand, follow-up on the labelling and/or a pre-audit.

Moreover, this scheme allowed for the possibility of a risk distribution model between the purchaser and the provider, with the provider's remuneration depending on the extent of the achieved reductions in the length of patient stays (UniHa, 2017[14]).

The framework agreement was awarded in 2017, and the first contract within the agreement has already been signed by the Toulon Hospital Centre.

Source: (UniHA,(n.d.)[15]); (UniHa, 2017[14]).

Bringing about organisational improvements

Procurement activities can have an impact on the organisation of the healthcare system, such as the amount and handling of the waste generated and the maintenance of the medicine inventory (including drug storage, stability and shelf life). In this regard, procurement must focus not only on the products to be acquired, but also on the use that the institution is going to make of them.

For example, a drug which is frequently purchased by IMSS can be acquired in two presentations: monodose or a ten-dose package. The ten-dose package entails a lower cost per dose than the monodose alternative. However, opening the ten-dose package means that the expiry date of any unused doses is shortened. Since, in IMSS's experience, no more than one or two doses are generally used at a time, the purchase of ten-dose packets of the drug usually entails significant waste and represents the least cost-effective option in the long run even though at first sight the cost per dose is lower.

Procurement practices can help reduce waste in these situations by taking expiry dates into account and drafting tender specifications that require the provision of a product as a monodose.

In particular, it is advisable to consider the extent to which IMSS's use and care delivery methods and patterns may affect the products' cost, as well as whether the products in question may support the easing and streamlining of internal processes. In this regard, some of the aspects that may be taken into account when drafting the tender documents include whether the products can be easily stored in an environment that guarantees their stability and supports a longer life cycle; the products' expiry date; the inventory costs; and what levels of waste will be generated (Box 6.6).

Box 6.6. Tenders for wound care products in Sweden

In Sweden in 2012, the Stockholm County Council (SCC) issued an innovative procurement procedure aimed at accounting for the total cost of providing care to patients using different competing wound-care products.

Under the tender documents, suppliers were required to calculate the total cost of treatment for each of three hypothetical cases with their own products, using a calculation model provided by the SCC. The model accounted for such aspects as the unit cost of wound care dressings, the necessary number of dressing changes, the time that needed by clinical personnel to change dressings (and the subsequent labour costs), and the likelihood of subsequent complications.

Eventually, the contract was awarded to the bidder that had proposed the highest unit price: this bidder had successfully provided evidence that its products entailed the lowest total cost of care over time.

Source: (Gerecke, Clawson and Verboven, 2015$_{[10]}$).

Some procurement transactions, and particularly those related to medical devices, have the potential to affect the healthcare system's expenditures by reducing operative costs. For instance, energy-efficient products, even if possibly higher priced at face value, can bring economic advantages to healthcare institutions by reducing their energy consumption, even if this aspect is not apparent from a simple assessment of the unit price (Box 6.7). The opposite can be true for a product that has a *prima facie* lower price, but whose low energy efficiency can constitute a hidden additional cost.

Box 6.7. Energy self-sufficiency through procurement in Poland

The hospital of Such Beskidzka in Poland sought to find a solution to the excessive sunlight that flooded a building facing south, which was the source of thermal discomfort for patients. Solutions included installing air conditioning in the hospital wards or installing shades to cover the windows and block the sun (EcoQUIP, 2016[16]).

However, the hospital went a step beyond by taking part in the EcoQUIP procurement project. Through an innovative procurement solution, the hospital achieved its main objective while at the same time achieving significant energy savings: the fixed outward blinds chosen to block the sun were also covered with solar panels, which allowed the hospital to achieve energy self-sufficiency with no exploitation costs (European Commission, 2016[17]).

The cost of cooling hospital wards by means of air conditioning would have amounted to around EUR 23 260/year; the innovative panels avoided this cost, while generating additional energy savings of over EUR 14 000/year for the hospital. Therefore, this innovative procurement solution helped the Such Beskidzka hospital save more than EUR 37 000 every year compared to a traditional, non-innovative solution such as the installation of air conditioning (Kautsch and Lichoń, 2015[18]).

Source: (EcoQUIP, 2016[16]); (European Commission, 2016[17]); (Kautsch and Lichoń, 2015[18])

Finally, good organisational practices can help avoid medicine stock outs. These can pose a public health hazard, in particular when essential drugs used to treat life-threatening conditions are unavailable. Procurement practices that do not seek to guarantee medicine availability can have pernicious effects on public health, namely deteriorating the medical condition of patients or causing hospitals to become overcrowded. Moreover, stock outs can involve extraordinary costs arising from the urgent need to purchase products at very short notice. Procurement practices can and should aim at guaranteeing the availability of necessary products.

IMSS has taken a positive step in this direction by implementing integrated services schemes, whereby health services such as haemodialysis are outsourced along with the medicines and medical devices necessary to perform them. Integrated services are an alternative for contracting medical services for the performance of diagnostic or therapeutic procedures, such as laboratory services, minimally invasive surgery, blood bank, dialysis and haemodialysis services, as well as for the procurement of ambulance rental or maintenance services. These schemes, coupled with the use of multiannual contracts, have helped IMSS's medical units to provide uninterrupted medical care.

These issues signal the need to move towards value-based procurement to ensure that procurement activities can not only achieve the best value for money, but also bring substantive improvements across the entire healthcare delivery system. One of the conclusions of the 2017 OECD Health Ministerial Meeting was that "people-centred care should better guide the course taken by health care in the future" (OECD, 2017[1]). By identifying the healthcare elements that can be indirectly affected by procurement practices, IMSS can capture these considerations and integrate them in the design of its procurement strategies.

However, the effects of procurement policies and practices can even extend beyond the provision of healthcare services to policy areas such as innovation, environmental protection or support to SMEs. Part III of this report will pick up that thread, describing in detail how IMSS purchasing power can influence the achievement of broader policy goals.

Proposals for action

The opportunity areas identified above suggest that IMSS can take a number of measures to continue to improve efficiencies and save money:

Assess the impact of IMSS's procurement strategies on savings

- Monitor the financial impact of procurement strategies and identify alternative options which can sustain benefits over time, such as multi-annual contracts for large consolidated tenders.
- Eliminate sources of inefficiencies in IMSS's procurement strategies that are costing it money, for example by standardising contractual provisions to avoid compliance costs which would be ultimately transferred by suppliers to participating institutions.
- Ensure that tender documents maximise savings by focusing on functional specifications rather than on detailed technical requirements.

Ensure a level playing field in IMSS's procurement

- Identify and remove entry barriers, notably for smaller Mexican suppliers of generic medicines, by expanding the bidding period to account for production lead times.
- Open the market strategically to suppliers through a comprehensive assessment of the benefits and risks of dividing tenders into lots while mitigating the risk of collusion amongst bidders.
- Increase the attractiveness of procurement procedures by developing tailored tender documentation and further promoting international competition in public tenders.

Use procurement to achieve achieve IMMS objectives and increase operational efficiencies

- Improve patient experience by defining procurement strategies which not account for the technical performance and price of goods and services, but also their impacts on treatments.
- Reduce the average length of patient stay by one day to save hospitalisation costs and maximise IMSS operational efficiencies.
- Use IMSS's procurement practices to contribute to holistic healthcare objectives.

Notes

[1] Reservation clauses allow for some tenders to be excluded from the application of free trade agreement rules.

[2] Those listed in fractions I, II, IV and V of art. 42 of the LOPSRM and fractions I, II, IV, V, VIII and XX of art. 41 of the LAASSP.

References

Albano, G. and C. Nicholas (2016), "The law and economy of framework agreements: designing flexible solutions for public procurement", *Cambridge University Press*, http://assets.cambridge.org/97811070/77966/frontmatter/9781107077966_frontmatter.pdf. [2]

EcoQUIP (2016), *Delivering efficiency, quality and sustainability in healthcare through innovation procurement*, EcoQUIP, http://www.ecoquip.eu/uploads/pdfs/EcoQUIP%20-%20Delivering%20efficiency,%20quality%20and%20sustainability%20through%20innovation%20procurement%20-%20case%20study%20based%20report.pdf. [16]

European Commission (2016), *Innovative public procurement can lower pressure on health budgets*, http://ec.europa.eu/growth/content/8945-innovative-public-procurement-can-lower-pressure-health-budgets_en (accessed on 05 November 2017). [17]

Gerecke, G., J. Clawson and Y. Verboven (2015), *Procurement, the unexpected driver of value-based health care*, The Boston Consulting Group and MedTech Europe, http://www.medtecheurope.org/sites/default/files/resource_items/files/BCG-Procurement-Dec-2015.pdf. [10]

IMSS (2017), "Strategy to foster competition in public procurement", *La Jornada*, http://semanal.jornada.com.mx/ultimas/2017/07/20/presenta-imss-estrategia-para-mejorar-competencia-en-licitaciones. [5]

IMSS (2017), *Statistical report 2016 (in Spanish) Memoria Estadística 2016*, http://www.imss.gob.mx/conoce-al-imss/memoria-estadistica-2016 (accessed on 27 November 2017). [12]

Investigación Farmacéutica (2017), *Major results of the consolidated tenders 2017, (Principales Resultados de los Fallos de CC 2017)*. [3]

Istad, K. (2016), *Big picture thinking can save money | Medtech Views*, http://medtechviews.eu/article/big-picture-thinking-can-save-money. [11]

Kautsch, M. and M. Lichoń (2015), *Cost-effective and low carbon solutions to maintain the thermal comfort of patients*, European Commission and EcoQUIP, http://www.ecoquip.eu/uploads/pdfs/Case%20Study%202%20-%20Cost%20effective%20and%20low%20carbon%20solutions%20to%20maintain%20the%20thermal%20comfort%20of%20patients.pdf. [18]

Management Sciences for Health (2012), *MDS-3: Managing Access to Medicines and Health Technologies*, Management Sciences for Health, Arlington, VA, http://www.msh.org/sites/msh.org/files/mds3-jan2014.pdf. [6]

New Zealand Ministry of Business Innovation and Employment (MBIE) (2017), *Government Model Contracts*, http://www.procurement.govt.nz/procurement/for-agencies/government-model-contracts (accessed on 04 December 2017). [4]

OECD (2012), *OECD Recommendation on Fighting Bid Rigging in Public Procurement - OECD*, http://www.oecd.org/competition/oecdrecommendationonfightingbidrigginginpublicprocurement.htm. [8]

OECD (2015), *OECD Recommendation of the Council on Public Procurement*, http://www.oecd.org/gov/ethics/OECD-Recommendation-on-Public-Procurement.pdf. [7]

OECD (2015), *Health at a Glance 2015: OECD Indicators*, OECD Publishing, Paris, http://dx.doi.org/10.1787/health_glance-2015-en. [13]

OECD (2017), *The next generation of health reforms. Ministerial statement*, OECD Health Ministerial Meeting, 17 January 2017, http://www.oecd.org/health/ministerial/ministerial-statement-2017.pdf. [1]

Ofcom (2017), *Ofcom sets rules for mobile spectrum auction*, https://www.ofcom.org.uk/about-ofcom/latest/media/media-releases/2017/ofcom-sets-rules-for-mobile-spectrum-auction. [9]

UniHA((n.d.)), *Qui sommes-nous ?*, http://fournisseurs.uniha.org/qui-sommes-nous/index.html (accessed on 10 July 2017). [15]

UniHa (2017), *Communiqué de presse. Une offre unique et novatrice à l'hôpital public*, http://www.uniha.org/index.php?tg=fileman&id=162&gr=Y&path=ZDoc+Page+Publique&sAction=getFile&idf=14347. [14]

Chapter 7. Safeguarding integrity and managing risks in IMSS procurement

A sound internal control system and effective risk management are critical elements for achieving IMSS's objectives and safeguarding integrity in its procurement processes. This chapter explores the strengths and opportunities for improving the strategies that drive IMSS's internal control and risk management activities. In particular, IMSS could clarify its risk management objectives for procurement, including sharpening the focus on fraud and corruption risks. The chapter also highlights how IMSS and internal control bodies could improve tools and clarify roles for managing risks in procurement processes. Priorities include making improvements to its risk assessment processes and increasing management ownership of the internal control system.

Public procurement is a high-risk activity because of the volume and regularity of purchases, and the often complex nature of processes to procure goods and services. Fraud, corruption and abuse can all unravel the fabric of integrity within procurement processes. Strategic and operational risks – such as inefficiencies in the tendering process, delays in delivery or substandard contract performance – can also undermine the achievement of policy and programme objectives.

The effectiveness of the internal control and risk management system in Mexico's Institute of Social Security (IMSS) therefore has a direct bearing on its success in achieving its strategic goals. As the largest public purchaser of pharmaceuticals and other medical supplies in Mexico, this is particularly relevant for IMSS's procurement activities. Risk managers, internal auditors and other stakeholders in IMSS's internal control system play critical roles in not only safeguarding integrity, but also ensuring that procurement activities operate effectively and efficiently for the benefit of citizens.

In 2013, the OECD reviewed IMSS's public procurement activities, and reported on IMSS's efforts to design and implement an effective internal control system for its procurement processes (OECD, 2013[1]). Since this review, IMSS has made improvements to manage risks and strengthen internal controls, in line with Mexican and international standards. For instance, it has developed dedicated units to lead risk management activities, such as risk assessments, and it has incorporated specific procurement risks into its risk matrices. While it has taken steps to improve risk management, it could tailor these activities further to address specific procurement risks, particularly the risk of fraud and corruption.

Building on the OECD's 2013 review, this chapter assesses ongoing challenges and risks facing IMSS, and offers recommendations for IMSS to manage risks more proactively. This includes making integrity objectives clearer in its risk management strategy, and improving efforts to monitor and evaluate the effectiveness of the internal control system.

The chapter begins with an overview of internal control and risk management in IMSS, including its application of government-wide standards. It then identifies ways that IMSS could improve its risk assessments and related guidance, as well as enhance management ownership over the internal control system. Finally, the chapter offers considerations for the SFP and Mexico's Supreme Audit Institution, as key stakeholders of the internal control system, to improve their support of IMSS's initiatives so as to better manage procurement risks. These considerations include clarifying roles and improving co-ordination. The recommendations in this chapter demonstrate the linkages between managing risks and institutional goals, recognising that citizens are the ultimate beneficiaries of a sound internal control system and risk management function.

Overview of internal control and risk management in IMSS

Internal control and risk management in the Mexican Government is grounded in the SFP's Manual of Internal Control System (*Acuerdo por el que se emiten las Disposiciones y el manual Administrativo de Aplicacion General en material de Control Interno,* or MAAG-CI), published in the Official Gazette on 2 November 2016. The MAAG-CI introduces the System of Institutional Internal Control (SCII) as Mexico's internal control and risk management framework for federal public entities. IMSS, as an autonomous government institution, is subject to the requirements outlined in the MAAG-CI and the SCII. The SCII has the following three components (see Box 7.1 for additional details):

1. The Standard Model of Internal Control (*Modelo Estándar de Control Interno*, or MECI).
2. The Institutional Risk Management (*Administración de Riesgos Institucionales*, or ARI).
3. The Institutional Development and Control Committee (*Comité de Control y Desempeño Institucional*, or COCODI).

Box 7.1. The System of Institutional Internal Control and its components

As outlined in the SFP's Manual of Internal Control System (MAAG-CI), the System of Institutional Internal Control (SCII) can be defined as a set of processes, mechanisms and other organisational elements which interact with each other (Mexico's Ministry of Public Administration, 2016[2]). An institution can apply the SCII at various levels, including planning, organisation, execution, direction, information and monitoring of its management processes. This is to ensure that the decision making is conducted in a manner that supports and promotes continuous improvement, quality, efficiency, compliance with the law, and the achievement of the institutional goals and objectives in an ethical and integral environment.

One of the three components of SCII, the Standard Model of Internal Control (MECI), is aligned with the Integrated Framework on Internal Control in the Public Sector (Marco Integrado de Control Interno en el Sector Público, or MICI), developed by Mexico's Supreme Audit Institution (Auditoría Superior de la Federación, or ASF). MECI, according to SFP officials, was an attempt to harmonise the internal control standards of SFP and ASF. MECI includes three different levels of control: strategic, executive and operational. The framework is built around the following components, drawing from the Internal Control-Integrated Framework by the Committee of the Sponsoring Organisation of the Tredway Commission: the control environment, risk assessment, control activities, information and communication, and monitoring activities.

The five components of MECI are structured around 17 principles, which are meant to aid officials in developing an effective internal control system. A successful integration of the principles contributes to the effective operation of the overarching components, and consequently to the effective operation of the overall internal control system within the entity. Moreover, the principles are meant to assist in making informed judgements when evaluating the maturity and degree of implementation of various components. When applying the framework, managers should be aware that they are expected to develop appropriate and tailored controls, since these are not articulated in MECI.

In addition to MECI, MAAG-CI also introduced the Institutional Risk Management (ARI), which provides a risk management framework and methodology. Specifically, the ARI outlines the activities an entity should undertake in order to identify, evaluate and mitigate corruption risks.

Source: (Mexico's Ministry of Public Administration, 2016[2])

IMSS's Directorate of Administration, and a team within it referred to as the Coordination of Modernisation and Competitiveness (MC), are responsible for directing the development, issuance and updating of policies, norms, procedures and guidelines related to regulations and internal control, among other areas. Other actors support the internal control system in IMSS. These include the Internal Control Office (*Órgano Interno de Control*, or OIC), an extension of the Ministry of Public Administration (SFP). The standards for internal control in Mexico assign a major role to the OICs to contribute to internal control and risk management activities.

The MAAG-CI requires federal public entities to produce an annual risk management matrix and an action plan, referred to as the Working Programme of Risk Management (*Programa de Trabajo de Administracion de Riesgos*, or PTAR). Within IMSS, the PTAR is developed and signed by the Director General, the Internal Control Coordinator (ICC) and the Risk Management Liaison. This is in line with the MECI, which assigns responsibility for monitoring the functioning of the internal control system to the heads of government institutions (i.e. IMSS's Director General), or when appropriate, the Governing Bodies (Mexico's Ministry of Public Administration, 2016[2]). MECI also requires the Director General to agree on the risk management methodology with the ICC. The latter is responsible for co-ordinating, implementing and monitoring PTAR activities, including the risk matrix and action plans, as well as progress reports and an annual report on risk behaviour.

The MC conducts risk assessments of a number of IMSS's services, which it documents in its Quality and Patient Safety Plan. As the title of the plan suggests, these risk assessments focus on risks and challenges that could affect the quality of medical care and patient safety, such as handling hazardous materials, as well as the management and use of medicines (IMSS, 2016[3]). The MC focuses its assessments on operational risks, and it co-ordinates with other IMSS directorates, as well as the OIC, to provide methodological support and follow up to other directorates in their own assessments.

Each directorate, including the procurement function, is responsible for analysing risks that are relevant to its area. In general, IMSS's approach reflects a "specific risk approach", whereby risks are identified within specific units. This is in contrast to a risk factor approach, which involves identifying risk factors shared across most, if not all, units within the institution (Wright, 2013[4]). According to officials, IMSS relies heavily on MECI, ARI and SFP's manual, described in Box 7.1 above, to structure its risk assessments, following the steps outlined in Figure 7.1 below. As a result of this process, for the 2017 calendar year, IMSS identified 13 strategic and operational risks linked to 47 risk factors in total across a range of activities included in its work plan for 2014-2018. For instance, as a strategic risk, IMSS identified a failure to digitalise paperwork and services that can improve the quality of services provided to citizens ((IMSS, 2017[5]); see Chapter 3). Other risks focused on health services, such as the risk of poor implementation of measures to prevent diseases, leading to increased mortality rates during hospital stays.

Figure 7.1. The risk assessment process based on ARI

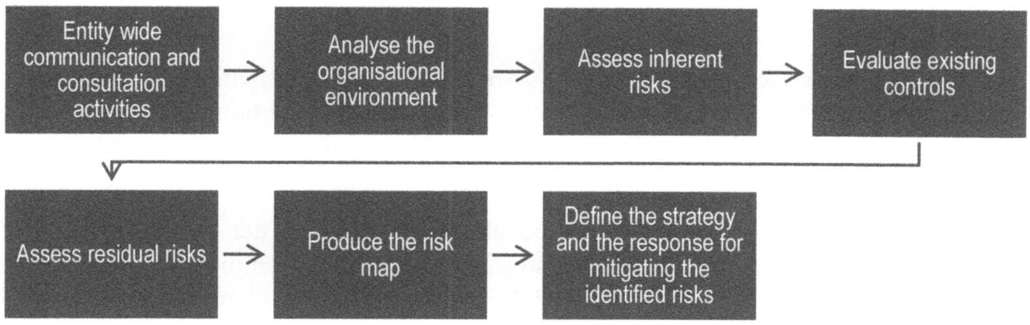

Source: (OECD, 2017[6])

The CABCS (Co-ordination of Procurement of Goods and Contracting for Services area or *Coordinación De Adquisición de Bienes y Contratación de Servicios*) co-ordinates IMSS's procurement function, and is responsible for assessing risks related to procurement activities. With the support of the MC, the CABCS identifies risks in the procurement cycle using the process described above. It assesses the probability and impact of risks, and determines whether control activities are sufficient for mitigating risks within a defined risk tolerance (see next section for more on risk tolerance). The MC analyses progress towards addressing these risks, and others, on a quarterly basis. The MC also consolidates the risks into a single matrix, graphic and PTAR. The matrix functions much like a risk registry (Box 7.2) and as such, IMSS's risk assessment process reflects the experience of other countries.

Box 7.2. Development and management of risk registers – example of the Irish Health Service Executive (HSE)

The Health Service Executive develops risk registers in order to manage its risks and to obtain a high-quality overview of the services' risk status at a certain point in time. The risk register serves as a powerful tool for risk tracking, and outlines the overall system of risks and the status of risk mitigation actions.

Each line manager is responsible for developing a risk register in his/her area of responsibility. Once completed, the register is shared with all employees of the entity in a clear and comprehensible manner, while taking into consideration their level of training, knowledge and experience.

An action plan is the critical part of a risk register. It is developed to address the additional controls required to reduce the risk to a satisfactory level. Supplementary controls that cannot be managed at the service level should be transferred to the next level of management. HSE acknowledges that for various reasons not every risk can be eliminated. Consequently, at any stage of the process it may be decided to 'live with' or accept a certain level of risk. When a risk cannot be entirely eliminated, it must be recorded in the risk register along with a list of controls aiming to reduce it to an acceptable level. These risks will be then monitored on a regular basis.

Four elements have been identified as prerequisites for developing a sound risk register:

1. **Availability of risk expertise**. Staff supporting the process need suitable training and education.
2. **Use of approved support materials and tools**. To ensure consistency throughout the process, a number of approved documents and tools are to be used when developing a register.
3. **Commitment and ownership.** Visible commitment from senior management is the key success factor in the process.
4. **Availability of site support**. Administrative support is required for organising workshops and overall co-ordination.

Since risk assessment is a dynamic process, risks and their control measures should be continuously reviewed, monitored and revised where necessary. Monitoring can be conducted at service level, at service area level, or for independence assurance.

Source: (Irish Health Service Executive, 2009[7])

Ensuring effective risk management strategies and implementation

IMSS could improve its risk management strategy for public procurement by clearly defining its goals and objectives, particularly those related to fraud and corruption risks.

The approval and signature of the Director General for the PTAR, discussed above, demonstrates a high-level commitment to risk management and internal control within IMSS. It also helps to set the tone from the top with regards to management's expectations for standards of conduct and communicating the importance of internal control, as required in the SCII. However, IMSS's Strategic Work Plan for 2016-2018 omits any reference to the importance of internal control and risk management for the effectiveness, efficiency and integrity of IMSS's activities, including procurement. Other key documents like the PTAR and risk matrix also do not explicitly mention corruption, fraud or integrity.

The OECD’s 2013 report on the IMSS, *Public Procurement Review of the Mexican Institute of Social Security: Enhancing efficiency and integrity for better health care*, recommended that IMSS establish a procurement risk management policy that was aligned with broader organisational objectives. The policy would aim to define and communicate IMSS's approach to risk, and provide high-level guidance on institutional processes and procedures for mitigating risks (OECD, 2013[1]). IMSS has yet to implement this policy; however, as an alternative, it could consider defining and incorporating integrity objectives into its work plans, the PTAR and guidance that discusses its procurement activities. This would help to demonstrate to managers and employees the importance of corruption and fraud risk management in this high-risk area.

In particular, IMSS could define clear objectives that explicitly emphasise the importance of a culture of integrity, and managing the risks of fraud and corruption. By making a reference to integrity and combating corruption at the strategic level, and highlighting high-risk areas like procurement, IMSS can further set a high-level tone that is conducive to effective fraud and corruption risk management. This would also help IMSS to better align with MECI, which now includes a principle dedicated to managing fraud and corruption risks, noting that entities should consider the potential for fraud when assessing risks to the achievement of objectives (Mexico’s Ministry of Public Administration, 2016[2]). Box 7.3 offers examples of strategic objectives dedicated to integrity from the United States.

Box 7.3. Defining integrity objectives: the approach of the United States' Centers for Medicare and Medicaid Services

The Centers for Medicare & Medicaid Services (CMS) is a federal agency within the Department of Health and Human Services (HHS) responsible for administering the Medicare, Medicaid and the Children Health Insurance Program. When developing its strategy, CMS ensures that it is well aligned with the strategic plan updated by HHS every four years. This allows for an integrated implementation approach and for the most current priorities to be duly reflected in the CMS strategy.

CMS defines its strategic plan in a comprehensive manner, outlining the agency's vision, mission and goals, as well as strategic objectives and desired outcomes. CMS's strategic objectives determine what improvements are required to achieve specific results, and thus help monitor whether progress has been made. With the assistance of the Strategic Planning and Management Council, the agency has identified strategic objectives covering the following organisational perspectives: organisational capacity, internal processes, financial stewards, and customers and stakeholders.

According to the CMS strategy, Objective 6.0, Strengthen Program Integrity, supports financial stewardship while helping to maximise value and effectiveness within the available resources. Improvements in financial stewardship subsequently help achieve the desired outcomes for customers and stakeholders, supporting the agency's overall goals and vision.

The CMS's strategy further describes the "Strengthen Program Integrity" objective through the following features and elements:

- enhanced financial accountability due to appropriate federal and state oversight of Medicaid expenditures;
- co-operation with law enforcement
- improving bad actor detection, identifying improper payments, refining enrolment processes
- taking into account policy levers and anti-fraud mechanisms at an early stage of regulation development
- improving the proactive stance through effective programme oversight and overall risk management
- enhancing enforcement through compliance and oversight activities
- improving prevention of fraud, waste and abuse through a targeted screening process
- effective risk management and strategic investments leading to high impact and return
- improved audit processes reduce audit frequency incompatibilities
- consolidated and well-aligned data are used for decision making
- improving collaboration with States on executing the healthcare delivery reform
- maintaining CMS's accountability, reliability and transparency by providing decision makers with access to its financial information
- proactive and coherent agency programme integrity activities.

Moreover, the importance of integrity is further underscored by being listed in the

CMS strategy as one of its core values by which they live. This emphasises its commitment to the highest standards of ethical behaviour and honesty.

Source: (CMS, 2016[8])

When defining integrity objectives, IMSS could also ensure they are echoed in the sub-objectives of IMSS's functional activities, particularly procurement. Sub-objectives relate to IMSS's functional activities and its departments, including its procurement and contracting activities. Management is responsible for linking entity-level objectives to specific sub-objectives, and co-ordinating across IMSS (Committee of Sponsoring Organizations of the Treadway Commission (COSO), 2013[9]). By strengthening this link, IMSS could more clearly articulate the value of internal control and risk management activities for achieving goals, objectives and outcomes. This could also enhance management ownership of these activities, as discussed further below.

To complement its efforts to create a culture of integrity, IMSS could further emphasise messages that focus on integrity values as opposed to rules.

In Mexico, the three years since the onset of major anti-corruption reforms in 2014 have seen considerable advances in public sector integrity and accountability. Beginning in early 2015 with the issuance of executive orders by the President of Mexico (focusing primarily on managing conflicts of interest), Mexico has undergone a series of reforms aimed at strengthening accountability and integrity in government. The federal government has also replaced its previous ethics code (*Código de Ética de la Administración Pública Federal*, DOF 31/julio/2002) and Integrity Rules (*Lineamientos de integridad y comportamiento ético, a través de Comités de Ética*, DOF 6/marzo/2012) with the new Ethics Code and Rules of Integrity (*Código de Ética y Reglas de Integridad*, DOF 20/08/2015). All public entities at the federal level are required to update their own organisations' codes accordingly. The reforms included four initiatives to strengthen management in public procurement processes, including (OECD, 2017[6]):

- **Protocol for Procurement Officials' Behaviour** (Protocolo de actuación en materia de contrataciones públicas, otorgamiento y prórroga de licencias, permisos, autorizaciones y concesiones). This is included in the General Law on Administrative Responsibilities (Ley General de Responsabilidades Administrativas). See chapter 5 for further discussion.
- **A registry of federal public administration public servants involved in public procurement processes** (Registro de servidores públicos de la Administración Pública Federal que intervienen en procedimientos de contrataciones públicas), including classification according to their level of responsibility and their certification.
- **An online publication of sanctioned suppliers,** specifying the reason of the sanction.
- **Increased collaboration with the private sector** to reinforce transparency in procurement procedures and decision making, and to reinforce integrity through the involvement of citizens in the identification of vulnerable processes and procedures, and the development of co-operation agreements with chambers of commerce and civil society organisations.

To comply with these new integrity requirements, IMSS established a "Code of Conduct and Prevention of Conflicts of Interests of IMSS Public Officials", which was approved by the Technical Council in December 2015. The Technical Council is responsible for issuing the guidelines that govern IMSS officials, such as those related to preventing acts of corruption. An annex to the Code of Conduct includes Integrity Rules for the Exercise of Public Service, and contains a section entitled "Public Procurement, Licenses, Permits, Authorisations and Concessions." This section states that the officials who participate in procurement processes must: 1) act with transparency, impartiality and legitimacy; 2) focus their decisions based on society's requirements and interests; and 3) ensure the best conditions for the government. It also describes which behaviours would violate these rules.

In addition, the Law of Social Security (LSS), the Internal Regulation of the IMSS (*Reglamento Interno del Instituto Mexicano del Seguro Social*, or RIIMSS), and the Internal Working Regulation of the Collective Work Contract (*Reglamento Interior de Trabajo del Contrato Colectivo de Trabajo*) for 2015-2017 jointly state, according to IMSS officials, that employees are bound to follow, when complying with their obligations, "the principles of responsibility, professional ethics, excellence, honesty, loyalty, impartiality, efficiency, warmth and quality in services provision and in health care to right-holders." It also notes that "they shall be subject to civil or penal responsibilities which they might incur as persons in charge of providing a public service."

While the Protocol of Conduct for Public Servants in Public Procurement helps to raise the profile of procurement as a high-risk area, it is largely based on rules instead of values (OECD, 2017[6]). This notion is reflected in the above laws and regulations. A compliance-based approach emphasises prevention of fraud and corruption through the establishment of enforceable standards and telling officials what to do. In contrast, a values-based approach aims to inspire integrity and induce behavioural changes through awareness-raising about ethics, values and the public interest. The former approach risks undermining motivation and morale if officials feel they are mistrusted or perceived to be corrupt. For this reason, OECD's Recommendation of the Council on Public Procurement, referred to in Box 7.4 below, emphasises the importance of not creating undue fear of consequences (or risk-aversion) in the procurement workforce or supplier community (OECD, 2015[10]).

Box 7.4. Integrity and OECD Recommendation of the Council on Public Procurement

III. RECOMMENDS that Adherents preserve the integrity of the public procurement system through general standards and procurement-specific safeguards.

To this end, Adherents should:

i) Require high standards of integrity for all stakeholders in the procurement cycle. Standards embodied in integrity frameworks or codes of conduct applicable to public sector employees (such as on managing conflict of interest, disclosure of information, or other standards of professional behaviour) could be expanded (e.g. through integrity pacts).

ii) Implement general public sector integrity tools and tailor them to the specific risks of the procurement cycle as necessary (e.g. the heightened risks involved in public-private interaction and fiduciary responsibility in public procurement).

iii) Develop integrity training programmes for the procurement workforce, both public and private, to raise awareness about integrity risks, such as corruption, fraud, collusion and discrimination, develop knowledge on ways to counter these risks, and foster a culture of integrity to prevent corruption.

iv) Develop requirements for internal controls, compliance measures and anti-corruption programmes for suppliers, including appropriate monitoring. Public procurement contracts should contain "no corruption" warranties, and measures should be implemented to verify the truthfulness of suppliers' warranties that they have not and will not engage in corruption in connection with the contract. Such programmes should also require appropriate supply-chain transparency to fight corruption in subcontracts, and integrity training requirements for supplier personnel.

Source: (OECD, 2015[10])

Fostering a culture that is conducive to risk management and that encourages management ownership over the internal control system requires officials who are motivated and do not feel treated as threats themselves. As such, IMSS could consider emphasising a values-based approach in its messaging and training on the code of conduct and ethics. Currently, risk management and internal control activities in IMSS are largely the responsibility of select teams and the OIC, with others involved on an ad-hoc basis for risk assessments and other activities. However, risk management and responsibility over the internal control system should permeate across the organisation, vertically and horizontally. By emphasising values-based approaches, IMSS would help to advance this idea. Moreover, sharpening the focus on integrity values in the procurement cycle would bring IMSS more into line with international standards, including the OECD's Recommendation of the Council on Public Procurement.

IMSS could further develop its strategy and activities for more systematically monitoring and evaluating the effectiveness of the internal control system and risk management activities.

While the IMSS Director General has the ultimate responsibility for the internal control system, according to MECI, other actors throughout the institution play critical roles, as detailed in IMSS's 2017 Organisational Manual of the Directorate of Administration (IMSS, 2017[11]). The Directorate of Administration, and the MC within it, is responsible for directing the development, issuance and updating of policies, norms, procedures and guidelines related to regulations and internal control, among other areas. In addition, the directorate has the duty to establish mechanisms to assess the state of the internal control system and risk management processes.

Numerous international standards exist for internal control and risk management, such as the International Standards Organisation's (ISO) 3100, *Risk Management: Principles and Guidelines*, which calls for planned monitoring and evaluation as part of the risk management process (ISO, 2009[12]), as shown in Figure 7.2. In line with the ISO standards, the MAAG-CI requires management to evaluate results and prepare quarterly progress reports and an annual report for the PTAR. In addition, according to the manual, management should evaluate and document the results of self-assessments and independent evaluations to determine whether internal control is effective and appropriate (Mexico's Ministry of Public Administration, 2016[2]). Management must also identify changes that have occurred in internal control, which may have resulted from institutional changes or changes to its environment.

Figure 7.2. International standards for risk management

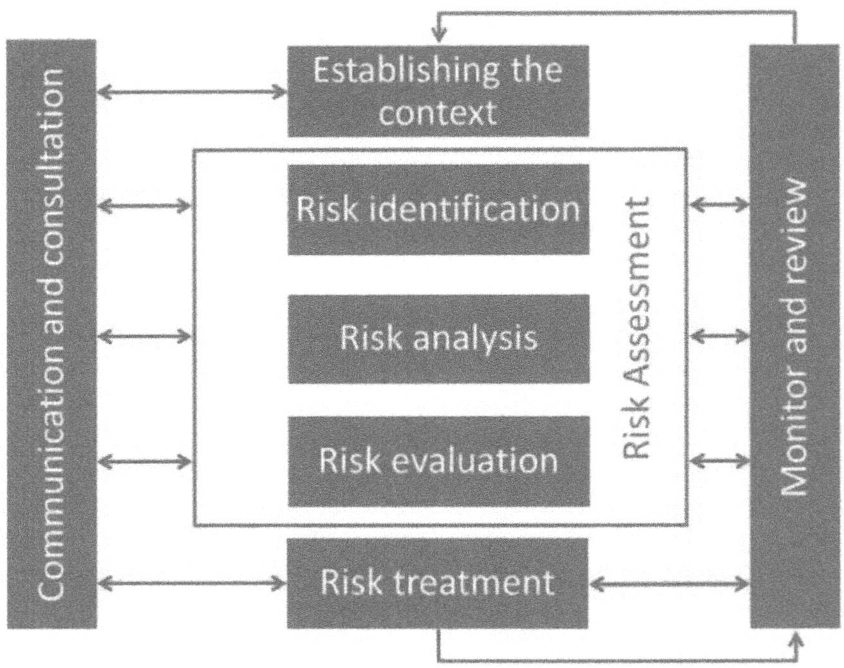

Source: Adapted from (ISO, 2009[13])

During interviews, IMSS officials described several activities to assess the internal control system and risk management activities, but they largely focus on evaluation rather than monitoring, and do not take into account the range of factors that could influence these functions. For instance, IMSS publishes an annual evaluation report that focuses on financial risks in the PTAR (*Evaluación de los Riesgos Financieros Considerados en el Programa de Administración de Riesgos Institucionales*). In addition, officials noted that they take into account audit findings by SFP and the Mexican Supreme Audit Institution (*Auditoria Superior de la Federación*, ASF) in order to determine where processes are failing. Based on these reviews, IMSS conducts "root cause" analyses, aimed at addressing vulnerabilities and improving policies and procedures. IMSS could more systematically and strategically evaluate these processes in order to better understand opportunities for improving its internal control system and risk management.

The SFP communicates requirements and offers guidance on the timing and objectives of monitoring and evaluation in its Manual of Internal Control System, the MAAG-CI. However, it is not explicit about the purposes and potential areas for evaluation. According to ISO 31000, *Risk Management – Principles and Guidelines* (ISO, 2009[12]), IMSS's monitoring and review processes should encompass all aspects of risk management in order to:

- ensure controls are effective and efficient in both design and operation
- obtain further information to improve risk assessment
- analyse and learn lessons from events (including "near-misses"), changes, trends, successes and failures
- detect changes in the external and internal context, including changes to risk criteria and the risk itself, which can require revision of risk treatments and priorities
- identify emerging risks.

IMSS could improve its monitoring and evaluation by going beyond financial risks to look at all aspects of the risk management process. This could include reviews of both the external and internal contexts that can affect IMSS's ability to pursue its objectives (Figure 7.3). In line with IMSS's strategic objectives, the MC and CABCS could take steps to improve evaluations of how CABCS assesses risks, and tailor these factors to procurement, keeping in mind the above purpose of evaluations.

Figure 7.3. External and internal contexts for evaluation of risk management activities

Evaluations of the context can include (but is not limited to):

- the cultural, social, political, legal, regulatory, financial, technological, economic, natural and competitive environment,
- whether international, national, regional or local;
- key drivers and trends having impact on the objectives of the organization; and
- relationships with, and perceptions and values of external stakeholders.

Evaluating the internal context can include (but is not limited to):

- governance, organizational structure, roles and accountabilities;
- policies, objectives, and the strategies that are in place to achieve them;
- capabilities, understood in terms of resources and knowledge (e.g. capital, time, people, processes,
- systems and technologies);
- information systems, information flows and decision making processes (both formal and informal);
- relationships with, and perceptions and values of, internal stakeholders;
- the organization's culture;
- standards, guidelines and models adopted by the organization; and
- the form and extent of contractual relationships.

Source: (ISO, 2009[12])

Improving risk assessments related to public procurement

IMSS could improve its risk assessments related to public procurement by sharpening the focus on corruption and fraud risks, as well as other strategic and operational risks that can affect the entire procurement cycle.

IMSS conducts risk assessments for a number of different areas; however, it could strengthen its assessments of its procurement functions. The risks related to the procurement cycle identified by IMSS are valid, but incomplete. IMSS primarily focuses on strategic and operational risks in the procurement cycle. It could consider additional risks, particularly those related to fraud and corruption, to ensure a thorough account of both the risks and control activities in place.

During interviews, IMSS and OIC officials highlighted a number of risks that could influence the effectiveness and efficiency of the procurement process, including insufficient planning, lack of knowledge to prepare contract requirements, and lack of collaboration between the contracting and petitioning areas, among others. However, for 2017, the risk matrix and PTAR explicitly refers to procurement risks in only two out of the 13 overall risks identified, and excludes many of the risks that officials highlighted.

One risk identified in the PTAR is the lack of co-ordination of processes for making consolidated purchases; both CABCS and the Co-ordination of Supply Control are noted as the risk owners. In addition, IMSS identifies projects that exceed their scheduled completion date as a risk. IMSS highlighted the poor detection of pensioners' deaths as a potential risk, but it does not link this to integrity, fraud or corruption. For instance, the risk of individuals who steal the identities of deceased pensioners in order to obtain goods and services that they would otherwise be ineligible to access. Neither the matrix nor the PTAR make explicit reference to risks related to fraud, corruption or integrity in any of IMSS's activities, including procurement.

Officials explained that IMSS involves various units in its assessments of procurement risks, including teams responsible not only for procurement, but also market research, control and product users. To increase the focus on fraud and corruption risks, IMSS could ensure that those who are at the frontline in preventing fraud and corruption are involved in the risk assessment (e.g. contracting officers), as well as external entities, such as contractors, ASF and regulators. Complaints, similar entities and social witnesses can also help identify risk (see Chapter 5). Interviews, surveys and focus groups are just some approaches that IMSS could use to gather information and input from these stakeholders. IMSS could also analyse individual tenders for risks. This approach could cover all phases of the procurement cycle, including pre-tendering, tendering, and post-award phases (see Table 7.1 for further discussion of such risks in the procurement cycle).

Table 7.1. Integrity, corruption and fraud risks across the procurement cycle

Risks in the pre-tendering phase	Needs assessment	• Lack of adequate needs assessment • Influence of external actors on officials' decisions • Informal agreement on contract
	Planning and budgeting	• Poor procurement planning • Procurement not aligned with overall investment decision-making process • Failure to budget realistically or deficiency in the budget
	Development of specifications/requirements	• Technical specifications are tailored for a specific company • Selection criteria is not objectively defined and no established in advance • Requesting unnecessary samples of goods and services • Buying information on the project specifications
	Choice of procurement procedure	• Lack of procurement integrity for the use of non-competitive procedures • Abuse of non-competitive procedures on the basis of legal exceptions: contract splitting, abuse of extreme urgency, non-supported modifications
Risks in the tendering phase	Request for proposal/bid	• Absence of public notice for the invitation to bid • Evaluation and award criteria are not announced • Procurement information is disclose and made public
	Bid submission	• Lack of competition or cases of collusive bidding: o cover bidding o bid suppression o bid rotation o market allocation
	Bid evaluation	• Conflict of interest and corruption in the evaluation process through: o Familiarity with bidders over time o Personal interests such as gifts or future/additional employment o No effective implementation of the "four eyes-principle"
	Contract award	• Vendors fail to disclose accurate cost or pricing data in their price proposals, resulting in an increased contract price (i.e. invoice mark-ups, channel stuffing) • Conflict of interest and corruption in the approval process (i.e no effective separation of financial, contractual and project authorities) • Lack access to records on the procedure
Risks in the post-award phase	Contract management/ performance	• Abuses of the supplier in performing the contract, in particular in relation to its quality, price and timing: o Substantial change in contract conditions to allow more time and/or higher prices for the bidder o Product substitution or sub-standard work or service not meeting contract specifications o Theft of new assets before delivery to end-user or before being recorded o Deficient supervision from public officials and/or collusion between contractors and supervising officials o Subcontractors and partners chosen in an on-transparent way or not kept accountable
	Order and payment	• Deficient separation of financial duties and/or lack of supervision of public officials leading to: o False accounting and cost misallocation or cost migration between contracts o Late payments of invoices • False or duplicate invoicing for good and services not supplied and for interim payment in advance entitlement

Source: (OECD, 2016[14]).

As noted in the table above, bid rigging (i.e. collusive tendering) is also a major risk that can affect the tendering phase. Bid rigging occurs when "businesses, that would otherwise be expected to compete, secretly conspire to raise prices or lower the quality of goods or services for purchasers who wish to acquire products or services through a bidding process" (OECD, 2009[15]). IMSS may be particularly vulnerable to this, given the current features of the consolidated tenders it leads. Indeed, a high volume of procurement coupled with repetitive tendering processes and little changes in the scope of those tenders from one year to another could expose them to bid-rigging practices. Bid rigging and corruption can occur simultaneously and they can reinforce each other, but they each have key elements that make them distinct. For instance, bid rigging is a horizontal relationship between bidders that restricts competition; in public procurement it harms the public purchaser. Corruption involves a vertical relationship between one or more bidders and one or more procurement officials. That is, a procurement official can receive bribes or rewards at the expense of the public purchaser (or the public in general) in exchange for currying favour with a particular firm (OECD, 2012[16]). While differences exist in the nature of the schemes, the control activities for managing the risk of both bid rigging and corruption can complement each other.

In addition to risks of fraud and corruption, several risks of strategic and operational importance to the procurement cycle are also overlooked in IMSS's current risk assessment. These may be a result of poor performance or mistakes, rather than breaches of integrity. Examples include bid challenges and complaints, poor quality of products, failure of suppliers, and inadequate contractual terms and management. Moreover, a large part of IMSS's public procurement function is highly decentralised, yet key decisions and strategies related to the procurement function have been centralised. Centralised procurement can entail risks that include market concentration and development of monopolistic structures, fit-for-purpose risks from over-standardisation of requirements, and responsiveness risks to developments in pricing and medical technology. By honing its assessments of the additional strategic and operational risks related to the procurement cycle, IMSS could intervene to prevent or mitigate the impact of these risks on procurement performance.

IMSS could further define risk tolerances to more effectively allocate resources and determine control activities.

The MAAG-CI requires federal public entities to define their risk tolerance relative to their strategic objectives. It further calls for the risk owners to monitor risks, using indicators, to ensure that they remain within predetermined tolerance levels (Mexico's Ministry of Public Administration, 2016[2]). In the event that risks exceed tolerance levels, the risk owner must report this change to the Director General and the ICC. The MAAG-CI makes explicit reference to corruption risks, yet it notes that entities do not have to define a risk tolerance for corruption risks (Mexico's Ministry of Public Administration, 2016[2]). Presumably, this is because SFP is attempting to convey that managers should have zero tolerance of any risks that could undermine the integrity of the institution.

Risk tolerance can be defined as "the acceptable level of variation in performance relative to the achievement of objectives" (Government Accountability Office, 2015[17]). This definition underscores the idea that risk management is not only about minimising threats, but also exploiting opportunities. For instance, IMSS may identify medical equipment that it wishes to procure at a discount price. Risk tolerance can help IMSS to determine whether controls in place are effective enough (relative to the tolerance) to justify increasing its purchase volume to take advantage of the lower price. Figure 7.4 below illustrates the practical application of risk tolerance in aiding managers to understand risk exposure and whether additional controls are needed. It depicts the relationship between inherent risks, residual risks and risk tolerance.

Figure 7.4. The relationship between inherent risks, residual risk and risk tolerance

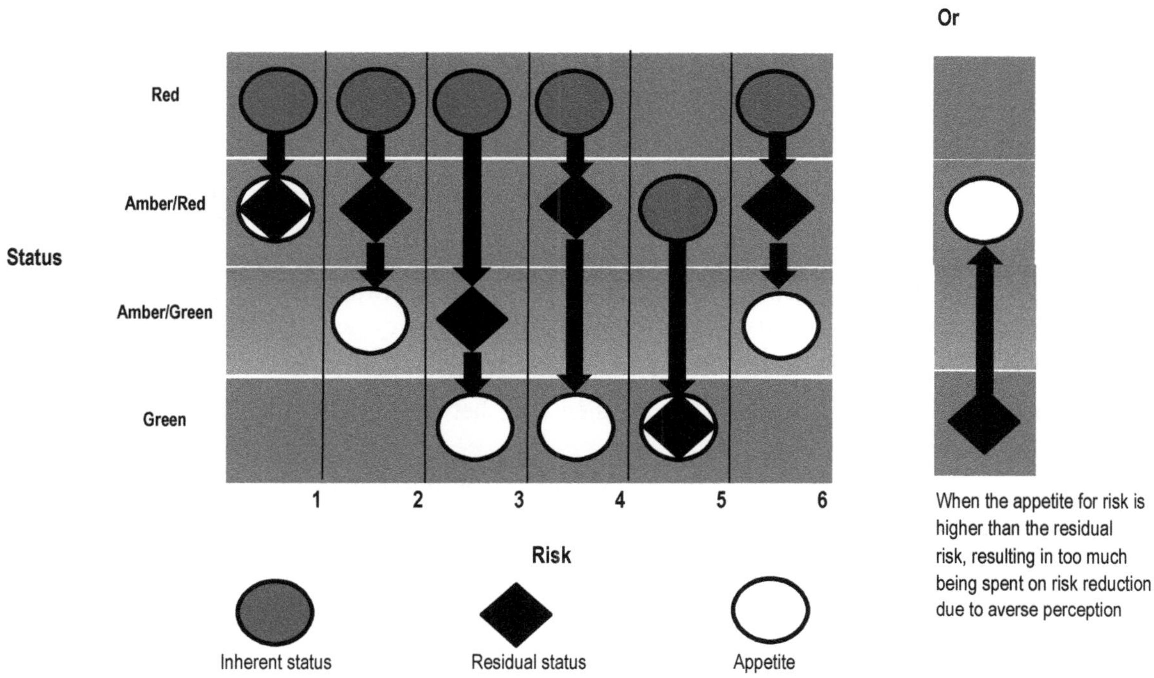

Source: (UK HM Treasury, 2006[18])

Risk tolerance is a critical element of effective risk assessments because it can help IMSS to make risk-based decisions about mitigation strategies. In addition, as IMSS officials have expressed the need to improve the balance between controls and efficiency in procurement process, further defining risk tolerance and providing guidance on how it is used could help IMSS to make better decisions on whether to add or reduce controls.

In 2014, IMSS strengthened its risk management framework, and incorporated risk tolerance into its assessment process. IMSS address risk tolerance in two ways. The first is in the risk matrix, where it notes the tolerance for each of the 13 risks on a scale of low, moderate, high and extreme. The second is in the PTAR, where IMSS notes an "indicator associated with risk tolerance," which links to one of the 47 risk factors IMSS has identified. For instance, the risk of uncoordinated processes when making consolidated purchases (one of the 13 risks) includes three risk factors, each of which is assigned an indicator for risk tolerance. The use of risk tolerance in the matrix and PTAR are positive signs of IMSS's attempts to incorporate this concept into decision making for determining control activities.

However, IMSS could improve its use of risk tolerances and guidance to ensure that they become more than a box-ticking exercise in response to requirements. For instance, IMSS does not define its tolerance of corruption and fraud risks, citing zero tolerance for such risks. Zero tolerance of corruption and fraud is an effective message for conveying an overall commitment to integrity; however, reducing such risks to zero has little practical value for the purposes of managing risks. As discussed, there is need to balance controls with efficiency, innovation and other business objectives, and this is true of the procurement cycle. IMSS could develop a meaningful risk tolerance for corruption and fraud risks in procurement processes in order to make informed decisions about control activities. For example, when procuring urgently needed medical equipment, IMSS could define a "low" tolerance instead of a "very low" tolerance, with the practical effect being expedited procurement procedures for historically high-performing suppliers.

IMSS could improve its guidance and tools for conducting risk assessments related to procurement and advancing new forms of analyses on tenders and processes.

According to ISO 31000, risk management activities should be documented in order to help improve methods, tools, and overall processes (ISO, 2009[13]). In addition, OECD's Recommendation of the Council on Public Procurement calls for government entities to not only publicise risk management strategies, but also to raise awareness and knowledge about the integration of risk management into the procurement cycle (OECD, 2015[10]). It makes the following recommendations for achieving this:

- engaging in communication to strengthen trust between stakeholders and control activities
- organising awareness campaigns and events on the importance of integrating risk management activities into daily business practices
- providing training sessions and workshops to inform relevant public procurement entities about their risks and ways to handle the identified risks,
- circulating periodic messages using various media (e.g. newsletter, promotional poster, brochures, videos, handbook, etc.) to relevant stakeholders on the existing risk management strategies
- disseminating best practices of risk management case studies from leading organisations
- inviting public procurement entities to relevant conferences and seminars on risk management strategies.

IMSS has invested considerable resources in developing sound risk management practices and assessments, in line with the MAAG-CI and international standards. However, according to officials, it has yet to develop specific guidelines or tools to aid in identifying, monitoring and reporting risks at various stages of the procurement process. Without such guidance, a heavy burden is placed on the MC to co-ordinate, consolidate and standardise risk management practices, including risk assessments. Additional guidance for public procurement officials would help IMSS to advance a more coherent and informed approach to identifying and managing risks in individual contracts. In doing so, IMSS could draw on the experience of the Australian government (Table 7.2).

Table 7.2. Australian guidance for identifying and managing procurement risks

Sources of Risk	Examples of Risk
Contract management capability	• Failure to have sufficiently skilled and experienced resources to effectively manage the contract(s) • Lack of recognition of the importance of contract management • Failure to act on contractor underperformance
Contractor performance	• Failure to provide contract deliverables on time, to the agreed quality standards • Failure to adhere to the agreed budget • Failure to comply with all contract provisions, for example, privacy, security, recordkeeping • Fraud and/or unethical conduct by the contractor
Changes in circumstances and/or requirements	• Contract changes not dealt with as contract variations • Contractor not prepared to agree to contract variations to accommodate changes in entity requirements • Changes in circumstances not managed in a timely manner
Stakeholder relationships	• Stakeholders not consulted and/or kept informed about contract performance • Changes in stakeholder expectations not communicated to contract manager • Differing and/or conflicting stakeholder expectations

Source: (Australia National Audit Office, 2012[19])

In developing the guidance, IMSS could consider explaining the processes and defining key terms reflected in the ARI, including the risk matrix, risk map and PTAR. These documents are meant to be tools for risk managers, and there are linkages between them that IMSS could clarify. For example, the risk matrix appears to include an assessment of inherent risks (risks in the absence of measures to address risks) and residual risks (risk exposure after applying mitigation strategies to address the risk). The residual risks are then depicted in the risk map – a standard two-dimensional representation of individual risks according to probability and impact. The PTAR then offers additional information on mitigation measures for these risks. The guidance could explain these linkages between, as well as the individual risk concepts within each to help guide and educate managers.

Improved risk assessments and guidance can also offer additional opportunities for IMSS to use the results for more advanced data analyses, particularly of tenders. Officials noted that IMSS collects information on a range of procurement risks and intends to expand its efforts to retroactively understand how tenders were carried out. IMSS could use the data it has collected on procurement risks to conduct additional analyses of individual tenders in order to aggregate risks across different procuring entities (see Box 7.5 for an example). The usefulness of this analysis depends on the quality and standardisation of the risk assessments, which in turn depend on having sufficient guidance for carrying out the process.

Box 7.5. Data-mining to identify corruption in public procurement in the European Union

In recent years, a team of sociologists has developed a new system to identify potential corruption in public procurement in Europe. The research team developed a "Corruption Risk Index" (CRI) to mine available information on public procurements to identify potential corruption issues.

To develop the CRI, the lead researcher spoke with experts on public procurement to identify 13 "red flags" that could indicate corruption in an individual contract or tender. These red flags included very short tender periods (e.g., a tender issued on a Friday and awarded the following Monday), very specific or suspiciously complex tenders compared with others in the field, tender modifications leading to bigger contracts, inaccessible tender documents, and very few bidders in highly competitive markets.

The flags were then weighted to determine a risk ranking for each contractor or firm. In a proof-of-concept conducted using data from Hungary, Slovakia, and the Czech Republic, the research team found that firms with a higher CRI score made more money than firms with lower CRIs, and were also more likely to have politicians involved as either managers or owners and to be registered in tax havens.

Source: (University of Cambridge, 2015[20]).

Clarifying roles and improving co-ordination

IMSS could take steps to increase management ownership of the internal control system and risk management policies and processes, including targeted trainings and messaging for procurement officials.

SFP's standards emphasise the importance of internal control and risk management, placing responsibility squarely on managers of government entities (Mexico's Ministry of Public Administration, 2016[2]). For instance, MECI calls for a specific corruption risk management function within government institutions as part of its risk management efforts. It also requires managers to develop a programme and policy to promote integrity and corruption prevention, involving training, disseminating a code of ethics and conduct, and whistleblowing mechanisms. These reforms are in line with international standards, and reflect the principles and practices outlined by the Institute of Internal Auditors, the Committee of the Sponsoring Organisation of the Treadway Commission (COSO) and others (Figure 7.5).

Figure 7.5. The three lines of assurance model

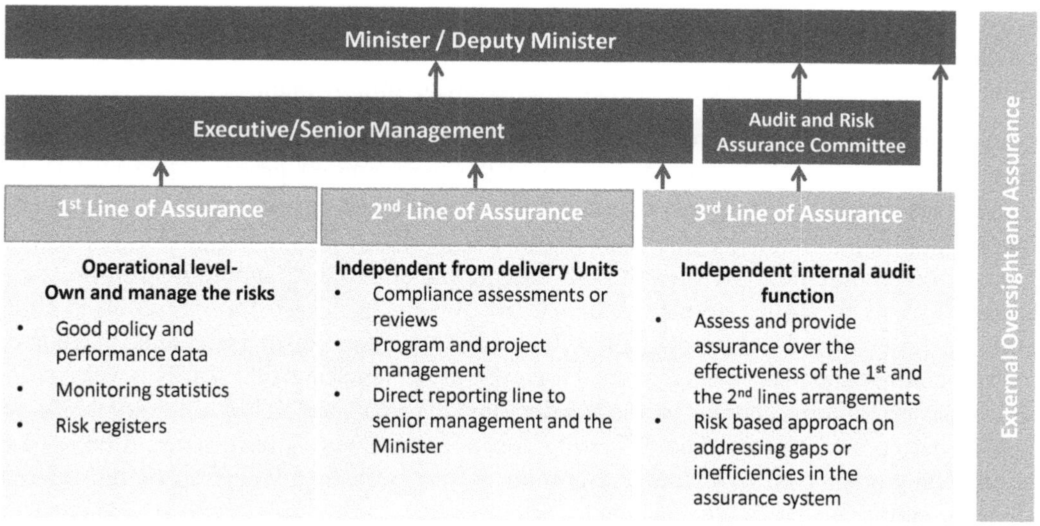

Source: Adapted with inputs from a. Federation of European Risk Management Associations (FERMA)/European Confederation of Institutes of Internal Auditing (ECIIA) Guidance on the 8th European Company Law Directive on Statutory Audit DIRECTIVE 2006/43/EC – Art. 41-2b, 2010, b. Institute of Internal Auditors (IIA): Three Lines of Defence Model, 2013, and c. Assurance Maps Presentation, PIC EU-28 Conference 2015.

IMSS has taken concrete measures to institutionalise the internal control system and risk management functions in line with SFP's SCII and IIA's three lines of defence. In IMSS, the contracting authority represents the first line of defence, while other units make up the second line of defence (e.g. the Change Management and Competition Unit). The OIC is the third line of defence. In addition, the MC has a sub-unit, called the Technical Coordination of Evaluation and Control (TCEC), which is entirely dedicated to improving IMSS's internal control system and risk management.

Among its many responsibilities, the TCEC designs strategies, practices and mechanisms for strengthening internal control and risk management, including following up on recommendations by OIC and the ASF. The TCEC plays the critical role of developing, implementing and evaluating the Internal Control Work Program and the PTAR. The TCEC, among other activities, is also responsible for promoting formalisation, standardisation and cross-cutting approaches, tools, methodologies and trainings for effective implementation of internal control and risk management in IMSS.

While IMSS has taken steps to institutionalise internal control and risk management as part of the overall management system, it could improve management's ownership of these functions, particularly those related to procurement processes. The challenges IMSS faces in strengthening management ownership are, in part, a function of existing policies and the structure of the internal control system in Mexico. This arrangement designates the SFP and the OICs with a mandate that blurs the division between the lines of defence. In particular, interviews with IMSS officials suggested that there is an over-reliance on the OIC to detect corruption and fraud. The omission of corruption and fraud risks in the risk matrix and PTAR further suggests the need for managers to take ownership of these functions.

In 2013, OECD reported that there is a perception within IMSS that the internal control and risk management functions, including those for preventing corruption, are the responsibility of the OIC (OECD, 2013[1]). To continue addressing this issue, IMSS could take steps to ensure that these functions are not seen as administrative or routine, but instead as a valuable exercise for advancing procurement objectives and broader institutional goals. Further defining and linking objectives and sub-objectives, as previously discussed, could help in encouraging ownership by management.

In addition, IMSS could develop targeted training dedicated to exploring and building knowledge about the first line of defence in the procurement process. The OECD has already recommended various communication strategies, awareness campaigns and training to promote management ownership (OECD, 2017[6]); (OECD, 2013[1]). Targeted training for procurement officials at both federal and state levels would help to tailor the messages so as to induce greater management ownership. These training courses could build on those carried out by the SFP, which offers courses for procurement officials on internal control and risk management. However, it is important that IMSS develops and leads its own training courses to further demonstrate that the OIC is not responsible for the internal control system. The following core messages and activities could be used in training or guidance to help create a culture of management ownership of the internal control system:

- **Making the business case for management ownership** – IMSS could improve its messaging for linking the internal control system to the success of the procurement cycle. Internal control activities are critical for the effectiveness and efficiency of procurement processes; without them, there is little assurance that goals and objectives have been accomplished. IMSS could convey the importance of internal control and risk management activities not only for preventing fraud and corruption, but also for ensuring that procurement processes are performing as expected.
- **Addressing the behavioural aspects required to induce change** – Management ownership has a strong behavioural component linked to individuals' beliefs, habits and motivations. IMSS could consider approaches for changing behaviours that first identify resistance to change, and that then develop strategies for overcoming any barriers. Change management models and "pull" strategies, such as those described in Box 7.6, could be used to encourage managers to take responsibility for the internal control system.
- **Demystifying and personalising the internal control and risk management functions** – Procurement officials may not actually realise that many of the assessments and checks they conduct are actually control activities. For instance, requiring quotes before purchasing equipment without a competitive bidding, while a common procurement procedure, is effectively a control to minimise risks of over-spending and to promote cost-consciousness. By identifying and defining officials' existing contributions to the internal control system, IMSS can reframe staff's perceptions about their daily contributions to an effective internal control system. This could also help to reinforce the notion that the OIC is not responsible for control activities or risk management.

Box 7.6. Change management paradigms to strengthen management ownership of an internal control system

Various factors can undermine the effective implementation of internal control and risk management, including institutional legacies, failure to understand complexity and a lack of leadership support. Institutionalisation also has a strong behavioural component involving the beliefs, habits and motivations of individuals. Common behavioural elements when faced with change include (Stoop, 2016[21]):

- feeling threatened by change, as a result of consequences on power structures, prestige, individual opportunities, or careers
- a lack of understanding of the need for change or the implications of the change
- not having confidence in the promoters of change.

There are myriad change management models that could be applied to improving management ownership, and ultimately the internal control and risk management functions. For instance, in the 1950s, renowned psychologist Kurt Lewin suggested that effective change requires successful completion of a three-step process of "unfreezing" the existing behaviour, moving to a new level and "refreezing" at the new level (Hayes, 2014[22]). Over the years, the process has evolved in different contexts to include concrete activities for each step. Lewin's theory argues that "pull" strategies, whereby restraining forces are removed to strengthen a culture of integrity, are more effective than "push" strategies (i.e. outside pressure for change), because they are more likely to increase commitment and result in permanent change (Hayes, 2014[22]).

Another pre-eminent change management model, developed by Harvard University Professor John Kotter, employs an eight-step process (Kotter, 1996[23]):

1. Create a sense of urgency
2. Build a guiding coalition
3. Form a strategic vision and initiatives
4. Enlist a volunteer army
5. Enable action by removing barriers
6. Generate short-term wins
7. Sustain acceleration
8. Institute change

Other change theory models exist that can help entities to address these issues, and understand "where they are" and "where they want to go" with regards to management ownership and building a culture of integrity. One of the benefits of applying change management paradigms is that they can be flexible enough to be tailored to the individual contexts of institutions. They also are based on the notion that change is not an end state that can be reached through programmed steps, but rather an ongoing process (Paton and McCalman, 2008[24]). Within IMSS, change management can help to bridge theory, as defined in new standards and guidelines, with practice. It also provides insights on how to manage resistance to change, which could include the following techniques (adapted from (Stoop, 2016[21])):

- demonstrate that the status quo cannot be maintained and why
- collect information concerns and rationale for the current situation, and provide factual responses

- understand and use resistance to change for making improvements
- engage those who are promoting change
- create new perspectives that are sustainable, rooted in the medium and long-term, not only the short term.

Source: (OECD, 2017[25])

IMSS and the OIC could take steps to clarify the roles and responsibilities for risk management and the internal control system. This could include auditor's statements of independence.

The OIC's basic structure consists of the Head of the OIC, the Responsibilities Head, the Auditing Head and the Complaints Head. Even though the OIC operates as IMSS's internal audit unit, it reports directly to SFP, not to the IMSS General Director. In 2013, the OECD recommended that IMSS establish an internal control committee in line with the SCII, which suggests that entities create an Institutional Development and Control Committee (*Comité de Control y Desempeño Institucional*, or COCODI) to monitor the implementation of the internal control system (OECD, 2013[1]). As this is not a requirement, IMSS decided not to set up a COCODI.

OIC's presence in IMSS is organised into six areas: i) Audit for the Development and Improvement of Public Management (*Auditoria para Desarollo y Mejora de la Gestión Pública*); ii) Internal Audit (*Auditoría Interna*); iii) Responsibilities (*Área de Responsabilidades*); iv) Complaints (*Área de Quejas*); v) Special Contingency Audit for Medical Services (*Auditoria Conatención Especial A Servicios Médicos*); and vi) Regional Co-ordination (*Coordinación de Vinculación Operativa*) (IMSS, 2017[26]). Two of these areas (Internal Audit and Special Contingency Audit for Medical Services) conduct audits across IMSS, including procurement, construction, cross-cutting and revenue audits. In addition to the OIC areas, delegates and incumbent public commissioners (DC) contribute to monitoring and control within IMSS.

According to officials, the recent anti-corruption reforms have not led to specific changes in the internal audit functions, but the division of labour between the various entities responsible for audit has been clarified in order to ensure proper implementation, including by contracting authorities. Nonetheless, existing manuals, OIC training activities, as well as IMSS's and OIC's responses to the OECD's questions during this review suggest the need for further clarification of the roles and responsibilities in the internal control system. For instance, OIC's *Manual of Organization of the Internal Control Body for IMSS* notes that the Audit for the Development and Improvement of Public Management is responsible for "carrying out the risk assessment that may hinder the achievement of the goals and objectives of the Mexican Social Security Institute." As noted in Figure 7.6 below, international standards suggest that entities responsible for auditing should, at most, facilitate the identification and evaluation of risks. To preserve their independence, audit entities should avoid designing or implementing processes that could be the subject of audits. Segregated responsibilities from management, clear and formally defined responsibilities and working in an unbiased way, are all key elements of international standards for preserving the independence of audit entities (INTOSAI, 2010[27]; INTOSAI, 2010[28]).

While other divisions in IMSS have the responsibility for risk management and conducting risk assessments, statements such as those found in the OIC's manual raise questions as to the extent and appropriateness of the OIC's involvement in conducting risk assessments. In addition, such manuals are communication tools for both IMSS and the OIC. Therefore, care should be taken to clearly define OIC's roles vis-à-vis other entities within IMSS with responsibilities for risk management and internal controls. IMSS and the OIC may find IIA guidance instructive for assessing and clarifying internal audit roles in IMSS's risk management activities (Figure 7.6).

Figure 7.6. The role of internal audit in risk management

Core internal audit roles with regards to enterprise risk management (ERM)	Giving assurance on the risk management process
	Giving assurance that risks are correctly evaluated
	Evaluating risk management processes
	Evaluating the reporting of key risks
	Reviewing the management of key risks
Legitimate internal audit roles with safeguards	Facilitating identification and evaluation of risks
	Coaching management in responding to risks
	Coordinating ERM activities
	Consolidating reporting on risks
	Maintaining and developing the ERM framework
	Championing the establishment of ERM
Roles internal audit **should not undertake**	Setting the risk appetite
	Imposing risk management processes
	Management assurance on risks
	Taking decisions on risk responses
	Implementing risk responses on mangaement's behalf
	Accountability for risk management

Source: Adapted from (The Institute of Internal Auditors, 2009[29])

Responses from IMSS and OIC officials to the OECD's questionnaire further suggest the need to ensure clear roles and responsibilities of actors in the internal control system. For example, officials said the OICs are in charge of implementing the governmental control and evaluation system. This perception of the OICs' role threatens to undermine management ownership of the internal control system, as well as the OIC's own efforts to institutionalise responsibilities for managing risks within IMSS, including procurement officials.

The OIC should further clarify its roles and responsibilities in its manual, guidance and trainings. Without this clarification, IMSS and the OIC could blur the lines between the three lines of defence, described above, and create duplicative, overlapping and fragmented internal control and risk management activities. Moreover, potential independence issues arise in the absence of clear roles and responsibilities between operational teams and the internal audit function, as defined by international standards. For instance, the OIC carries out a number of training courses for procurement officials, including a course called the "Importance of the promotion of good practices in public contracting for improvement of public management". When conducting such courses, the OIC should avoid prescriptive guidance on how to implement internal control and risk management activities, so it is not in a position where it is auditing the very policies and practices it helped to design. To further protect the OIC from threats to its audit independence, the OIC could consider implementing internal auditor statements of independence.

The SFP/OICs and ASF could strengthen collaboration in order to more effectively provide coherent oversight over IMSS procurement processes.

In 2017, the OECD reported on the different models for internal control and risk management produced by the SFP and Mexico's supreme audit institution, *Auditoría Superior de la Federación* (ASF) (OECD, 2017[25]). As noted, the SFP developed its own internal control and risk management framework called the System of Institutional Internal Control (SCII), accompanied by a risk management tool (Administración de Riesgos Institucionales, or ARI) and guidance for the OICs. In addition, in 2014, ASF developed the Integrated Framework for Internal Control in the Public Sector (*Marco Integrado de Control Interno en el Sector Público*, or MICI), as well as the Automated System for Risk Management (*Sistema Automatizado para la Administration de Riesgos*, or SAAR), which is an electronic platform accompanied by two self-assessment guides to aid practitioners in managing risks.

In 2017, OECD recommended further harmonisation of these standards developed by the SFP and Mexico's supreme audit institution, recognising the potential to cause confusion among auditors and auditees, and leaving government entities more vulnerable to fraud, waste and abuse (OECD, 2017[30]). SFP and ASF officials confirmed that two separate models were being used when auditing IMSS's activities, citing a lack of co-ordination between these internal and external audit entities.

Co-ordination between SFP and ASF has a number of benefits, including reduced risks of fragmentation, overlap and duplication, as well as better coherence between audit findings (e.g. avoiding contradictory recommendations and findings). Effective internal and external audit co-operation, including information sharing, can also reduce the audit work of the respective entities. A joint study by the European Organisation of Supreme Audit Institutions and the European Confederation of Institutes of Internal Auditing offers insights into how external and internal audit entities can strengthen co-ordination (Box 7.7)

Box 7.7. The International Organisation of Supreme Audit Institutions' guidelines for internal control standards for the public sector

In 2014, the European Organisation of Supreme Audit Institutions (EUROSAI) and the European Confederation of Institutes of Internal Auditing (ECIIA) jointly published a study that explored the mechanisms and challenges for co-operation and co-ordination between external and internal audit entities. The report presented results from a survey of 25 supreme audit institutions (SAIs) and 42 public sector entities, all members of the ECIIA responsible for the internal audit function.

The report showed that most of the SAIs surveyed align with international standards regarding co-ordination and co-operation with internal audit institutions. Most of them refer to the International Standards for Supreme Audit Institutions (ISSAIs), International Standards on Auditing (ISA) and INTOSAI's GOV standards, such as ISSAI 1610, ISA 610, INTOSAI GOV 9140 and INTOSAI GOV 9150. Only a minority of SAIs surveyed have explicit, written internal rules, such as auditing manuals, standards, guidance, procedures or checklists, documenting and formalising the co-ordination and co-operation channels.

Co-ordination and co-operation between SAIs and internal auditors was often described as "informal", which can make it difficult to assess or ensure the quality of co-ordination. The most common benefits of co-operation and co-ordination cited include:

- promoting good governance by exchange of ideas and knowledge
- more effective and efficient audits based on a clearer understanding of the respective audit roles with better co-ordinated internal and external audit activity resulting from co-ordinated planning and communication
- refined audit scope for SAIs and internal auditors.

However, almost half of the responding SAIs stated they experience risks or identify potential risks in relation to co-ordination and co-operation. A majority of SAIs pursued co-ordination and co-operation largely in the following areas:

- evaluating the audited entity's internal control framework and risk-management arrangements
- evaluating the entity's compliance with laws and regulations
- documenting the entity's systems and operational processes.

Source: (EUROSAI and ECIIA, 2014[31]).

One key area where ASF and SFP could improve co-ordination is early in the audit programming and planning processes. Both the SFP and ASF have their own sets of criteria for risk-based audit programming related to the procurement cycle. The risk criteria include the volume of procurement, performance indicators, reports in the media and complaints from suppliers, among others. Co-ordinating early and refining these criteria could help ASF and SFP to ensure effective coverage of the audit universe, avoid duplicating efforts and identify complementary audit subjects. In addition, audit entities can be effective inducers of change through their recommendations and audit findings. With better co-ordination between ASF and SFP, and using each other's work as inputs for programming and planning, IMSS is more likely to benefit from audit work to address the issues described above. This could include improving management ownership of internal control systems in the procurement process, and better management of risks in the procurement cycle.

Proposals for action

Within IMSS, various stakeholders contribute to the design and implementation of an effective internal control system. This chapter has explored the activities involving IMSS staff, the OIC and the ASF, covering four lines of defence (including external audit). The first set of recommendations focus on strategic initiatives for IMSS, followed by other recommendations to improve the tools and culture of risk management. Finally, the OIC and ASF also have opportunities to improve internal control and risk management to enhance IMSS's procurement processes:

Ensuring effective risk management strategies and implementation:

- Improve IMSS's risk management strategy for public procurement by clearly defining its goals and objectives, particularly those related to fraud and corruption.
- Emphasise messages that focus on integrity values as opposed to rules to complement efforts to create a culture of integrity.
- Develop IMSS's strategy and activities for more systematically monitoring and evaluating the effectiveness of the internal control system and risk management activities.

Improving IMSS's risk assessments related to public procurement:

- Sharpen the focus on corruption and fraud, as well as other strategic and operational risks that can affect the entire procurement cycle.
- Further define risk tolerances to more effectively allocate resources and determine control activities.
- Improve IMSS's guidance and tools for conducting risk assessments related to procurement and advancing new forms of analyses on tenders and processes.

Clarifying roles and improving co-ordination:

- Increase management ownership of the internal control system and risk management policies and processes, including organising targeted trainings and messaging for IMSS's procurement officials.
- Clarify the roles and responsibilities among the SFP, IMSS's OIC and the ASF for risk management and the internal control system, potentially including auditors' statements of independence.
- Strengthen collaboration among SFP/OICs and ASF in order to more effectively provide coherent oversight over IMSS's procurement processes.

References

Australia National Audit Office (2012), *Developing and Managing Contracts: Getting the right outcome, achieving value for Money*, Commonwealth of Australia 2012, http://www.anao.gov.au. [19]

CMS (2016), "CMS Strategy: The Road Forward 2013-2017", https://www.nadona.org/wp-content/uploads/2016/05/CMS-Strategy.pdf (accessed on 14 November 2017). [8]

Committee of Sponsoring Organizations of the Treadway Commission (COSO) (2013), *Internal control-integrated framework.* [9]

EUROSAI and ECIIA (2014), "Coordination and Cooperation between Supreme Audit Institutions and Internal Auditors in the Public Sector", http://www.eciia.eu/wp-content/uploads/2014/05/EUROSAI_ECIIA_Joint_Paper_05052014.pdf. [31]

Government Accountability Office (2015), *A Framework for Managing Fraud Risks in Federal Programs*, http://www.gao.gov/assets/680/671664.pdf. [17]

Hayes, J. (2014), *The theory and practice of change management*, Palgrave, United Kingdom, https://he.palgrave.com/page/detail/The-Theory-and-Practice-of-Change-Management/?K=9781137275349#. [22]

IMSS (2016), *Norm that establishes the dispositions for the implementation and maintenance of the institutional model for competitiveness, [Norma que establece las disposiciones para la implementacion y mantenimiento del modelo insticucional para la competivedad], 1000-001-003*, http://www.imss.gob.mx/sites/all/statics/pdf/manualesynormas/1000-001-016_0.pdf. [3]

IMSS (2017), *Organisational manual of the directorate of administration, [Manual de organazación de la dirección de administración], 1000-002-001, validated 22 June 2017*, http://www.imss.gob.mx/sites/all/statics/pdf/manualesynormas/1000-002-001_1.pdf (accessed on 15 November 2017). [11]

IMSS (2017), *Risk matrix and working programme of risk management, [Programa de trabajo de administracion de riesgos].* [5]

IMSS (2017), *Manual of organization of the internal control body, [Manual de organazación del órgano interno de control en IMSS], 0900-002-001, validated 2 February 2017.* [26]

INTOSAI (2010), *INTOSAI GOV 9100 – Guidelines for Internal Control Standards for the Public Sector*, http://www.intosai.org/issai-executive-summaries/view/article/intosai-gov-9100-guidelines-for-internal-control-standards-for-the-public-sector.html (accessed on 22 November 2017). [27]

INTOSAI (2010), *INTOSAI GOV 9140 – Internal Audit Independence in the Public Sector*, http://www.intosai.org/issai-executive-summaries/view/article/intosai-gov-9140-internal-audit-independence-in-the-public-sector.html (accessed on 22 November 2017). [28]

Irish Health Service Executive (2009), *Developing and Populating a Risk Register Best Practice Guidance*, http://hse.ie/eng/About/Who/OQR010_20090422_v_11Developing_and_populating_a_Risk_Register_BPG.pdf. [7]

ISO (2009), *ISO 31000:2009 - Risk management -- Principles and guidelines*, https://www.iso.org/standard/43170.html (accessed on 14 November 2017). [12]

ISO (2009), *ISO 31000 Risk management*, https://www.iso.org/standard/43170.html. [13]

Kotter, J. (1996), *Leading Change*. [23]

Mexico's Ministry of Public Administration (2016), *Agreement on the Manual for Internal Control ("Acuerdo por el que se emiten las Disposiciones u el manual Administrativo de Aplicacion General en material de Control Interno")*, https://www.gob.mx/cms/uploads/attachment/file/174036/acuerdo-disposiciones-manual-CI.pdf (accessed on 14 November 2017). [2]

OECD (2009), *OECD Guidelines for Fighting Bid Rigging in Public Procurement: Helping governments to obtain the best value for money*, https://www.oecd.org/competition/cartels/42851044.pdf. [15]

OECD (2012), *Session III Improving Effective Public Procurement: Fighting Collusion and Corruption*, https://one.oecd.org/document/DAF/COMP/LACF(2012)15/en/pdf (accessed on 14 November 2017). [16]

OECD (2013), *Public Procurement Review of the Mexican Institute of Social Security: Enhancing Efficiency and Integrity for Better Health Care*, OECD Public Governance Reviews, OECD Publishing, Paris, http://dx.doi.org/10.1787/9789264197480-en. [1]

OECD (2015), *OECD Recommendation of the Council on Public Procurement*, http://www.oecd.org/gov/ethics/OECD-Recommendation-on-Public-Procurement.pdf. [10]

OECD (2016), *Preventing Corruption in Public Procurement*, http://www.oecd.org/gov/ethics/Corruption-in-Public-Procurement-Brochure.pdf. [14]

OECD (2017), *Brazil's Federal Court of Accounts: Insight and Foresight for Better Governance*, OECD Public Governance Reviews, OECD Publishing, Paris, http://dx.doi.org/10.1787/9789264279247-en. [25]

OECD (2017), *OECD Integrity Review of Mexico: Taking a Stronger Stance Against Corruption*, OECD Public Governance Reviews, OECD Publishing, Paris, http://dx.doi.org/10.1787/9789264273207-en. [6]

OECD (2017), *Mexico's National Auditing System: Strengthening Accountable Governance*, OECD Public Governance Reviews, OECD Publishing, Paris, http://dx.doi.org/10.1787/9789264264748-en. [30]

Paton, R. and J. McCalman (2008), *Change Management: A Guide to Effective Implementation, Third Edition*, SAGE Publications, London. [24]

Stoop, P. (2016), *Concepts for facilitating and managing change: challenges in institutional and organisational development, with respect to the processes of regionalisation of a Supreme Audit Institution, presentation*. [21]

The Institute of Internal Auditors (2009), "IIA Position Paper: The Role of Internal Auditing in Enterprise-Wide Risk Management", https://na.theiia.org/standards-guidance/Public%20Documents/PP%20The%20Role%20of%20Internal%20Auditing%20in%20Enterprise%20Risk%20Management.pdf (accessed on 14 November 2017). [29]

UK HM Treasury (2006), *Thinking about risk - Managing your risk appetite: A practitioner's guide, November 2006*, http://webarchive.nationalarchives.gov.uk/20130107005526/http://www.hm-treasury.gov.uk/d/tar_practitioners_guide.pdf (accessed on 14 November 2017). [18]

University of Cambridge (2015), *Mining for Corruption*, https://www.cam.ac.uk/research/features/mining-for-corruption (accessed on 26 October 2017). [20]

Wright, R. (2013), *The Internal Auditor's Guide to Risk Assessment*, The Institute of Internal Auditors Research Foundation, Altamonte Springs, FL.. [4]

Part III. Leveraging on IMSS procurement power to achieve broader policy objectives

Chapter 8. Assessing the impact of IMSS procurement on national policies

As the largest health provider in Mexico, IMSS is an unavoidable actor of the national health system and represents a considerable source of revenue for the private sector. Therefore, this chapter explores the role of IMSS in the Mexican health system and how the entity could use its procurement to maximise the effectiveness of national health policies. In addition, considering the national impetus given to the support of small and medium-sized enterprises (SMEs) which are the backbone of the Mexican economy, this chapter assesses the measures implemented by IMSS to facilitate SMEs access to its procurement opportunities.

The statistical data for Israel are supplied by and under the responsibility of the relevant Israeli authorities. The use of such data by the OECD is without prejudice to the status of the Golan Heights, East Jerusalem and Israeli settlements in the West Bank under the terms of international law.

Aligning procurement strategies with national health policies

IMSS leadership in health procurement advocates for an enhanced role in framing national policies

At 3.2% of gross domestic product (GDP) (Figure 8.1), Mexico's public health expenditure is one of the lowest in the OECD, with the OECD average at around 6.5%. This low rate of health expenditure may explain Mexico's below-average performance in many health indicators, such as life expectancy, infant mortality, overweight and obesity rates (see Chapter 1). In 2005 the OECD provided recommendations in six areas to enhance Mexico's healthcare system (OECD, 2005[1]): 1) ensuring adequate funding of the health system; 2) tackling the remaining barriers in accessing services for those not covered by social security; 3) encouraging greater efficiency of health care providers; 4) encouraging greater productivity of health care professionals; 5) promoting the quality and the effectiveness of care; and 6) improving the governance of the system. Since then and despite health reforms, significant efforts are still required to address the major health issues facing the country (OECD, 2016[2]).

The National Development Plan *(Plan Nacional de Desarrollo)* for 2013-2018 defines the national priorities, divided into five main objectives: 1) Peace in Mexico; 2) Inclusive Mexico; 3) Quality of the Mexican education system; 4) Prosperous Mexico; and 5) Mexico with a global responsibility. These objectives are to be achieved through strategies and action plans for the relevant sectors. For example, the Sectoral Health Programme (SHP) for 2013-2018 (Mexican Health Ministry, 2014[3]), has been translated into development plans for each part of the health system, including IMSS.

Figure 8.1. Public health expenditure as a share of GDP, 2013 (or nearest year)

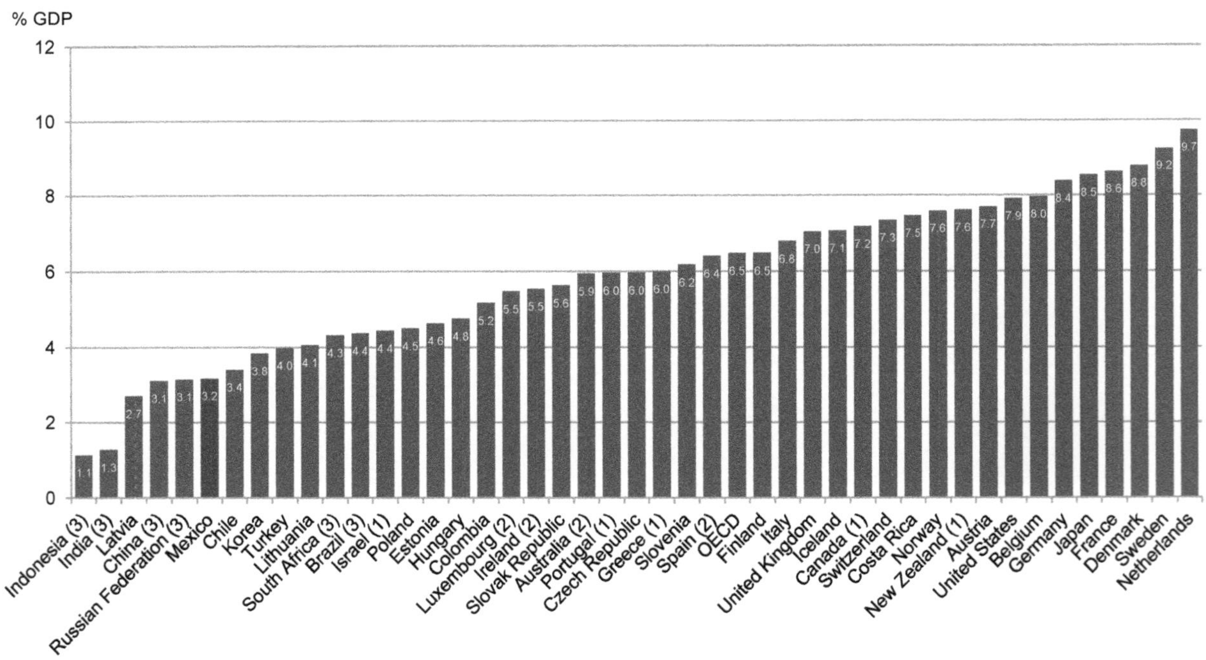

Note: Excluding investments unless otherwise stated. 1. Preliminary estimates. 2. Data refers to 2012. 3. Including investments

Source: (OECD, 2016[2])

The Health Ministry is in charge of co-ordinating the national health system, establishing and conducting national health policies, and co-ordinating healthcare service programmes of entities of the federal government. It is also in charge of co-ordinating the Sectoral Health Programme.

Like the National Development Plan, each sectoral programme includes objectives, strategies and action plans. The SHP includes six objectives:

1. Consolidating actions for the protection, promotion of health and prevention of diseases
2. Ensuring the effective access to qualitative healthcare services
3. Reducing the risks affecting the population's health in all activities
4. Closing the existing gaps in provision of healthcare services between different social groups and regions of the country
5. Ensuring the generation and effective use of health resources
6. Advancing the national universal health system under the stewardship of the Health Ministry.

Many of the strategies and action plans derived from the SHP are linked to procurement by health entities (Box 8.1).

Box 8.1. Examples of strategies and action plans of the sectorial Health Plan linked to procurement

Strategy 1.5. Increase access to sexual and reproductive health with special focus on teenagers and vulnerable populations

1.5.5 Ensure the supply of contraceptive methods and for the prevention of HIV and other STDs

Strategy 2.6. Ensure access to medicines and medical supplies for a qualitative health

2.6.1. Strengthen the supply chain of medicines and medical supplies in public health institutions

2.6.2. Increase the supply of medicines and biological products according to local needs

2.6.3. Implement medical distribution programs that align the incentives of the institutions of all participants

2.6.4. Encourage the rational use of medical prescription

Strategy 2.7. Implement the National Strategy for the Prevention and Control of Overweight, Obesity and Diabetes

2.7.5. Ensure timely and complete supply of medicines and medical supplies

Strategy 5.5. Encourage efficient spending on medicines and medical supplies

5.5.1. Promote the release of generics to reduce health spending

5.5.2. Promote the consolidated procurement of medicines and medical supplies among public sector institutions

5.5.3. Encourage coordinated procurement of medicines and medical supplies between the federation and federative entities

5.5.4. Consolidate the price negotiation process of medicines and medical supplies with current and single source patent

5.5.5. Monitor the efficiency in spending allocated to the procurement of medicines and health supplies

5.5.6. Apply innovative procurement schemes and supply of medicines to ensure their supply

Source: (Mexican Health Ministry, 2014[3])

The effective implementation of this sectoral programme is however hindered by the fragmentation of the health system and the multiplicity of health providers (see Figure 8.2). Besides increasing inequalities in access and quality of care, this also affects the co-ordination of procurement strategies whose outcomes ultimately contribute to health care services.

Figure 8.2. Landscape of the Mexican Health system

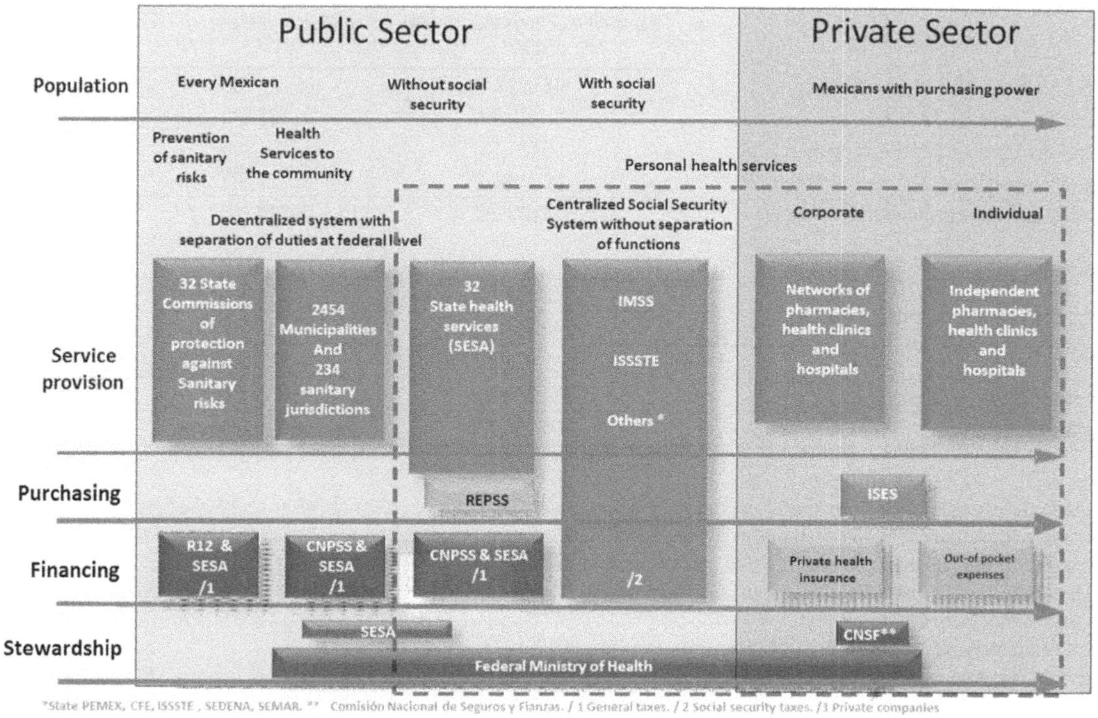

Source: (OECD, 2016[2])

IMSS is the largest health provider in the country, covering around 59 million regular beneficiaries and 12 million IMSS-Oportunidades beneficiaries (a federal programme providing preventive health services free of charge for rural and marginalised urban communities), representing together more than 50% of the Mexican population. IMSS is also the largest contracting authority in terms of expenditures, spending more than 40% of all public sector health expenditures (Table 8.1). It is also the largest employer in the healthcare system, employing 65 115 doctors and 95 387 nurses and running more than 264 hospitals (OECD, 2016[2]). In IMSS, on average 500 000 consultations, 50 000 emergencies and 4000 operations are dealt with every day.

Table 8.1. Health expenditure in Mexico, 2013

	Expenditure (thousand current pesos)	Coverage (people)	Per capita expenditure (current pesos)
Budget line 12 (Ramo 12: Minsitry of Health)	118 893 910	65 527 283	1 814
Budget line 33 (Ramo 33: FASSA[1])	67 679 092	65 527 283	1 033
Budget line 19 (Ramo 19: IMSS-Prospera)	9 881 767	11 891 406	151
States' health expenditure	28 217 527	65 527 283	431
Total federal and state expenditure for people without social security[2]	**224 672 296**	**65 527 283**	**3429**
IMSS	208 586 381	59 511 963	3 505
ISSSTE[3]	49 832 292	12 630 569	3 945
PEMEX[4]	12 866 306	755 346	17 034
Total social security	271 284 979	72 897 878	3 721
Total public sector	495 957 275	138 425 161	7 150

Note:

1. FASSA: Federal contributions to health services (*Aportaciones Federales para los Servicios de Salud);*
2. Population without social security includes those affiliated to Seguro Popular, those covered by IMSS-Prospera and those without any public health insurance who can get care at Ministry of Health and states' facilities.
3. ISSSTE: *Instituto de Seguridad y Servicios Sociales de los Trabajadores del Estado,* The State's Employees' Social Security and Social Services Institute,
4. PEMEX: *Petróleos Mexicanos.* Population corresponds to 2012.
5. Figures exclude expenditure reported by the Ministry of Defence (*Secretaria de la Defensa Nacional-SEDENA*), the Ministry of Navy (*Secretaria de Marina-SEMAR*), Insurance institutions specialised in health (*Instituciones de Seguros Especializadas en Salud-ISES*) and Social Security Institute for the Mexican armed forces (*Instituto de Seguridad Social para las Fuerzas Armadas Mexicanas- ISSFAM)*, which together represent 5.4% of total public expenditure.

Source: (OECD, 2016[2])

Therefore, IMSS is a major contributor to the healthcare system – not only in providing healthcare services, but also in gathering information on health indicators and healthcare performance. Given its importance, IMSS has a role to play in both implementing and supporting national health policies. It could be beneficial for the effectiveness of Mexican health policies to consider IMSS not only as an implementing entity, but also as a stakeholder participating in the development of health policies.

In the United Kingdom, for example, the National Health Service (NHS) is responsible for the provision of health services and for the procurement of related goods and services. Considering its purchasing power and role in the UK's health care system, the NHS not only ensures the effective application of national health policies, but also participates in their design and implementation (see Box 8.2 for an example).

Box 8.2. The NHS National Diabetes Prevention Programme

The NHS Diabetes Prevention Programme (NHS DPP) is a joint commitment from NHS England, Public Health England and Diabetes UK, to deliver at scale, evidence based behavioural interventions for individuals identified as being at high risk of developing Type 2 diabetes.

Type 2 diabete is preventable and there is strong international evidence that behavioural interventions can significantly reduce the risk of developing the condition, through reducing weight, increasing physical activity and improving the diet of those at high risk. Diabetes treatment currently accounts for around 10 per cent of the annual NHS budget.

The NHS DPP is led by Public Health England and was developed by a delivery team from NHS England, Public Health England, and Diabetes UK. The programme is overseen at a strategic level by the NHS Prevention Board, and programme governance is provided by the NHS Diabetes Programme Board.

Prior to deciding on the type of programme, the University of Sheffield was commissioned to develop a NHS DPP return on investment tool to assist sites in understanding the costs, savings and health benefits likely to be produced by implementing the NHS DPP. The report took into account several variables with the main elements being the cost of the programme per participants and the programme effectiveness. Based on several scenarios of costs proposed by bidders, it concluded that with an average cost range of GBP 155-350 (equivalent tariff range approx. GBP 250-560), the net cumulative financial impact over five years of the DPP represented a cost between GBP 37m and 113m, excluding implementation costs and assuming a base case effectiveness. Over a 20-year horizon the net cumulative financial impact of the DPP is a saving of between GBP 4m and 80m depending on final average costs (excluding implementation costs).

The report further estimated that during the first five years the DPP is estimated to save a cumulative 700-1,100 Quality Adjusted Life Years (QALYs) depending on programme effectiveness. Over the long term, the 20-year horizon estimates between 13,000-21,000 cumulative QALYs saved. This translates to 14,000-21,000 cases of diabetes prevented or delayed in the first five years of the programme, for an initial five-year cohort of 390,000 participants enrolled in the programme. Assuming base case effectiveness, for every 100,000 people enrolled in the NDPP the cumulative impact over the following five years is approximately 4,500 diabetes diagnoses prevented or delayed.

Based on these preliminary impact assessments, the NDPP team ran in late 2015 a national commercial procurement to select four framework providers to deliver the NDPP nationally. Potential providers were required to bid against criteria set by the NDPP national team, and submit their intervention models to ensure these were in line with the national service specification. Bids were evaluated by an expert panel from NHS England, Public Health England (PHE) and other key stakeholder organisations.

Source: Adapted from (NHS England, 2016[4])

To support the implementation of national health policies, IMSS could leverage on strategic public procurement

Besides its contribution to shape national health policies, IMSS could use its procurement operations as a strategic tool for the implementation of public policies. Indeed, public procurement is a key lever for improving the value that IMSS can deliver to patients through medical care and pharmaceutical products. In line with the SHP, IMSS developed its own institutional programme for 2014-2018, which has 5 central objectives,[1] 29 strategies and 129 action lines aimed at building a universal national health system and expanding the access to social security, and more generally enhancing the healthcare system and ensuring the effectiveness of national healthcare policies (IMSS, 2014[5]).

Many strategies and actions in the programme directly aim to enhance the procurement process (Box 8.3). While many others are not directly linked, they will still require a procurement process. For example, Strategy 1.1 aims to increase beds by building new hospitals in zones lagging behind. The effective implementation of this strategy through effective procurement operations in all IMSS entities will help to improve the efficiency of the system.

Box 8.3. Example of strategies and action plans linked to procurement in IMSS's institutional programme for 2014-2018

Strategy 1.3: Favouring consolidated tenders in order to guarantee better prices

- Implement mechanism to determine goods and services to procure through consolidated tenders taking into account their characteristics, use and frequency.
- Promote consolidated tenders with other entities of the health sector.

Strategy 3.1 Rationalising and optimising administrative and operational expenses to strengthen priority programmes

- Implement austerity measures and administrative and operational expenditure restraints
- Enhance the procurement methods for goods, services and public works
- Strengthen the supply chain for therapeutic goods and for the provision of integrated services
- Optimise the use of spaces and institutional buildings.

Strategy 3.6: Optimising the use of resources for medical care

- Control and evaluate the adequate and efficient prescription of drugs
- Apply the diagnosis-related groups (GRD) to enhance the health, economic and financial management of hospitals
- Strengthen the substitution of drugs favouring the use of those with the lower price while ensuring security and similar efficiency.

Source: (IMSS, 2014[5])

When analysing the various strategies and action aiming to create a universal national health system and their links with public procurement, three categories can be identified: 1) strategies to optimise processes through procurement methods, such as consolidated tenders; 2) strategies to optimise financial and physical resources, such as promoting substitutes for medicines and optimising the use of space; and 3) strategies to control the use of resources, such as the adequate and efficient prescription of drugs.

Among the different national health strategies which translate into IMSS's institutional programme, universal access to medicines concentrated recent efforts. Indeed, in line with the National Action Plan (Plan Nacional de Desarrollo) for 2013-2018, universal access to healthcare – and more specifically to medicines – is one of Mexico's national objectives. One major step towards achieving this would be to substitute expensive patented drugs with generic drugs. This policy had been endorsed by IMSS by developing the strategy 3.6 of its institutional programme for 2014-2018 where the entity has to strengthen the substitution of drugs favouring the use of those with the lower price while ensuring security and similar efficiency.

A recent report from the Mexican Competition Authority noted that penetration rates of generic drugs in Mexico when patents are no longer in force are considerably lower than in other countries, meaning Mexican families are missing out on substantial benefits (COFECE, 2017[6]). For example, two years after the entry of the first generic, the penetration of generic drugs reaches 21.4% of the market, compared to 89% in the US for the same period. Among the causes of this low penetration rate, the report points to the relatively low number of generic drugs available and identifies entry barriers in consolidated tenders for small generic manufacturers.

If the penetration rate were to double, this would save Mexican families MXN 2,252 million per year. Considering its buying power and influence amongst health institutions in consolidated tenders, IMSS should consider all available strategies which would help to increase the number of generic drugs. As discussed in Chapter 6 extending the duration of the bidding period and the production lead-time could act as strong incentives for small generic manufacturers to participate in tenders.

Fulfilling IMSS's potential as a source of revenue for the private sector

To widen economic benefits for companies of all sizes IMSS could build on its purchasing power

Although health spending is below the OECD average in Mexico, the procurement volume is still significant and can be used to achieve several policy objectives at the national level but also at the entity level. It represents a considerable source of revenue for the private sector. Thus, IMSS's strategic decisions could shape the economic growth of suppliers in IMSS's markets.

The OECD Recommendation on Public Procurement calls on countries to include secondary policy objectives in their public procurement policies, such as sustainable green growth, innovation, standards for responsible business conduct and the development of small and medium-sized enterprises (OECD, 2015[7]). This section will focus on the role of procurement in developing Mexico's small and medium-sized enterprises.

In many countries, small and medium-sized enterprises (SMEs) are the backbone of the economy, representing more than 90% of all firms in most OECD countries (Figure 8.3).

The role of public procurement in giving access to markets can enhance SMEs' performance. Recognising the important role that the public sector can play as a purchaser of goods and services, as well as the critical role of SMEs in the economy, governments are increasingly using public procurement to promote, develop and support local SMEs (see Box 8.4 for a Korean example). This is also the case for Mexico.

Figure 8.3. Share of enterprises by number of employees in OECD countries

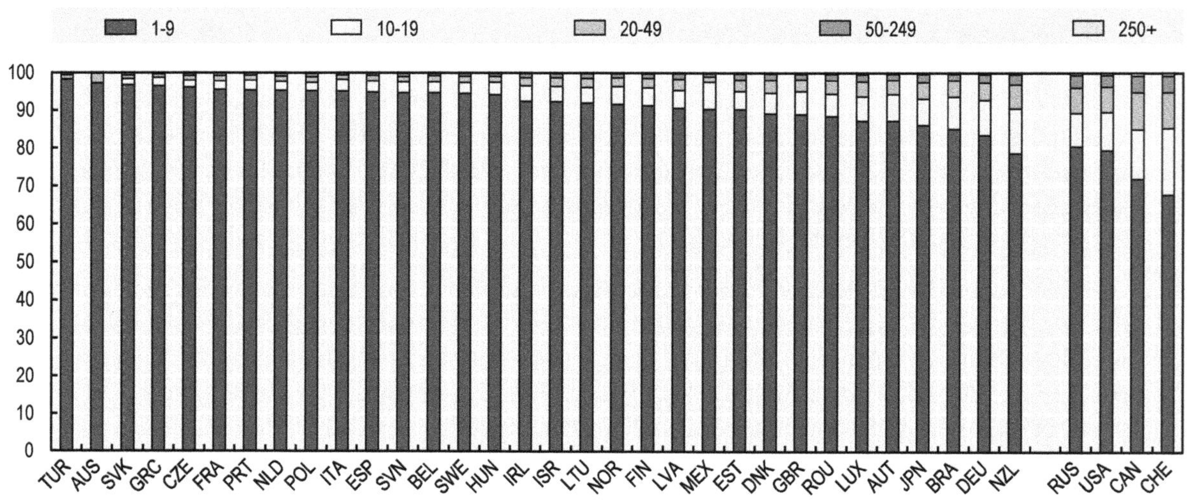

Note: CAN, USA, RUS: data do not include non-employers.
Data for CHE exclude enterprises with less than 3 persons employed
AUS, TUR: size cass 1-9 refers to 1-19
AUS: size class 20-49 refer to 20-199, 250+ refers to 200+; JPN: 50-249 refers to 50-299, 250+ refers to 300+;
AUS, CAN, ISR, NZL, RUS: data refer to 2015, MEX: 2013, JPN: 2011
KOR, MEX data refer to establishments.
GBR data exclude small unregistered businesses; these are both self-employed without VAT or PAYE administrative basis and incorporated businesses with one employee, as the latter are likely to be owners/workers in the business.
Source: (OECD, 2017[8])

Box 8.4. Korea's support for SMEs

Support for SMEs in Korea is a strong priority, given the make-up of the economy. There are approximately 3.3 million SMEs in Korea, while there are only 2 900 large businesses: SMEs make up 99.9% of Korean businesses. The Public Procurement Service (PPS) implements the government's policies for increasing public purchases from a variety of types of entities, including small and medium-sized businesses, local businesses, women-owned businesses and other social enterprises.

The legal basis of support of SMEs requires the heads of public institutions to provide small and medium-sized businesses with increased opportunities to receive orders when they intend to make procurement contracts for goods, services and construction works.

A recent change, which took effect on 1 January 2015, now defines SMEs solely in terms of sales volume (either annual or average). In addition to the criteria for being included as an SME, there are specific factors that can exclude an enterprise from SME status, including total assets exceeding USD 423.8 million.

A business must be deemed independent in ownership and operation (not a subsidiary of a large enterprise) with respect to the relevant laws and regulations.

Article 4 of the Enforcement Decree of the Act on Facilitation of Purchase of Small and Medium Enterprise-Manufactured Products and Support for Development of their Markets sets an annual purchasing goal for SME-manufactured products of 50% or more of total purchasing value.

An SME set-aside programme is run in co-operation with the Small and Medium Business Administration (SMBA). Under this programme, SMBA designates specific products for SMEs, and currently there are 207 products with this designation. For these products to be designated as competitive products, only SMEs that directly manufacture such products are invited to participate in competitive tenders.

Source: (OECD, 2016[9])

While the primary objective of public procurement is to deliver goods and services necessary to accomplish government missions in a timely, economical and efficient manner, countries are increasingly using it as a governance tool to achieve broader objectives. Considering the structure of the private sector in most countries around the world where SMEs make up a large share of the economy, efforts directed towards the promotion of their economic growth are commonly pursued and actions to strengthen SMEs business environment include opening access to public markets (Figure 8.4).

Figure 8.4. SME business environment: A conceptual framework

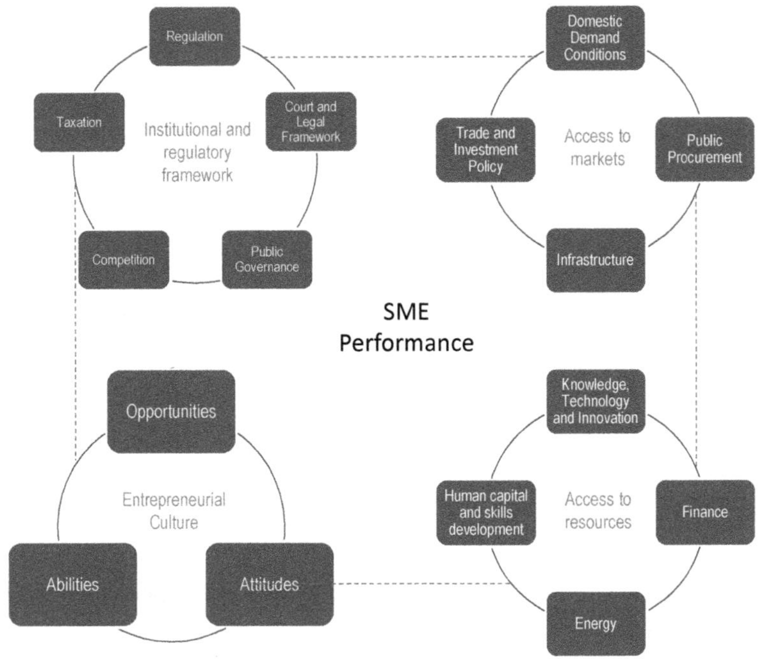

Source: (OECD, 2017[10])

As part of efforts carried out to ease SMEs' access to markets governments and entities develop and implement several measures to enhance SMEs' participation in public procurement. Box 8.5 offers a description of some of these measures.

Box 8.5. Measures for enhancing SME participation in public procurement

- Put in place a specific legislative provision or policy (e.g. set-aside, bid preferences) to encourage participation from SMEs in procurement
- Remove barriers to SME access to public procurement by:
  - disseminating information on bids online
  - offering possibility to submit bids online
  - dividing contract into lots
  - simplifying administrative procedures for SMEs.
- Offer training and capacity building to SMEs, by:
  - making documentation or guidance focused on SMEs available online,
  - providing capacity-building programs and workshops for SMEs to help new entries into the public procurement marketplace
  - developing dedicated call centres for answering questions from SMEs.
- Apply preferential fees or financial incentives:
  - offering preferential financial treatment (e.g. waiving fees) for SMEs
  - providing tender documents at a lower price for SMEs
  - reducing the payment deadlines for SMEs.

Source: (OECD, 2016$_{[11]}$)

At the national level, there is no stand-alone policy to support SMEs access public procurement opportunities. However, the Mexican procurement legal framework includes provisions to support their access and development through several mechanisms (see next section). These include joint bidding and subcontracting arrangements, set asides, allotment strategies, and favouring awards of contracts to SMEs in the case of a tie between two or more suppliers. When preparing its procurement plan, IMSS assesses the estimated procurement value for each need, as well as the procurement value directed to SMEs. According to IMSS's 2017 procurement plan, approximately MXN 15 billion will be allocated to SMEs, representing around 18.7% of the total procurement value. This information is reported on the webpage of the Ministry of Economy dedicated to enhancing SMEs' participation in federal public procurement. The page also includes a section reporting on progress made by entities from the federal government in implementing this provision. In July 2017, IMSS had reached 51% of its target, while other entities like the State's Employees' Social Security and Social Services Institute (ISSSTE) had reached 47% and the Health Ministry 73% of their annual targets.

Although this information is relevant, in order to tailor specific procurement strategies to enhance SMEs' participation, it is also crucial to have information on each procurement procedure (open tender, restricted tender, direct award, etc.) or type, such as consolidated tenders.

When demand is aggregated into high-volume contracts, it is possible that SMEs could be excluded from the procedures, since they often have limited production capacity and reduced access to credit, which makes competition for these types of contracts less suitable for them than for larger firms. In the case of IMSS's consolidated procurement, this concern applies particularly to procedures involving medical devices which is characterised by the presence of several SME suppliers – more so than in other markets where IMSS carries out consolidated procedures, such as for medicines. Therefore, IMSS recently initiatives implemented by IMSS for the procurement of medical devices such as launching two tenders, one at the international level and the other at the national level with a higher procurement value aiming at giving access to local suppliers, in particular SMEs.

Yet, IMSS's experience finds higher non-compliance rates among SMEs than among larger companies, presumably due to the SME's lack of capacity to satisfy the high-volume demand created by consolidated procurement. In this context, shipping and delivery costs proposed by SMEs also tend to be higher than those offered by larger companies, since SMEs have access to less extensive delivery networks than their larger competitors. SMEs' limited access to credit also makes them vulnerable to the delays in payment that can be a common feature of IMSS's consolidated procurement procedures (Chapter 4).

To assess the potential of IMSS's procurement opportunities for attracting SMEs, the authors have analysed detailed information on suppliers' participation in procurement opportunities (Figure 8.5). In the ten consolidated tenders launched in 2016 to procure medicines and healing material, on average 60% of bidders were large firms. Yet this analysis only takes into account the size of the awarded bidders and does not compare the amounts awarded to the size of suppliers. Doing so would complement this analysis and enable IMSS to identify bottlenecks as well as opportunities for improvement by tailoring strategies on a case-by-case basis. Indeed targeted and specific efforts are required in order for IMSS to enhance SME participation in its procurement process.

Figure 8.5. Share of micro, small, medium and large enterprises bidding for all consolidated tenders launched by IMSS in 2016

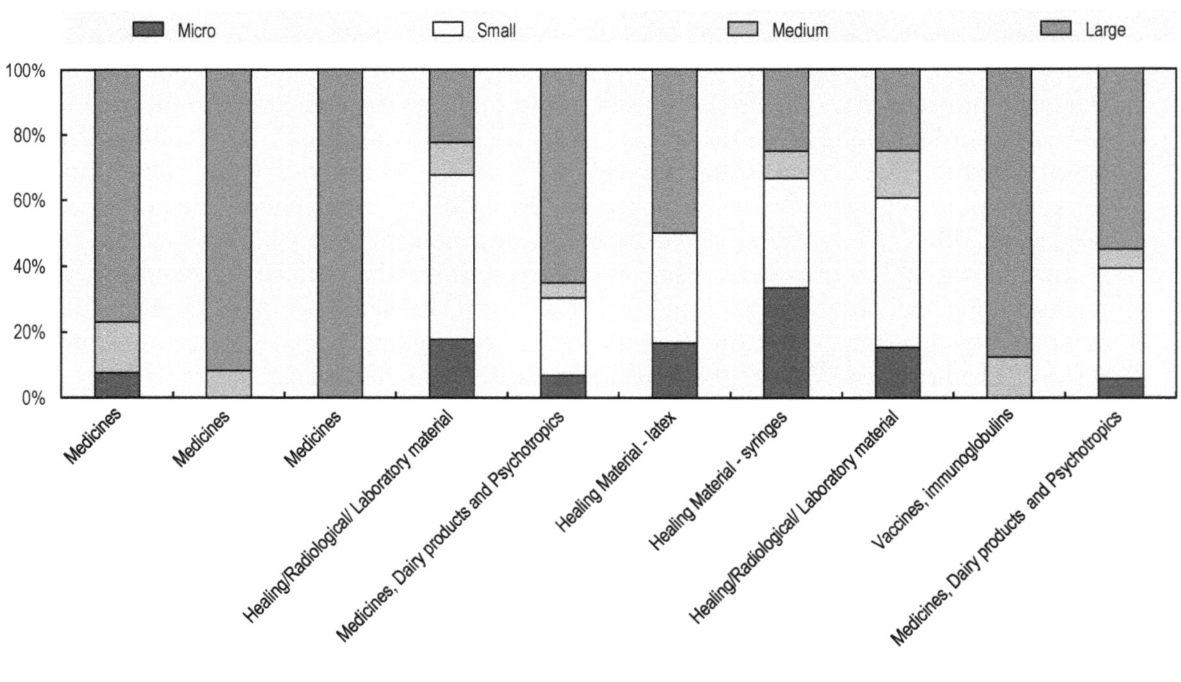

Source: Analysis based on CompraNet

To enhance SMEs participation in IMSS procurement opportunities, the institute could implement various procurement strategies going beyond thresholds imposed by the law

The legal framework, and in particular Article 23 of the Regulation of the Public Procurement law (*Reglamento de la Ley de Adquisiciones, Arrendamientos y Servicios del Sector Público*- RLAASSP), mandates contracting authorities to allocate to SMEs 50% of their procurement volume which is spent through restricted tenders or direct award (i.e. exceptions to open tenders provided for in Article 42 of the Public Procurement law (*Ley de adquisiciones, arrendamientos y servicios del sector público* - LAASSP). Yet Article 42 mentions that these exceptions cannot exceed 30% of the annual procurement budget, which means that through this procedure SMEs will receive a maximum of 15% of procurement volume of each entity. As described in Table 8.2, 21% of IMSS's procurement volume was awarded to SMEs in 2016.

Table 8.2. Share of IMSS procurement volume and contracts allocated to SMEs, 2014-2016

Year	Share of procurement volume awarded to SMEs	Share of contracts awarded to SMEs
2014	16%	20%
2015	16%	34%
2016	21%	28%

Source: Data provided by IMSS

In the absence of detailed information and assuming that the use of this set-aside through exceptions to open tenders is fully seized by the IMSS (15% of its procurement volume), one can estimate that only 6% of the procurement volume spent through open tenders was awarded to SMEs in 2016 and only 1% in 2014 and 2015. Therefore, IMSS could benefit from monitoring closely the use of the set-aside provisions included in the legal framework.

When procuring large volumes such as in consolidated tenders, or in the case of complex procurement, the market structure and concentration might not be adapted to effective competition and to participation by market players of smaller sizes. This may harm the efficiency and inclusiveness of the system. The Competition Authority (COFECE) has voiced concerns about the negative impact of consolidated tenders on SMEs.

To overcome barriers to SMEs participation, contracting authorities can implement a variety of strategies and policies including:

- enabling competitors of different sizes to participate through joint bidding and subcontracting arrangements
- reducing the size of the contract by dividing it into lots.

The different strategies and policies are discussed in turn below. For each of them market analysis will play a crucial role since it will identify SMEs' capacity to participate in procurement opportunities and therefore inform decisions to implement the most appropriate strategies.

Joint bidding

Joint bidding refers to the practice of two or more supplier submitting a single bid. The main objective of this mechanism is to enable suppliers with limited capacity (human, technical and geographical) to participate in a tender that they would not be able to bid for alone. When implementing this mechanism, however, contracting authorities might need to be vigilant of the risks of bid rigging (OECD, 2012[12]).

In Mexico, the LAASSP and RAASSP allow for firms to submit joint bids for all open tenders, and in specific cases for restricted tenders, when the contracting authority finds it appropriate to enhance SMEs' participation. The process to be followed by the different suppliers is described in Article 44 of the RAASSP. SMEs may choose to combine their resources with other firms (SMEs or not) and present a joint offer in a procedure in which they would have been unable to take part on their own. However, this option seems to be underused: only one joint bid has been identified in all the consolidated tenders launched in 2016, and it was not awarded a contract.

Considering the extent of market concentration in certain product categories such as in medical devices, joint bidding could help to diversify IMSS's supply base and to attract more SMEs. IMSS could promote the use of joint bidding among suppliers by further insisting on the existence of this possibility in its tender documentation and through meetings with chambers of commerce and business associations.

Subcontracting

SME participation can also be fostered through subcontracting arrangements. Indeed, for large contracts, SMEs might not be in a position to be a prime contractor, performing the whole contract; However subcontracting can still provide SMEs with opportunities to perform a share of the contract (OECD-SIGMA, 2016[13]) . Again, the Mexican regulatory framework foresees this possibility in Article 3-VI of the LAASSP. Subcontractors need to provide the same documentation as the winner of the contract. IMSS has not shared information with the review team on how many of its contracts have subcontracting arrangements. An analysis of those contracts could help to tailor specific strategies, for instance according to contract size, to enable the direct participation of subcontractors in procurement opportunities. In addition, in Mexico, subcontractors are not paid directly, which can put them in a difficult financial situation. IMSS could consider promoting the use of subcontracting arrangements and assessing the feasibility of paying subcontractors directly.

Allotment strategies

Dividing large contracts into lots can bring on board more SMEs, but requires taking several factors into account. These include the possibility of achieving economies of scale, and the market structure in terms of participants and their degree of specialisation. The size of each lot will determine the potential economic operators who can participate. Article 39 of the LAASSP states that it is possible to award one contract/lot to more than one supplier. This mechanism has been implemented by IMSS for some procurement procedures, including consolidated tenders. Open tenders are divided into lots or "*partidas*". This procedure is called simultaneous procurement ("*abastecimiento simultaneo*") and requires fixing the rules in advance governing the share of the contract to be awarded to each lot and under what conditions. As mentioned in the LAASSP, entities implementing this mechanism will need to take into account recommendations from COFECE on mitigating the risks of collusion. IMSS should consider increasing its division of contracts into lots while taking into account market analysis outcomes and COFECE and OECD's recommendations.

By adopting more systemic measures easing access to public markets, IMSS could increase the attractiveness of its procurement operations for SMEs

Aside from these strategies, another element which often acts as an impediment to small businesses participation in public tenders is the extent of resources, both human and financial, required to submit an offer. These include the fees and red tape necessary for firms to submit the bidding documents, as well as the required monetary guarantees. To minimise the adverse impact of these procedural steps, the costs and administrative burden associated with the preparation of bids should be kept to a minimum.

The first type of costs that can be minimised are those directly related to submitting the bid itself: the payments for obtaining the tender documentation and financial guarantees, such as performance bonds, to ensure the satisfactory execution of the contract by the awarded bidder. When used disproportionately, bonds can represent an administrative and financial obstacle to SMEs participating in public procurement opportunities.

Although access to tender documentation is free of charge in Mexico, performance bonds representing 10% of the bid can be required. As discussed in Chapter 3, the requirement to provide this financial guarantee can be waived in specific instances, such as previous satisfactory performance (art. 48 of the LAASP). Yet the benefit of the exemption cannot be granted as such to SMEs. IMSS could consider applying targeted efforts to reduce the value of the guarantee for SMEs, or exempt them from providing it, in order to enhance their participation in procurement opportunities.

Advanced payments can also play an important role in facilitating entry to the market for SMEs that have limited access to credit. This holds true in Mexico, where SMEs' average interest rate in 2015 was around 9% - one of the highest in OECD countries. Many contracting authorities in OECD countries allow SMEs to receive advanced payments. These can enable firms to perform their contract despite needing to buy expensive inputs. Under Article 13 of the LAASSP, contracting authorities can provide advanced payments to suppliers. When it comes to SMEs and when the manufacturing time exceeds 60 days, this article mandates contracting authorities to provide advanced payments ranging between 10 to 50% of the procurement value. Mexico's legal framework enables the provision of advanced payments, but they need to be guaranteed, which undermines the benefits of the system. While there is a mandatory aspect in case of long manufacturing time, this article doesn't prevent IMSS to voluntarily apply advance payments to other situations such as contracting with SMEs. IMSS could therefore consider implementing this mechanism when contracting with SMEs, even when the manufacturing process is shorter than 60 days.

In Mexico, three instruments have been developed through the Productive Chain Program (*Programa Cadenas Productivas*) for suppliers of the federal government (including IMSS) by Nacional Financiera, a local development bank. Through this programme suppliers can obtain 1) immediate liquidity based on the invoice's value through a financial transaction called electronic factoring; 2) loans (up to approximately USD 6,9 million); and 3) letters of credit which can be used to provide performance bonds. IMSS could benefit from promoting these mechanisms or developing other specific instruments for its SME suppliers.

Additional ideas for alleviating the financial burden on suppliers and in particular SMEs can be found amongst large contracting authorities or central procurement agencies in many OECD countries (Box 8.6).

Box 8.6. Financial support initiatives for SMEs in OECD countries

Reverse factoring in France

In addition to the advanced payment foreseen in the French public procurement law, UGAP, a French Central Purchasing Body (CPB) operating in many sectors including the medical sector, developed a solution called "reverse factoring" for its suppliers. The CPB does not provide financing to its suppliers; the mechanism consists of negotiating financial interest rates to be paid by suppliers to a financial institution for those willing to receive an anticipated payment and being paid in 2 days on average instead of the standard 30 days.

Given its procurement power, the interest rates negotiated by the CPB following an open tender are much more advantageous than the interest rates that a single supplier could get in the financial market. The CPB does not have any financial interest when suppliers are using this mechanism.

UGAP's suppliers can adhere to this solution on a voluntary basis and can use it for all their invoices, or on a case-by-case basis depending on their financial needs.

Instant contract payments in Korea

PPS, the Korean procurement agency, provides special financial support to SMEs involved in public contracting. SMEs are entitled to an upfront payment of up to 70% of the value of a government contract. For some contracts for goods – including orders against unit-price contracts, lump sum contracts for goods valued up to KRW 500 million, or at the request of the end-user for other goods contracts – the business is entitled to instant payment upon presentation of the invoice. In these cases, payment is made from PPS's special account and then reimbursed by the end-user. Though central government entities are entitled to a payment period of up to five days, instant payment allows SMEs to receive payment within as little as four working hours.

Source: (UGAP, 2017[14]); (OECD, 2016[9])

Besides direct financial costs, indirect costs also stem from the various forms and administrative documentation which need to be submitted along with the technical and financial proposal. The time or cost necessary to request them could hinder SMEs from participating in public tenders. Some countries, such as Spain (Box 8.7) have attempted to streamline their tendering procedure, for example by using the same application forms or asking for the same type of information in different tenders. Mexico's legal framework does not include such measures, and suppliers have to submit the administrative documentation for every tender. The SFP is the entity in charge of the federal public procurement system including the management of CompraNet, the e-procurement system. As a policy maker, it is the entity in charge of detailing the practical steps to carry out procurement procedures which are defined in the legislative environment. As such, it has the potential for devoting efforts to streamline as much as possible tendering procedures.

Box 8.7. Self-declarations to reduce red tape in Spain

In 2013, Spain introduced measures intended to support and facilitate participation of SMEs in public procurement. SME bidders can now provide contracting authorities with a self-declaration, rather than numerous documents certifying their legal, social and fiscal situation.

This self-declaration is sufficient for public works contracts worth under EUR 1 million and for goods and services contracts worth under EUR 90,000. Only the winning bidder is required to provide the documentary evidence and contracting authorities will not conclude contracts with bidders unable to do so.

These measures are consistent with recent EU Directives on Public Procurement, which note that: "Many economic operators, and not least SMEs, find that a major obstacle to their participation in public procurement consists in administrative burdens deriving from the need to produce a substantial number of certificates or other documents related to exclusion and selection criteria. Limiting such requirements, for example through use of a European Single Procurement Document consisting of an updated self-declaration, could result in considerable simplification for the benefit of both contracting authorities and economic operators"

Source: (OECD, 2014[15])

The OECD recommends opening public markets to competitors of all size including SMEs. Countries have developed a wide array of measures supporting SMEs in their public procurement systems such as making documentation or guidance focused on SMEs available online, providing capacity-building programmes and workshops for SMEs, as well as developing dedicated call centres for addressing their questions (Box 8.5).

In Mexico, SMEs might lack the capacity to understand and to deal with public procurement processes. A survey by the National Institute of Statistics and Geography shows that on average 80% of staff working in SMEs lack a higher education degree (Figure 8.6), suggesting a need to strengthen staff capacity in several areas including public procurement.

IMSS could offer training and capacity building for SMEs on the public procurement process, in particular the use of e-procurement tools, as well as on the exact needs of the public sector and how they can contribute to the system. Offering training for suppliers on different aspects of IMSS's procurement procedures could encourage greater participation in open tenders. SFP does provide training in how to use CompraNet to potential suppliers to the public sector. IMSS could benefit from promoting this training amongst its suppliers and bidders.

Figure 8.6. Level of education of staff by enterprise size.

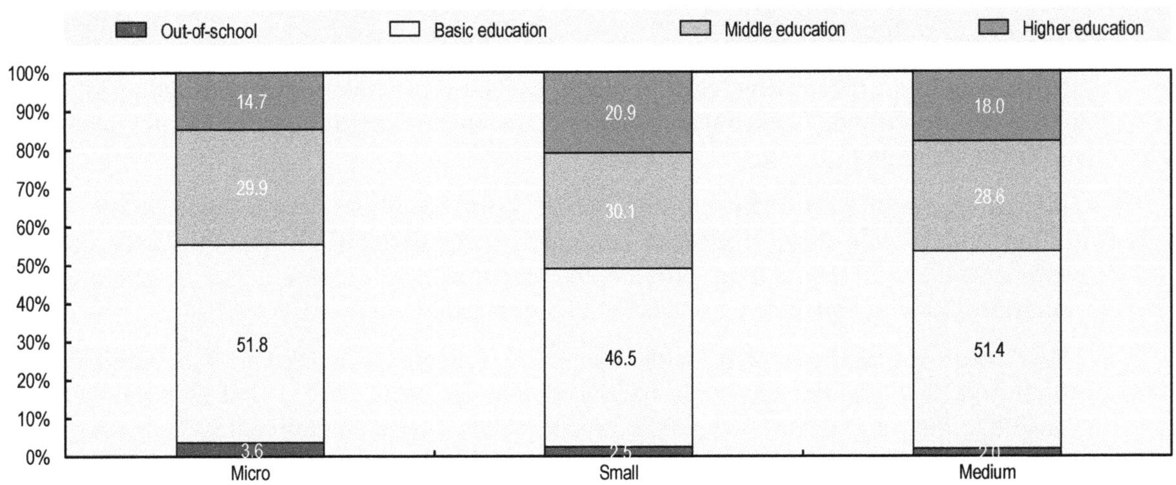

Source: (INEGI, 2016[16])

Given the specificities of the health sector and the procurement volume in IMSS tenders, it could also develop dedicated training programmes in areas that bidders in IMSS procurement processes find challenging. For example, in response to the situation on joint bidding described above, training could pave the way for SME suppliers to present joint bids when they cannot bid on their own, while providing them with guidance to avoid contract performance problems.

IMSS could work on identifying other problem areas, for instance those raised in the clarification meetings, and design training for suppliers on these issues. The training could be offered in the form of in-person training sessions, by means of an online website, as a written guidance document, or with the intermediation of business chambers (see OECD examples in Box 8.8).

Box 8.8. Supplier training in Italy and Sweden

Supplier training desk in Italy

In Italy, MSMEs (micro, small and medium enterprises) tend to participate in lower value public procurement tenders. Their participation in tenders worth from EUR 100,000 to 300,000 corresponds to 65%, whereas in tenders worth EUR 1 to 5 million it decreases to 51%, and to 30% for tenders with a value higher than EUR 5 million.

Italy has strengthened its co-operation with suppliers by setting up Supplier Training Desks within the offices of National Enterprise Associations. Here, experts from the central purchasing agency (Consip) provide training and assistance to local businesses, and in particular MSMEs on the use of electronic procurement tools.

This project has been well received and attended by MSMEs. Since the beginning of the project, more than 2 250 MSMEs have been supported by the Supplier Training Desks and qualified for the public e-marketplace for low-value purchases through e-catalogues (MePA). Today, SMEs represent the highest percentage of enterprises using the MEPA.

Online assistance in Sweden

The Swedish Competition Authority (SCA) has created an online interactive tool providing companies with guidance on when and in what form they can co-operate and submit joint procurement bids. The SCA had noticed that companies found it difficult to draw the line between competitive and anti-competitive and/or illegal co-operation, and saw an opportunity to pair its enforcement work with more preventative outreach measures by assisting companies at an earlier stage.

The guide features frequently asked questions, such as, "Can we co-operate in this particular tender?", or "When am I allowed to use a competitor as a subcontractor?". It also contains information on the consequences of illegal co-operation. Throughout the guide, "pop-up windows" give the user more detailed information about specific questions or examples based on real cases. Eventually, the user is given an indicative answer on whether the situation in question is likely to be permitted or not, subject to the need to seek legal advice in case of uncertainty

Source: (OECD, $2014_{[15]}$)

Proposals for action

As the largest health provider in Mexico, IMSS is a central actor of the national health system and represents a considerable source of revenue for the private sector. Building on efforts made by IMSS since the last review, the institute could further align its procurement strategies with national health policies and further implement measures to facilitate SMEs access to IMSS procurement opportunities.

Aligning IMSS procurement strategies with national health policies

- At the federal level, further contributing to framing national health policies by closely interacting with the Ministry of Health.
- Contribute to national healthcare objectives such as universal access by defining specific procurement strategies supporting these endeavours. For example, IMSS could design procurement processes which would increase the penetration rate of generic drugs, thereby providing the Mexican population with cheaper alternatives to patented drugs.
- Leveraging on strategic public procurement to ensure the effectiveness of national healthcare policies.

Fulfilling IMSS's potential as a source of revenue for the private sector

- Given the information available in CompraNet and in its own information system, track information on the size of suppliers submitting a bid, as well as the size of suppliers winning a contract, and link it with the identification of suppliers during the market analysis phase to assess the level of participation of potential suppliers and tailor specific procurement strategies to enhance SME's participation in IMSS procurement activities.
- Define procurement strategies to attract SMEs to participate in IMSS procurement opportunities for all categories including medicine and medical devices by:
  - monitoring closely the use of the set-aside provisions for SMEs included in the legal framework to disentangle the compliance with the legal framework from the rest.
  - promoting the use of joint bidding to diversify IMSS's supply base and to attract more SMEs especially for some product categories with a high market concentration such as medical devices , and;
  - defining allotment strategy and subcontracting arrangements in IMSS procurement opportunities while taking into account market analysis outcomes and COFECE's recommendations.
- Going beyond the legal framework and develop additional measures to increase SMEs' access to IMSS contracts, including:
  - exempting or reducing the value of guarantees for SMEs,
  - facilitating access to advanced payment for suppliers and ensuring timely payments as delays increasingly harm SMEs,
  - developing or promoting financial instruments and mechanisms aiming at supporting SMEs in Mexico
  - with the support of SFP streamlining tendering procedure in particular for the submission of administrative documentation
- In addition, IMSS could promote training provided by SFP among its suppliers and bidders, and develop a dedicated call centre to support SMEs during the tendering phase.

Note

[1] The objectives are 1) to contribute to the universal right to access healthcare; 2) to strengthen its revenues; 3) to increase productivity; 4) to enhance the healthcare model; and 5) to enhance economic and social benefits.

References

COFECE (2017), "Study on free market and competition in the expired-patent drug markets in Mexico", https://www.cofece.mx/cofece/ingles/attachments/article/38/Studies-drug%20markets_vF-BAJA.pdf (accessed on 21 November 2017). [6]

IMSS (2014), "IMSS institutional programme 2014-2018 [El programa institucional del Instituto Mexicano del Seguro Social 2014-2018]", http://www.imss.gob.mx/sites/all/statics/pdf/PIIMSS_2014-2018_FINAL_230414.pdf (accessed on 10 November 2017). [5]

INEGI (2016), "National survey on productivity and competitiveness of micro, small and medium enterprises", [Encuesta nacional sobre productividad y competitividad de las micro, pequeñas y medianas empresas]", http://www.inegi.org.mx/est/contenidos/proyectos/encuestas/establecimientos/otras/enaproce/doc/ENAPROCE_15.pdf (accessed on 10 November 2017). [16]

Mexican Health Ministry (2014), "Programa Sectorial de Salud 2013-2018 [Sectoral Health Programme 2013-2018]", http://www.omm.org.mx/images/stories/Documentos%20grandes/Programa%20Sectorial%20de%20Salud%202013-2018.pdf. [3]

NHS England (2016), "NHS Diabetes Prevention Programme", https://www.england.nhs.uk/ourwork/qual-clin-lead/diabetes-prevention/wave-2/ (accessed on 03 August 2017). [4]

OECD (2005), *OECD Reviews of Health Systems: Mexico 2005*, OECD Reviews of Health Systems, OECD Publishing, Paris, http://dx.doi.org/10.1787/9789264008939-en. [1]

OECD (2012), "Recommendation of the OECD Council on Fighting Bid Rigging in Public Procurement", Vol. 1159, http://www.oecd.org/daf/competition (accessed on 10 November 2017). [12]

OECD (2014), "Compendium of Good Practices for Integrity in Public Procurement: Meeting of the Leading Practitioners in Procurement", http://www.oecd.org/officialdocuments/publicdisplaydocumentpdf/?cote=GOV/PGC/ETH(2014)2/REV1&docLanguage=En (accessed on 10 November 2017). [15]

OECD (2015), "OECD Recommendation of the Council on Public Procurement", https://www.oecd.org/gov/ethics/OECD-Recommendation-on-Public-Procurement.pdf (accessed on 10 November 2017). [7]

OECD (2016), "Checklist for Supporting the Implementation of OECD Recommendation of the Council on Public Procurement: Balance", http://www.oecd.org/governance/procurement/toolbox/search/Checklist%2004%20Balance.pdf (accessed on 10 November 2017). [11]

OECD (2016), *OECD Reviews of Health Systems: Mexico 2016*, OECD Reviews of Health Systems, OECD Publishing, Paris, http://dx.doi.org/10.1787/9789264230491-en. [2]

OECD (2016), *The Korean Public Procurement Service: Innovating for Effectiveness*, OECD Public Governance Reviews, OECD Publishing, Paris, http://dx.doi.org/10.1787/9789264249431-en. [9]

OECD (2017), *Small, Medium, Strong. Trends in SME Performance and Business Conditions*, OECD Publishing, Paris, http://dx.doi.org/10.1787/9789264275683-en. [10]

OECD (2017), *Entrepreneurship at a Glance 2017*, OECD Publishing, Paris, http://dx.doi.org/10.1787/entrepreneur_aag-2017-en. [8]

OECD-SIGMA (2016), "Brief 33, Small and Medium-sized entreprises (SMEs) in Public Procurement", http://www.sigmaweb.org/publications/Public-Procurement-Policy-Brief-33-200117.pdf (accessed on 10 November 2017). [13]

UGAP (2017), *Collaborative advance payment solution [Solution collaborative de paiement anticipé]*, http://www.ugap.fr/solution-collaborative-de-paiement-anticipe_4468228.html (accessed on 10 November 2017). [14]

Chapter 9. Unlocking the potential for innovation in the Mexican health system through public procurement

This chapter focuses on the extent to which IMSS uses public procurement strategically to promote innovation and serve the institute's beneficiaries beyond the achievement of traditional public procurement objectives. The chapter complements the general analyses previously undertaken (see Chapter 8) by discussing IMSS's current efforts to put procurement for innovation into practice, namely to leverage its buying power as one of the largest healthcare providers in Mexico to foster innovation and other complementary objectives.

As previously discussed, strategic procurement involves a shift from a unidimensional mandate to a multifaceted one. Doing so can obtain value for money while supporting additional policy objectives, such as innovation, inclusion of SMEs in public markets (Chapter 8), and environmental protection. It can moreover help institutions avoid unnecessary duplication, while creating synergies.

In addition to discussing current efforts carried out by the institute to promote innovation into its procurement practices, the chapter also highlights various future avenues that IMSS can pursue for this purpose, focusing on three areas:

1. Exploring the potential for innovation in the health sector
2. Fully utilising the existing room for public procurement for innovation by targeting every day practice
3. Working towards a supporting framework for procurement for innovation

Innovation and procurement can improve healthcare services and productivity

A pressing issue shared by countries around the world is how to improve the cost-benefit balance of health care services, i.e. how can the ratio of outputs to inputs in health care be substantially improved?

The situation in many countries is of rising costs both for government and private players, while health outcomes fail to keep pace. Without changes, rising costs could overburden governments as an ageing population and new healthcare needs become too costly. Health costs also affect jobs because in a system with a high share of private pay for health care coverage, some employers will respond to rising costs by not hiring more workers, or at least constraining the take-home pay of those they retain.

Change is needed as many elements of health care systems are built around assumptions from a different time, when the reality and possibilities of new technologies and increasing regulatory complexity, did not exist. The move towards patient-centred healthcare, i.e. putting patients' expectations at the centre of the healthcare system, can also be seen as a result of this need for change. This is a shift away from a situation in which patients negotiate in a fragmented, confusing and sometimes seemingly uncaring system that is a product of accumulated accident and unintended consequences rather than design (Kaufmann, 2012[1]).

Research (OECD, 2015[2]) clearly suggests a positive link between innovation, efficiency and productivity growth and points to the crucial role of public policies, such as research and development incentives, in fostering innovation. With healthcare accounting for 9% of GDP on average in OECD countries (OECD, 2017[3]), the efficiency with which healthcare resources are used has a significant impact on overall productivity. The role of new technology and innovation in healthcare has been attracting increasing attention in this context. Better healthcare services, supported by effective procurement practices, have an impact on countries' economic development indicators, and notably on productivity. Indeed, measures to raise the rate of productivity growth in countries' economy have been a prominent element in economic policy debates.

While efficiency gains, i.e. achieving better results while using the same amount of resources, or achieving the same results by using fewer resources, can contribute to meeting these challenges, public procurement can further contribute to the provision of people-centred, high-quality care by fostering the achievement of policy goals such as the application and spread of innovation. Consequently, traditional procurement practices must evolve to unlock the potential of innovation.

Indeed almost all governments are recognising the potential to use public procurement strategically to support complementary policy objectives, such as innovation. Alongside sustainability and inclusiveness, innovation – which underpins jobs, productivity and growth – remains a policy imperative for all countries.

What is procurement for innovation?

Procurement for innovation refers to how governments and public entities can use their substantial buying power to create demand for innovation. Procurement for innovation involves harnessing innovation to facilitate the delivery of better solutions through procurement practices. It can refer to a range of activities – from framing purchasing practices in a more innovation-friendly way by e.g. using more performance-based specifications, to public authorities initiating the development of new solutions in collaboration with suppliers and research and development providers.

The majority of OECD member countries already use public procurement as a tool to pursue complementary policy objectives, including innovation. Environmental considerations continue to be the key policy objectives that are addressed through public procurement. Almost all OECD countries surveyed (29 countries) support green public procurement through various policies and strategies at the central level and those developed by specific procuring entities. As one of the main demand-side innovation policies, public procurement is used in the majority of OECD countries (24 countries) to support innovative goods and services (OECD, 2017[4]). Box 9.1 provides some examples of innovation in the health sector in the UK.

Innovation is about finding new and better ways of doing things (Semple, 2015[5]). For example, patients could be offered online access to health professionals that could solve basic primary-care concerns without the need to visit a doctor. Electronic solutions could also support patient self-management and control, for instance by means of online access to medical records, test results and appointment booking. Some innovations can result in immediate savings for public entities, whereas others will save costs in the long-term while requiring an initial investment.

Box 9.1. United Kingdom examples of innovations in health

Through "The Health Foundation" initiative, several projects were selected to compete under the headline "Innovating for Improvement". The aims were to identify projects to improve healthcare delivery and/or the way people manage their own health care by testing and developing innovative ideas and approaches and putting them into practice. The following projects were part of the competition:

- **Maternal risk assessment**: management by and with pregnant women, where they want and need it. 'SAFER' is a risk assessment tool that is used to assess antenatal risks and develop comprehensive clinical management plans. This project will involve testing this methodology and engaging pregnant women in its development and implementation, with the aim of creating a community-based model that will improve maternal outcomes.
- **Introducing tele-psychiatry into routine practice in an emergency department psychiatric service.** Tele-psychiatry uses video-conferencing to deliver mental health services from a distance. This project aims to improve patient satisfaction and reduce costs by trialling tele-psychiatry in three ways: to provide senior medical opinion on complex cases; to complete assessments at distance; and to provide follow-up home appointments using patients' own technology.
- **Home monitoring to support patients during chemotherapy.** This project involves the piloting of an innovative remote monitoring service for cancer patients who are measuring their white blood cells, haemoglobin, body temperature and self-reported symptoms in their own home, with the aim of improving patients' quality of life during chemotherapy and reducing the number of hospital visits.

Source: (The Health Foundation, 2015[6]).

Procurement for innovation can contribute to other social objectives

Often, the implementation of procurement for innovation responds to social challenges which would be difficult to tackle through procurement processes carried out as an administrative, tick-the-box, exercise. Examples of how innovation procurement has been used to address needs and challenges in the health sector and also to pursue other secondary policy objectives such as environmental performance can be found across Europe.

For example, in the Netherlands the Erasmus University Medical Centre wanted to find better solutions for its need to disinfect 70 000 hospital beds and mattresses annually. These solutions should ideally use less energy and water compared to common methods of manual cleaning. The medical centre presented its need to the market, challenging suppliers to provide it with innovative solutions. Principles of procurement for innovation, such as a series of market soundings and outcome-based specifications, were used to stimulate cross-supply chain interaction. In the end the contract was won by a small enterprise that provided a robotic solution featuring high-precision cleaning robots from the automotive industry (EcoQUIP, 2016[7]).

Box 9.2 offers other examples of types of public policy problems whose solutions have been supported by public procurement.

Box 9.2. Innovative procurement initiatives in Colombia

The National Development Plan (2014-2018) specifies procurement innovation as a cross-cutting strategy targeted to generate a higher economic and social value to enhance the conditions for the development of business activities. Several projects were developed, including the following pilots:

1. The Ministry of Information and Communication Technology (MinTic) acquired services for the development of a laboratory to develop management IT skills and information security. The purpose was to create scenarios to run security tests, cybersecurity and develop research in IT and information privacy. It is important to run tests of fictional scenarios to verify the quality of the current tools to protect information and to test new developments. Through this process, MinTic tests various security aspects in a safe and controlled environment. The direct beneficiary is the ministry itself, though other government agencies benefit from the developments too. In addition, Colombia seeks to encourage its youth to study IT; procurement for innovation in the IT sector is a good incentive for doing so.
2. The National Agency for Overcoming Extreme Poverty (ANSPE) identified the need for a programme that mixes technology and knowledge as a way to provide populations in extreme poverty with the tools and knowledge to generate income by developing soft skills. It therefore led the development and acquisition of an IT-based tool used to strengthen soft skills. Under this programme, innovation is created from the need to combine different strategies (educational, technological, etc.) to identify opportunities and knowledge to overcome poverty.
3. The *Empresas Públicas de Medellín* (the state owned enterprises of Medellín, or EPM) is undertaking a project to reduce wastewater by locating leaks. The project is looking through a procurement process for a system to control costs to be charged to the users within monthly bills and create awareness of the impacts of water consumption. The direct beneficiaries will be EPM and consumers. EPM will reduce its costs of finding water leaks; consumers will not pay for water lost. In fact, the costs for water lost due to leaks are transferred to consumers and has an important environmental impact. This will lead to awareness of water consumption and cost efficiencies.

Source: (OECD, 2017[8]).

Measures exist in Mexico to promote innovation through public procurement and IMSS could build further on existing procurement-related innovation policies and efforts.

When it comes to policies for innovation, governments have traditionally directed their efforts towards the supply side, creating conditions for the private sector that are favourable for innovation. Recently, however, "demand-side" policies to support innovation have also become prominent, increasingly recognising public procurement as a potential strategic instrument to encourage innovation.

Successful implementation of procurement for innovation requires an understanding of how innovation works, including the conditions that either enable or hinder it. It also requires an understanding of how these conditions can be created or modified in a procurement context, both at the organisational and at the operational level, with the aim of creating purchasing solutions that better meet identified needs.

An indispensable prerequisite for strategic public procurement is a legal and regulatory framework that allows for incorporating complementary policy objectives, such as innovation, into procurement policies. Countries use a variety of policies, strategies and other instruments for encouraging and developing procurement for innovation. While some countries – such as Canada, France, and the Netherlands – approach this task by developing a stand-alone action plan for procurement for innovation, other countries – such as Colombia, Spain and New Zealand – have procurement for innovation as a part of their general innovation or procurement strategy (OECD, 2017[8]).

Although IMSS does not currently have in place an institutional framework for innovation procurement, it has already taken steps in that direction (for example, see Box 9.3), laying what could be the foundations of an innovation procurement strategy. IMSS could build further on existing procurement-related innovation policies and efforts.

In 2013 President Enrique Peña Nieto instructed the Ministry of Economy to create a programme to drive innovation through public procurement. To fulfil this mandate, the Ministry of Economy will concentrate efforts on promoting innovation, especially within micro, small and medium-sized firms, and improving public services through innovative products and services. This will involve a three-phase plan:

1. Short term: design and pilot innovation on a small scale.
2. Medium term: implement the innovation programme in Federal Government.
3. Long term: promote a culture of innovation and scientific development (OECD, 2017[8]).

Box 9.3. IMSS's Innovation Olympics

The Innovation Olympics (*Olimpiadas de Innovación*) are an IMSS-organised contest for ideas and innovative projects for improving patient care in IMSS in different fields and professional disciplines. The competition is open to multidisciplinary teams, including at least one IMSS worker. With this initiative, IMSS seeks to capitalise on the Institute's talent pool in order to improve patient care.

The Innovation Olympics offer an opportunity for IMSS' procurement activities to promote innovation. As a start winning projects from the Olympics could be used as pilots for gaining more experience in the uptake of innovative solutions through procurement. Influenced by the set-up of the Olympics, this could be organised as cooperation involving procurement officials and the clinical or technical personnel with a first-hand knowledge about the needs. Depending on the project/concept it might also be suitable to conduct market consultations to work with suppliers to develop new solutions.

Source: Information provided by IMSS

Mexico's Innovative Development Program 2013-2018 (*Programa de Desarrollo Innovador 2013-2018*) (Secretaría de Economía, 2013[9]), developed by the Ministry of Economy, mentions national markets as one of its strategic targets. It aims to strengthen domestic and foreign demand (including public-sector demand) for innovative products, services and business models created in Mexico. The Special Program for Sustainable Production and Consumption 2014-2018, co-ordinated by the Environment and Natural Resources Ministry (SEMARNAT), includes among its objectives increased green public procurement (SEMARNAT, 2014[10]).

Several elements of the policy environment at the federal level include references to the pursuit of complementary objectives through procurement, including innovation and environmental considerations. The "Law for the Development of the Competitiveness of Micro, Small and Medium Enterprises" explicitly provides for public procurement processes to take into account certain complementary policy objectives. Article 14 of the Law of Rentals, Acquisitions and Services by the Public Sector (LAASP) provides for the option for giving preference to certain suppliers, such as small and medium-sized enterprises (SMEs) offering goods featuring innovative technology certified by the Mexican Institute for Intellectual Property (*Instituto Mexicano de la Propiedad Industrial, IMPI)*.

The Law on Public Works and associated services (LOPSRM) allows for the use of restricted invitation or direct acquisition mechanisms in the case of a strategic alliance formed to apply innovative technology to national infrastructure (including IMSS's infrastructure).[1] The ROPSRM (art. 99) allows for the possibility of modifying technical specifications if new technological advances justify them. In addition, the LAASP and the administrative manual include provisions for the substitution of goods and/or services by those with advanced technologies which comply with several environmental sustainability criteria, such as energy savings, low emissions of pollutants and/or gases, low water consumption and/or high reutilisation, or low generation of waste (Articles 18 and 20).

However, these provisions are exceptions to public tenders and are applied in a way that limits competition and also limits scope and impact. Elsewhere in the OECD there are ways to encourage and include innovation in open competition and more general scope. For example, under the European public procurement directives, methodological features of "innovation friendly" procurement, such as focusing on communicating needs and proposed functions, market engagement and use of performance based specifications, are possible (Box 9.4).

Box 9.4. "Innovation friendly" procurement in Norway

Political support for the potential of public procurement as an effective innovation instrument has been recently achieved in Norway. At the same time, Norway has a decentralised procurement system and highly independent procuring entities. Thus, to promote a more widespread application of procurement for innovation, the contracting authorities needed more support. As a result, a programme was established in 2010 dedicated to promoting procurement for innovation and for supporting contracting authorities in carrying out procurement in a more 'innovation friendly' way. The programme was a collaborative effort between the organisations representing the three major stakeholders in public procurement: the confederation for enterprises (suppliers), the association for local level procuring entities and the agency responsible for central procuring entities.

Since 2010, the programme has contributed to more than 100 projects using the procurement process as a strategic instrument to encourage innovation. The projects focus on several areas, including healthcare, digitalisation, building and the environment.

Another part of the programme's work is to initiate processes to scale up and co-ordinate individual local efforts that are of national interest, e.g. procuring welfare technology, knowledge exchange, improving market conditions and targeted efforts to develop new and better solutions for the public sector and citizens.

Evaluations of several of the projects show cost-savings, environmental benefits, and qualitative improvements in public sector services. Also noteworthy is the finding that suppliers involved in these "innovation friendly" procurements invest six times more in innovation than suppliers who have not been involved. This supports the argument for using public procurement as an effective demand-side innovation instrument for governments (Menon, 2015[11]).

Source: (National Programme for Supplier Development,(n.d.)[12])

However, procurement officers at IMSS currently make little use of Mexico's existing framework; the institute's day-to-day procurement practice does not seem to reflect the strategic goals set out in Mexico's Innovative Development Program 2013-2018 or the Health Sector Program 2013-2018 (Secretaría de Salud, 2013[13]).

Making IMSS procurement more innovation friendly

IMSS could build on the existing strategic priorities of innovation and health at the national level and translate them into its own procurement activities. In this way it could harness its substantial buying power in the marketplace to achieve better healthcare services and greater productivity.

It could use procurement for innovation strategically to address challenges such as:

- geographical differences in health care access and quality
- the need to respond to the changing healthcare needs of the Mexican population, including ageing, sedentary lifestyles, obesity and diabetes; to the transition from the prevalence of infectious diseases to degenerative ones; and to the need to promote preventive medicine
- the need for patients to assume co-responsibility for their health.

However, achieving these improved outcomes through innovative solutions identified in public procurement processes requires structuring procurement practices. Good practices employed by OECD countries to encourage public procurement for innovation include (OECD, 2017[8]):

- identifying the innovation objectives to be pursued through the use of public procurement in accordance with national priorities
- introducing the use of procurement for innovation in the legal and regulatory framework
- creating incentives for procurement for innovation
- considering the capacity and capability of the procurement workforce to support procurement for innovation
- putting in place professionalisation activities to equip procurers with adequate technical knowledge to conduct procurement for innovation, including risk management
- raising awareness on the part of procurers and potential suppliers
- establishing systems to monitor the impact of procurement for innovation and balance cost/benefits
- framing procurement needs through a thorough needs analysis involving relevant stakeholders, such as beneficiaries or employees, with the aim of encouraging collaboration in interdisciplinary teams
- carrying out a market consultation on the identified needs
- providing for flexibility to reframe needs and organise tendering process based on the information acquired with the aim of encouraging collaboration
- using performance-based specifications
- following up on the implementation of innovation during the contract period
- creating legal provisions or regulations to open up public procurement to innovative firms
- allowing for the preferential treatment of innovative companies (including purchasing assurance schemes, framework contracts for certified products).

Although these activities are listed in a loosely chronological order, different situations require different approaches. There is no one-size-fits-all approach to procuring the most innovative solution. Some of the listed activities can be combined, repeated or omitted depending on the specific circumstances, namely the type of product to be procured, the maturity of the market, the contract value, the ambition of the purchasing entity and the procurement skills available.

While overarching strategies can provide general guidance for the implementation of public procurement for innovation, it is also necessary to work on incorporating innovation considerations at each individual stage of the procurement cycle. It is helpful to divide the procurement process into the following stages in order to identify the opportunities for introducing innovation at each stage (Clement, Watt and Semple, 2016[14]):

- Pre-procurement
- Deciding on the procurement procedure
- Defining the subject of the contract (subject matter)
- Selection/exclusion of bidders
- Technical specifications
- Award criteria
- Contract management

IMSS could put procurement for innovation into practice throughout these stages, targeted to specific innovation priorities and balanced against capacity and efficiency constraints. Based on the existing legal and regulatory framework, measures could be particularly effective in the pre-procurement and planning phases, in the technical specifications, in the award criteria, and in contract management – either because they represent low-hanging fruit or build on existing measures (Clement, Watt and Semple, 2016[14]). This section contains a selected set of measures that could achieve good results in IMSS's specific context, without imposing an excessive burden on the institute's procurement system.

Embedding measures which support innovation throughout the procurement cycle

Considering innovation in the pre-procurement and planning phases could help IMSS exploring the potential availability of innovative solutions in the markets

The pre-procurement or planning phase is crucial to ensure the implementation of innovation objectives, as it can help IMSS explore the potential availability of innovative solutions to fulfil its needs. Currently, however, market research carried out by IMSS suffers from some limitations, as noted in Chapter 3. The following concrete measures could be beneficial (Clement, Watt and Semple, 2016[14]):

- Raise awareness amongst the requiring and contracting units of the importance of considering innovation as an essential component of market investigations. Currently even the fact that incorporating innovation objectives in the planning phase is an option seems to be largely unknown.
- Provide training and guidance material on including innovation objectives in needs analysis. Currently, requiring areas seem to work on the basis of needs for specific products, rather than needs for results.

One of the most crucial components of a procurement environment conducive to innovation is engaging with markets to gather information about industry trends and potential for innovation. For example, the purchase of medical devices would offer good opportunities for implementing innovation procurement. Medical devices are essential for the diagnosis, treatment and rehabilitation of diseases, and therefore play an important part in equipping IMSS to be able to deliver better healthcare services. Moreover, Mexico has a well-developed cluster of medical device suppliers, with exports valued at USD 7.7 billion in 2014, according to the Ministry of Economy (Secretaría de Economía, 2015[15]). This highly specialised supplier base has the potential to provide IMSS with innovative medical-device solutions, and IMSS could leverage its purchasing power to encourage this result.

IMSS has recently been engaging in a dialogue with suppliers on the consolidated purchases of therapeutic goods, holding weekly meetings with relevant business chambers to discuss the issues that most frequently hinder the contractual relationships arising from consolidated procurement. IMSS has worked to ensure that calls for tender and delivery conditions captured these market opinions.

Yet, it does not seem that this forum is successfully used to increase IMSS's awareness of new potential solutions to its needs. Pre-tender dialogues with suppliers and suppliers' meetings could also be used to flag up innovative solutions as well as obsolete products, and to explore how functional requirements and award criteria could be used future procedures so as to encourage innovation (see the sections below).

IMSS could frame technical specifications so as to encourage innovation and adapt award criteria

In IMSS, technical specifications are usually determined by the requiring area, with little input from the central purchasing unit that conducts the public procurement process. However, a smart definition of the technical specifications to be procured represents one of the most important aspects of designing a procurement procedure that not only helps IMSS achieve the best value for money, but also facilitates the pursuit of complementary policy objectives, such as fostering innovation.

In order to allow for technical specifications that facilitate procurement for innovation, the following measures could be implemented (Clement, Watt and Semple, 2016[14]):

- Train and guide procurers to draft technical specifications that include performance requirements and technical standards or certifications that take innovation objectives into account.
- Raise awareness within the requiring units on the importance of considering these performance requirements and standards.

Alongside improved technical specifications, functional requirements could allow suppliers to propose innovative solutions by requesting what needs to be achieved, rather than the way in which this is done. This can encourage the exploration of innovative solutions that deliver the results sought by IMSS, but at a lower cost or with added advantages (Box 9.5).

Box 9.5. Using functional requirements to promote innovation

In 2015 and 2016 IMSS used a medical strategy known as therapeutic substitution in its consolidated purchases. Under this programme, written protocols were set up for the substitution of certain medicines by other drugs that, despite being differently formulated, have similar therapeutic action and pharmacological activity, including secondary effects. Therapeutically equivalent medicines can therefore include different chemical components or the same one, but in different dosages or routes of administration.

Therapeutic substitution is especially useful when expensive, patented, new or single sourced medicines are prescribed. This strategy can be seen as a way of focusing on functional performance, namely on what is to be achieved rather than how it is to be done. Although this scheme only applied to a very specific set of goods, and is not a principle of horizontal application for the drafting of technical specifications as a rule, it sets a precedent and could offer learning experience for IMSS to extend the use of functional requirements across its entire procurement practice.

Source: Information provided by IMSS

IMSS is advised to include functional requirements in its technical specifications, so as to invite innovative offers and attract the highest possible number of bidders (including those offering substitute products), while increasing its chances of obtaining better value for money and deterring collusive practices. Moreover, functional requirements defined to support innovation can help deliver other complementary objectives, such as environmental-friendly solutions.

Capturing innovative dimensions requires an evaluation framework which allows for the comparative assessments of tenders according to several objectives. For example, procurement award criteria at IMSS are often based solely on price. However, they can also reward innovation and performance.

Following up on the measures laid out in Chapter 6, IMSS could (Clement, Watt and Semple, 2016[14]):

- Raise awareness among contracting and requiring units that the use of exceptions to public tendering should be as limited as possible to ensure a genuine competition ultimately supporting innovation.
- Raise awareness and provide training and guidance on the use of the points and percentages system to give extra weight to innovation considerations when selecting bidders. For example, a bidder whose product includes an innovative feature, such as increasing environmental performance, could receive more points than non-innovative alternatives.
- Publicly acknowledge outstanding procurement processes where smart award criteria have led to an efficient outcome in terms of both price and objectives of finding innovative solutions.

Adapting contractual relationships to the investments required to innovate would provide IMSS and its suppliers with more incentives to develop innovative products

As noted in Chapter 6, in many cases, IMSS could foster innovation by extending the duration of contracts stemming from procurement procedures. This is particularly relevant in the context of consolidated procurement. Short contract periods, such as the one-year contracts resulting from consolidated purchases, not only increase the administrative burden for IMSS's procurement officers, but can also be a barrier to innovation by failing to justify investments in innovation by firms. By extending the contract period to 2 or 3 years, IMSS could foster these investments by giving firms a reasonable period to recoup them, while at the same time increasing the transactional efficiency of its purchasing processes.

In general, longer contract periods also improve the possibility to include pro-innovation clauses, such as provisions allowing for the incorporation to the product of any innovations arising during the contract's validity period.

Skills and collaboration: to reap the benefits of procurement for innovation IMSS should invest efforts in developing the skills of its procurement workforce and increasing coordination with subject matter experts.

As well as adaptions to the procurement environment, effective procurement for innovation requires the skills and capacity to tackle the increasing complexity of the corresponding tenders. Building these in the procurement workforce is an essential condition for the success of procurement for innovation, since it is procurement officers who are in charge of implementing market engagement, using functional requirements, performance-based specifications, and diverse award criteria, as described above and in Chapter 6. Procurement officers must be trained to take innovation objectives into account throughout the procurement cycle.

A mind-set shift from zero risk tolerance to reasonable risk-taking would also help IMSS's procurement workforce to put procurement for innovation into practice. In this regard, IMSS should embrace the philosophy that although failure should be ideally avoided, it is also often part of the innovation process and can act as a learning opportunity. Strategic risk-management practices, embedded in a comprehensive framework (discussed in Chapter 7), could help IMSS mitigate many of the risks inherent to innovation.

Other participants in public procurement procedures can also play an important role in fostering procurement for innovation. Procurement officers can collaborate with firms and experts, who may provide input in the drafting of procurement documents, such as tender specifications. In this regard, models to create more inclusive teams would help IMSS encourage innovation through public procurement.

The active participation of clinical staff, namely the doctors and nurses in charge of providing patient care in practice, is also key for the implementation of innovative solutions. It is advisable that clinical staff be offered appropriate training to help them put the relevant innovations into practice.

In order to better provide training and guidance for the procurement workforce to implement innovation procurement, IMSS could deepen its collaboration with stakeholders such as other purchasing entities, innovation centres, or chambers of commerce, in order to establish a lasting culture of innovation (OECD, 2017[8]). The example from Chile in Box 9.6 illustrates how new models for collaboration between different stakeholders can have substantial impact on the professionalisation of procurement management.

Box 9.6. Innovative practice in Chile: workshops to improve regional public procurement

Experience indicates that while in general, procurement officers know the rules of public procurement, requests from technical areas are often carried out with inadequate time, or do not provide enough information for the procurement area.

In this initiative, two institutions with complementary expertise collaborated to contribute to the public procurement management of municipalities. ChileCompra provides technical and practical knowledge of public procurement. In addition, the project counted on the participation of the Comptroller General of the Republic (through its regional comptrollers), which provides legal and administrative knowledge. This joint effort is part of the advisory role of both institutions.

Both institutions hold practical workshops in each municipality for procurement officials and all relevant actors in municipal procurement, including requesting areas and municipal officers. This highlights the fact that public procurement is an institutional activity, where all efforts are relevant. For the first time, two institutions with complementary expertise in procurement management are working together. This synergy implies better quality workshops, in which solutions to everyday problems in public procurement can be found at the local level.

Source: (OECD, 2017[8]).

Proposals for action

To summarise, IMSS could build on its recent interest in fostering innovation to implement procurement for innovation. Several actions can be implemented by IMSS to make the most of the potential for innovation in the health sector so as to improve health services and increase productivity:

- Adapt evaluation mechanisms to capture innovative dimensions in suppliers' proposals.
- Design procurement processes to be innovation friendly. Innovation considerations should play a central role in the conduct of market investigations and needs assessments, as well as in the drafting of tender documents.
- Use multiannual contracts to encourage innovation (when appropriate) by offering bidders the possibility to recoup initial investments.
- Strengthen capacity building and awareness-raising exercises for IMSS procurement staff to give them the skills to put procurement for innovation into practice.
- Explore the possibility of pursuing secondary policy objectives when using public procurement for innovation since complementarities could be found that could generate additional value for IMSS.

Note

[1] In Fraction XIII of its Article 42.

References

Clement, S., J. Watt and A. Semple (2016), *A Guide to Implementing Sustainable Procurement The Procura+ Manual*, ICLEI – Local Governments for Sustainability, European Secretariat, http://www.procuraplus.org/fileadmin/user_upload/Manual/Procuraplus_Manual_Third_Edition.pdf. [14]

EcoQUIP (2016), *Delivering efficiency, quality and sustainability in healthcare through innovation procurement*, EcoQUIP, http://www.ecoquip.eu/uploads/pdfs/EcoQUIP%20-%20Delivering%20efficiency,%20quality%20and%20sustainability%20through%20innovation%20procurement%20-%20case%20study%20based%20report.pdf. [7]

Kaufmann (2012), *Valuing Health Care: Improving Productivity and Quality*, Kauffman - The Foundation of Entrepreneurship, Kansas city, https://scholarship.law.duke.edu/cgi/viewcontent.cgi?referer=&httpsredir=1&article=5220&context=faculty_scholarship. [1]

Menon (2015), *Procurement for innovation: An effective tool for the modernisation of public sector – if we facilitate for it and remove barriers*, http://innovativeanskaffelser.no/wp-content/uploads/2017/02/innovative-offentlige-anskaffelser-menon-rapport-mai-2015.pdf. [11]

National Programme for Supplier Development((n.d.)), *About Innovative Procurements*, http://innovativeanskaffelser.no/about/ (accessed on 01 December 2017). [12]

OECD (2015), *The Future of Productivity*, OECD Publishing, Paris, http://dx.doi.org/10.1787/9789264248533-en. [2]

OECD (2017), *Health at a Glance 2017: OECD Indicators*, OECD Publishing, Paris, http://dx.doi.org/10.1787/health_glance-2017-en. [3]

OECD (2017), *Government at a Glance 2017*, OECD Publishing, Paris, http://dx.doi.org/10.1787/gov_glance-2017-en. [4]

OECD (2017), *Public Procurement for Innovation: Good Practices and Strategies*, OECD Public Governance Reviews, OECD Publishing, Paris, http://dx.doi.org/10.1787/9789264265820-en. [8]

Secretaría de Economía (2013), "Programa de Desarrollo Innovador (2013-2018)", http://www.economia.gob.mx/files/prodeinn/Programa_de_Desarrollo_Innovador2013-2018.pdf. [9]

Secretaría de Economía (2015), *The Medical Device Industry in Mexico*, https://connect.innovateuk.org/documents/3112383/30824476/The+Medical+Device+Industry+in+Mexico/5e7a569b-e48a-4864-8caa-84a2624da543. [15]

Secretaría de Salud (2013), *Programa Sectorial de Salud 2013-2018, [Sectoral Health Programme 2013-2018]*, http://dof.gob.mx/nota_detalle.php?codigo=5326219&fecha=12/12/2013. [13]

SEMARNAT (2014), "Programa Especial de Producción y Consumo Sustentable 2014-2018", https://www.gob.mx/cms/uploads/attachment/file/30928/ProgramaEspecialdeProduccionyConsumoSustentable.pdf. [10]

Semple, A. (2015), *Guidance for Public Authorities on Public Procurement of Innovation*, Procurement of Innovation Platform, http://www.innovation-procurement.org/fileadmin/editor-content/Guides/PPI-Platform_Guide_new-final_download.pdf. [5]

The Health Foundation (2015), *Twenty-one Innovative Projects are Selected to Improve the Quality of Health Care*, http://www.health.org.uk/news/twenty-one-innovative-projects-are-selected-improve-quality-health-care. [6]

ORGANISATION FOR ECONOMIC CO-OPERATION AND DEVELOPMENT

The OECD is a unique forum where governments work together to address the economic, social and environmental challenges of globalisation. The OECD is also at the forefront of efforts to understand and to help governments respond to new developments and concerns, such as corporate governance, the information economy and the challenges of an ageing population. The Organisation provides a setting where governments can compare policy experiences, seek answers to common problems, identify good practice and work to co-ordinate domestic and international policies.

The OECD member countries are: Australia, Austria, Belgium, Canada, Chile, the Czech Republic, Denmark, Estonia, Finland, France, Germany, Greece, Hungary, Iceland, Ireland, Israel, Italy, Japan, Korea, Latvia, Luxembourg, Mexico, the Netherlands, New Zealand, Norway, Poland, Portugal, the Slovak Republic, Slovenia, Spain, Sweden, Switzerland, Turkey, the United Kingdom and the United States. The European Union takes part in the work of the OECD.

OECD Publishing disseminates widely the results of the Organisation's statistics gathering and research on economic, social and environmental issues, as well as the conventions, guidelines and standards agreed by its members.

OECD PUBLISHING, 2, rue André-Pascal, 75775 PARIS CEDEX 16
(04 2017 15 1 P) ISBN 978-92-64-19017-7 – 2018

www.ingramcontent.com/pod-product-compliance
Ingram Content Group UK Ltd.
Pitfield, Milton Keynes, MK11 3LW, UK
UKHW051500290926
15471UKWH00008B/1316

9 789264 190177